D1593100

Market Research
in the Internet Age

Market Research in the Internet Age

Leveraging the Internet for Market
Measurement and Consumer Insight

Robert W. Monster
Raymond C. Pettit

John Wiley & Sons (Asia) Pte Ltd

Other Wiley Editorial Offices

John Wiley & Sons, Inc., 605 Third Avenue, New York, NY 10158-0012, USA
John Wiley & Sons Ltd, Baffins Lane, Chichester, West Sussex PO19 1UD, England
John Wiley & Sons (Canada) Ltd, 22 Worcester Road, Rexdale, Ontario M9W 1L1, Canada
John Wiley & Sons Australia Ltd, 33 Park Road (PO Box 1226), Milton, Queensland 4064, Australia
Wiley-VCH, Pappelallee 3, 69469 Weinheim, Germany

ISBN: 0470-82064-0

Typeset in 10.5/13 points, Times Roman by Linographic Services Pte Ltd
Printed in Singapore by Saik Wah Press Pte Ltd
10 9 8 7 6 5 4 3 2 1

Contents

Foreword

INTRODUCTION

Market research is accustomed to change: the industry has been doubling in size every six or seven years for more than 30 years and shows little sign of stalling. During those years it has operated on a simple business model with a number of important advantages:

- it benefits from rapid change, deregulation, increased competition and market confusion – all of which are on the increase;
- it provides information and knowledge, a powerful management tool;
- it provides competitive advantage in the form of vital information with the spoils going to the one with the best information;
- it rides on the back of technology and benefits from rapid technical change.

Hence, market research (MR) is a model based on many drivers of the new economy.

Each new development in communications is quickly taken up and applied – so it was with telephones, PCs, scanning, networks, and now, of course, the Internet. Tomorrow it will certainly be mobile broadband and in fact almost any future improvement in communication technology.

However, while in the past these have created revolutions in the way that the market information industry collected, processed, and delivered its product, the Internet is and will do this "in spades." Today we are still riding the technology tiger, but it is running faster and we are not sure exactly where it will end up – it is very exciting, yet risky!

We may not know where it will end, but fortunately we know where we are. In the Internet debate on "content versus pipes," the question of should one own the deliverables or the highway, market information is undoubtedly at the "content" end. Thankfully, much of the content we produce gets out of date reasonably fast – it is slowly perishable and fortunately delivering it quickly gives considerable business advantage. So with the Internet's inherent one-to-one, and one-to-many linkages, we, in the market information industry, are in the expansion phase of a new era.

If this industry had been granted one wish to bring its business to the forefront of management the Internet would have been it. Market research is a feedback mechanism for marketing, in many respects market information and the Internet is a marriage made in heaven. Among those things that make our industry grow are:

1 the ability to deliver information faster;
2 the availability of bigger samples with greater accuracy and granularity;
3 the use of more varied ways to analyze the data;
4 the opportunity to lower costs.

In the history of market research innovation, the Internet delivers on all these more than any other technical change has done. Of course, researchers still need to have market insight, creativity, diligence, and so on, but these aspects are often the zero sum elements of the business, while the Internet is allowing us to make the whole cake bigger.

It is not for me to spell out here the benefits, changes, and innovations the Internet will bring with regard to:

• collecting data;
• processing databases;
• delivering intelligence and knowledge.

Indeed, the reader will find that this book is full of these insights. As a long-term observer and business leader in the field of market research, I believe that the combined effect that these developments are having will profoundly impact on the way in which companies, institutions, and executives function. How they request, organize, and distribute knowledge are in rapid evolution – "power to the middle manager and greater knowledge in the boardroom" are on the march.

Today, we are only a few years into this Internet-driven revolution. The highlighting of a few of the more foreseeable changes that the industry can expect may stimulate your reading of this excellent book.

ANSWERS BEFORE QUESTIONS!

Over the past few years we have moved to the age of having more data and more information than anyone can possibly handle. TNS' major clients can no longer even review all the data we produce for them, let alone analyze and interpret them. The Internet is taking this one stage further, whereby more and more databases are becoming accessible in real-time to more and more executives. The era of infinite databases that are available and linkable in real-time (even from a telephone) is approaching.

Hidden within these huge databases are the answers to many, maybe most, marketing issues. This includes such information as:

- How does advertising work?
- How does promotional activity function?
- What are the characteristics of products that ensure success?
- What part does "service" play in the mix and what values can we place on it?

We will have the data in abundance. The problem is knowing what databases and what sets of data to bring together, and precisely what questions to ask. As the Internet opens up more databases to more people, as the size of these databases increases, and as the ability to carry out fusion between them improves, so we will know that the answers will be "in there somewhere." The trick will be asking the right question to find the needle in the haystack. This fundamentally changes the way we think about the market information business. Traditionally, it was possible to say for most MR projects, "Just analyze everything by everything …". In the future we will need to think about what analyses we intend to conduct, what observations we link, and what theories we test, particularly as data become cheap, but insight and time becomes expensive.

FROM EXPERIMENT TO OBSERVATION

Traditionally, market research has relied heavily on experiments, tests, structured design, and all of the statisticians' armory. This was partly because of the huge cost of collecting data, and second, because of the huge cost and mathematical difficulty of analyzing many problems. The Internet is significantly reducing not just the cost of collecting data, but of having access to them in huge and varied volumes. At the same time, data-mining is taking the chore out of all aspects of regression and correlation, but correlation is not cause and regression is not reason.

We have known for many years that whatever small-scale experiments or tests to study the "human condition" we have set up, they have contained so much random noise and uncontrolled variables that we would never be sure of the reliability of what we measured.

Thanks to the Internet, computers, databases, and so on, we are moving from an experimental science, such as physics and chemistry, to observational sciences, like astronomy and biology. At last we have the ability to observe and analyze substantial quantities of consumer behavior as and when it happens; that is, to be able to observe events in quantity and investigate them in detail.

Pavlov knew and showed us many years ago the value of being able to know the results of your actions close to the event. The Internet will continue to change fundamentally the pace of learning, and therefore the pace at which marketing decisions are taken – this in itself will improve the quality of those decisions.

One example might suffice: today Taylor Nelson Sofres is able to tell media owners within minutes when a new advertising campaign breaks on their rival's channel or station. This Internet-enabled approach to information delivery gives the media sales teams the ability to immediately try to win back some of that lost business. In the past, the delay meant the money was spent and the business lost before competitors could react.

The move to market research becoming an observational science, in quantitative terms, moves focus from "what has happened" to "why," and to think on the modeling structures lying behind the events.

QUANTITATIVE BEFORE QUALITATIVE

In traditional research, one conducted a number of in-depth interviews with small samples of people in order to theorize. Once theories were developed, they could be "tested" on more reliable samples in the hope that the theories would be confirmed on larger segments of the population. The Internet will allow us to observe one-to-one and one-to-many. Increasingly, we know what people are doing, as they are doing it, and are able to monitor minute patterns of behavior (for example, clickstream data). This means that "quantitative research" is becoming cheaper, ever more accurate, and is arriving before qualitative analysis.

There have historically been endless debates that surrounded our industry. Some familiar examples include:

- Do people tell you the truth and answer questions honestly?
- Can they remember what they did, when and in what order?
- Do people know why they do things and can they verbalize such motivations?
- Does the environment and the situation in which the information is collected change people's replies?
- Are either being removed from the equation, or can they be more easily put to the test?

The Internet is starting to allow us simply to "short circuit" this by linking directly the actions we take with the consequent activity. Why ask "*what people did*" when you can observe even faster what they actually did? Why not study the motivations by looking at the consequences?

We have not yet even grasped where this quantum leap in observation will lead to, particularly as the Internet-enabled capability to observe becomes more mainstream.

We are moving from the age of theory and hypothesis to hands-on exploration. People do not learn to ride a bicycle by studying the theory of balance and gyration, nor do they learn how to watch television by understanding electronics. Having access to these devices, interacting with them to learn how they function, is enough to carry us to new places and new ideas. So it is with the Internet. The market information industry lives and grows through an ongoing process of more data, more analyses, and more interconnections of concepts. As a result, the industry is in a prime position to benefit from all aspects of the Internet's ability to automate, aggregate, and archive this abundance of raw material for knowledge.

FROM MARKET RESEARCH DEPARTMENT TO CORPORATE INTRANET

The Internet will liberate market data and information about the markets from the market research department "enclave." Traditionally, the problem of deciding the questions, the analysis, and the choice for inside knowledge were left to the market research department, to enthusiastic amateurs in the marketing department, or both. However, the Internet is easily capable of delivering this knowledge to "everyone" in the company as quickly and as easily as to the market research manager. This trend will continue as the marketing of products moves increasingly to one-to-one marketing, direct marketing, and other methods that disintermediate producer from buyer.

So it will be the person doing the marketing who will not only want the answers, but also be more likely to be the one generating the insight. Despite their frequent beliefs, claims, and hopes, researchers have no monopoly on insight and creativity. Increasingly, the market research process will be short-circuited and the research department's function will be changed from supplier reports to a new role of facilitator of market knowledge for the whole company.

Already, in many companies, the researchers are moving from people who collect and distribute the data, to people who set up the information systems and produce the models that will allow anyone and everyone in the company access to the company's knowledge base. Of course, much or most of this knowledge was "somewhere" in the company, but it is the Internet and its status as a common denominator on the employee's desktop that is allowing companies to find the knowledge, bring it together, and make it universally available.

IRI in America has its data available on the Internet and systems to allow immediate client access today. This has increased the number of users in the client companies by tenfold, and in the case of some companies by nearly 100 times. Not only that, but users are also no longer tied to accessing data from a PC with specially installed software. Now they can access from anywhere in the world and increasingly from a variety of devices.

FROM LIBRARY TO LAPTOP

With everybody in the company having access to all MR and marketing information, the data, insight, and ultimately the knowledge, will move from the library to the individual's laptop. Still, the place to look for most market research reports is in its traditional home: the library, the bookshelf, or at best the CD-ROM. However, the format is still broadly standardized and based on cross-tabs and numbers. While we are now moving to delivery of more and more data via the Internet, we are still a little way away from putting old research into the new Internet format, let alone turning old data into knowledge. In a few years market research libraries and filing systems will become part of our real-time systems and be available via the executive's laptops. In the background, Internet software suppliers are, of course, structuring intranets so that, when these data arrive, database fusion and data-mining will integrate them into the corporate customer relationship management and information system. In doing so, there is still the big step of turning this vast amount of interconnected data into real knowledge. Most research is still burdened by tables, descriptive text, and summaries. The increased speed of distributing information will at last force our industry to "cut the cackle" and "get to the bottom line;" that is, like the rest of the world, learn to package and deliver their results in short e-mails that communicate a few facts and a call for action. Could the new model of data delivery become one based on *Alert, alerted, acted*?

We can already see that the best market researchers are formulating new roles within the companies they serve. Examples include:

- information consultant;
- information strategist.

Increasingly, they see their job as ensuring that not only are all the databases and the market information placed into a web portal structure for the company, but that the right information is going to the right individuals in the right format – and fast.

My own company is already supplying its services through portals uniquely targeted to:

- fixed market consumer goods (FMCG) companies;
- healthcare companies;
- telecom and other companies.

Moreover, as noted above, this is increasingly this week's data, refreshed every few days and pre-analyzed to discover the key "alerts" that each individual executive needs. Given this decreasing half-life for data, why would a researcher bother to ever print and file an MR report again?

FROM MENU TO À LA CARTE

Steadily, as executives work with these new concepts, they are learning new insights they can get from the company's knowledge databanks. As alert systems are installed, executives are discovering new parameters that allow them to spot changes quickly and to avoid wasting time on irrelevancies. As more executives become familiar with the concepts of knowledge management, they will set up their PCs to be more functional to their needs.

For example, the TNS Household purchase panel data we supply around the world are used to be the repository of the marketing and sales department. The intranet is now encouraging other individuals to see the importance of such data in their job. This includes:

- human resources using the sales and brand share data to more rapidly adjust their staffing and recruitment activities;
- training managers to use it to spot who needs retraining and for what;
- research and development using it to more rapidly spot changes in customer preferences.

These may not be revolutionary concepts, but the Internet is allowing executives to react to data in real-time, while giving them the capability to do and manage their own research.

We can see an increasing number of companies in which knowledge is at the center of management. Such companies are moving this knowledge to the right individual rapidly in order to extract things that matter to him or her. This is where the Internet is taking us. These decisions will be taken with incredible speed and increasing accuracy.

The best researchers will take charge of knowledge management. Having solved the information logistics needs of the client, they will return insight creation back to the statisticians, modelers, interpreters, and creative thinkers in our profession – back to where the best and brightest in our industry have always been.

Researchers will see their job as getting back to:

- modeling the causes behind changes;
- forecasting the changes in people's motivations;
- leading the company into this new knowledge-driven territory.

I am sure you will learn a great deal more from this book about these projections, many of which are now in course. Wherever the tiger that we are riding takes us, it is, and will be, an exciting era for the enthusiasts in our industry.

Tony Cowling
Executive Chairman, Talyor Nelson Sofres, PLC
London
21 December 2001

Preface

WHY THIS BOOK IS UNIQUE

Market research – or "the systematic design, collection, analysis, and reporting of data and findings relevant to a specific situation facing the company"[1] – has greatly matured as an art and science during the past 50 years. Market research is now regularly conducted by mail, on the Internet, by telephone, in the mall, in the neighborhood, and around the world to obtain insightful and reliable information about people's perceptions, attitudes, and behaviors.

The focus of this book is on market research and how it is being influenced by the Internet and related enabling technologies, both domestically and across geographic borders. The book contains a number of features that make it unique:

- A visionary discussion of the industry through the eyes of leading practitioners and thinkers in the global market research space.
- A presentation of enabling Internet technology applied across the enterprise and around the world. The impact of technology-driven competitors and their solutions in customer relationship management, new media, and business intelligence are also examined.
- Real-world descriptions and case studies that demonstrate the global potential and ability to use the Internet as the unifying infrastructure to collect data from a plurality of sources that are integrated in real-time in order to support informed decision-making and risk management.
- Perspectives gathered from leading industry executives in North America, EMEA (Europe, the Middle East, and Africa), Asia, and Latin America. Original research includes results from a quantitative study, as well as executive interviews concerning the state of global market research and the effects of the Internet.
- Integration of practical guides for deploying multi-mode online research, evaluating online research vendors, and using online analytic and reporting tools.

A BRIEF HISTORY OF MARKET RESEARCH

The simple counting of, and accounting for, people, crops, animals, and land have been with us since the existence of the earliest human civilizations. Research, in the form of census surveys, commenced in England hundreds of years ago, and in the United States, the first president suggested a formal counting of the population to equip a new government with statistics about its people. In the intervening years, the development of scientific sampling and statistical methods based on the Gaussian, or normal, distribution powered the use of relatively sophisticated techniques in the survey and research process for the purposes of predictive sampling, particularly in polling.[2]

Documented use of research to inform marketing decisions was noted as early as 1879 in the United States.[3] A modern market ("commercial") research department was born in 1911 at the Curtis Publishing Company in Philadelphia. At around the same time, as businesses developed and codified marketing techniques, applied psychologists, who were focused on market research, studied such things as the wording of survey questions.[4] A few years later, Daniel Starch pioneered measures of advertising recognition and E.K. Strong introduced recall measures and scaling to the market researcher's growing toolkit.[5] Other major groups doing surveys at this time were the governments of many Western nations.[6]

As social science and market research advanced in the twentieth century, companies such as United States Rubber and Swift & Company established research departments. Schools, such as the Harvard Graduate School of Business (1911), and associations, such as the National Association of Teachers of Advertising (1915), began to develop "bureaus" and departments of "business research." Psychologists and sociologists at the Psychological Corporation, established in 1921, began, in nationwide surveys, to ask consumers about life, work, and public issues, but also such things as what cars they drove, what coffee they drank, and what cigarettes they smoked.[7] A.C. Nielsen entered the field of research in 1922, building on the work of Percival White, the author of the first application of scientific research to commercial problems.[8]

Nothing, however, epitomized the potential of "scientific" market research more dramatically than the widely reported story of the *Literary Digest*'s 1936 presidential poll. For 20 years the magazine had successfully forecast election results. In 1936 the *Digest* sent out more than 10 million ballots to people who had subscribed either to a telephone service or who owned a car. More than 2 million ballots were returned. The result, however, was a famous fiasco. The survey predicted that the Republican candidate, Alfred M. Landon, would beat Democrat Franklin D. Roosevelt by 20 percent. As we know, Roosevelt was re-elected that year by a landslide vote.[9]

The poor showing by the 1936 *Digest* poll stemmed from a failure to realize that the poll used a biased sample of potential respondents. At that time, telephone subscribers and automobile owners tended to be more affluent and to vote Republican, so less affluent and less educated voters partial to the Democratic candidate were severely underrepresented in the poll. In that same election, three newcomers to the polling business predicted the correct outcome of the 1936 election. George Gallup, acknowledged as one of the first true "scientific pollsters" (American Institute of Public Opinion), was able to predict the 1936 election of Franklin D. Roosevelt through the use of accurate sampling techniques. In addition, The Fortune Survey, conducted by Paul Cherington and Elmo Roper, and the Crossley Poll, under the direction of Archibald Crossley, predicted this same election accurately and correctly. The accomplishments of Gallup and others in achieving many accurate predictions contributed to the success and the gradual acceptance of polling in general. All achieved results were carried out by a means of personal interviews with a small but representative sample of voters – a model for the scientific data-collection and opinion-sampling that has been the foundation of market research to the present day.[10]

Although probability sampling was intensively developed as a result of the work done at government agencies, it was slow to be adopted by marketing and advertising researchers until after the 1948 United States presidential elections, which proved exceedingly difficult to predict. Concurrently, academic survey research centers were established, at the universities of Michigan and Chicago, and systematic studies began on the principles of creating reliable and valid survey questions. Dr. Robert Merton, a sociologist at Columbia University, became a pioneer in qualitative and focus group techniques. Knowledge about interviewing techniques was reasonably advanced by the 1950s. Surveys also became common in the social sciences in this era due to government and foundation funding and support, first in the United States and then in many other Western nations.[11]

MODERN MARKET RESEARCH EMERGES

The use of surveys in business and industry began to grow in the 1960s and 1970s, and blossomed dramatically in the 1980s and 1990s. This was due, in large part, to the availability of computers and software to do surveys and analyze survey results. Both qualitative and quantitative approaches to market research have flourished, each holding different value and importance, depending on the business need or research objective.

Today, business decision-makers at all levels are aware of the value of surveys and other forms of collecting customer knowledge and intelligence to the success of their business efforts. As reliable information has become more critical to managing organizations and making decisions, market research as a process has proliferated in many ways. In fact, market research is everywhere: carried out by professional market research firms; deployed in-house by internal market research departments; and increasingly enabled as a component of the analytic, measurement, or data-mining tools found in business, marketing, and customer relationship management (CRM) software solutions.

THE INTERNET AS ENABLING TECHNOLOGY

The Internet has revolutionized the computer, commercial, and communications world. It is simultaneously a worldwide broadcasting system, a mechanism for disseminating information, and a vehicle for collaboration and interaction between individuals and their computers. Manual Castells, a professor of sociology at the University of California at Berkeley, has written a highly acclaimed trilogy of books about the changes wrought by the Internet. His view of technological revolutions succinctly captures the essence of the Internet phenomenon:

> The historical record of technological revolutions ... shows that they are all characterized by their *pervasiveness*, that is by their penetration of all domains of human activity, not an exogenous source of impact, but as the fabric in which such activity is woven. In other words, they are *process oriented*, besides inducing new products.[12]

Commercialization of the Internet involved not only the development of competitive, private network services, but also commercial products implementing Internet technology. As early as the 1980s, vendors were incorporating standard transmission protocols into their products because they saw buyers for that approach to networking. Unfortunately, they lacked both tangible information about how the technology worked and how customers planned on using this new approach.

It was not long before a new phase of commercialization emerged. Prior to this, commercial efforts comprised of vendors providing networking products, and service providers offering users connection to quite basic Internet services. The Internet has now become a pervasive service, and focused on what has become a global information infrastructure to support an explosion of commercial services. This has been tremendously accelerated by the widespread adoption of web browsers and the underlying hypertext transfer protocol (http) that it uses to access information on the World Wide Web.

The web allows users, linked throughout the world, easy access to information. Many of the latest developments in technology have been aimed at providing increasingly sophisticated integration, e-commerce, and enabling services overlaid on basic Internet data communications. The fundamental Internet protocol, although it is more than 30 years old, will most likely be with us for the next 50 years. Therefore it is safe to assume that Internet-centric processes will have a long life span.

Since 1995, the commercial Internet has developed into an infrastructure that can support the practice of global market research. The main characteristics of the Internet – ubiquity, speed, and interactivity – are key attributes of this enabling technology that are driving a revolution in the way market research will be accomplished in the near future.

THE OUTLOOK FOR MARKET RESEARCH

Market research as an industry stands at the threshold of great change. Forces are at work that are reshaping the industry, molding it into a different form capable of meeting the challenges and opportunities made possible by the Internet and enabling technologies. In particular, it is the rapid rise of business globalization *increasingly driven by technological solutions* that will demand the formation of global market research organizations equipped to serve a client's most pressing needs.

Today, enabling technologies are available to allow market researchers to fill a tremendous gap that exists in the efforts to understand customers and consumers. Failure to recognize this need, to adapt to technological innovations, and to leverage market research's methodological strengths will result in an industry that may be submerged and relegated to being a component of larger, faster, and more efficient technology-driven solutions for business intelligence, marketing automation, advertising feedback, and customer relationship management.

WHAT THIS BOOK IS ABOUT

This book begins by describing the effects caused by the Internet on global market research today. Part 1 examines where we are currently, the arrival of numerous competitors on the scene, and the role of technological change, particularly the enabling effect of the Internet. Trends that will fundamentally reshape the global market research industry are presented and discussed in the context of three identifiable change categories.

The next part of the book presents the results of original research and in-depth personal interviews with many of the thought-leaders involved in global marketing, advertising, and research. Part 2 incorporates research results from the field, designed to measure the perspectives of leading research suppliers and buyers. In addition, insights have been distilled from discussions with leading forces in the top 25 global market research firms; new media companies; CRM software and consulting integration firms; and Global 100 corporations about the challenges, issues, and opportunities they envision in the future.

Part 3 of this book systematically explores and describes the components of a world-class technology-enabled model for deploying global market research online. Chapters 6 through to 11 provide extensive coverage of how enabling technology and web-based tools can be applied in managing global research using the Internet as the supporting communication infrastructure, including building and maintaining online panels, managing research projects, and reporting of results. The reader will learn how qualitative and quantitative research procedures, from start to finish, can be accomplished online.

A practical guide and overview for deploying a global online market research system is presented in Part 4. A number of key features are depicted through step-by-step walk-throughs that capture the essence of a comprehensive, organized, and integrated system. In addition, an inclusive evaluation checklist provides a useful way to size up potential online software solutions and services.

The book concludes with two scenarios and five predictions for global market research in the year 2005.

In summary, we stand at the threshold of a new age of global market research, shaped by new technologies, globally driven business thinking, and synergistic efforts to provide for the needs of a growing global business presence. Today, the market research industry is at a crossroad driven by the convergence of client need and enabling technology. The purpose of this book is to provide a roadmap from the present to the possible. We hope you enjoy the journey!

Robert W. Monster	Raymond Pettit
Founder and CEO	President
Global Market Insite, Inc.	ERP Associates

Notes

1   Kotler, P. 1983. *Principles of Marketing*. Prentice-Hall: Englewood Cliffs, N.J.
2   McDaniel, C. & Gates, R. 2002. *Marketing Research: The Impact of the Internet*. South-Western: Cincinnati, OH.
3   McDaniel, C. & Gates, R. 2002.

4   Chris Commins, "Market Research: A Brief History," *Strategy Magazine*, June 5, 2000, Brunico Communications.

5   McDaniel, C. & Gates, R. 2000.

6   For example, in the United States, the Department of Agriculture indirectly advanced survey methodology by developing complex procedures for drawing probability samples to predict crop yields. In England, Sir Ronald Fisher perfected most of what we know as the Analysis of Variance method through work on agricultural measurements.

7   Alan S. Kay, "The Roots of Market Research," www.destination.com, 2000, Freedom Technology Media Group.

8   McDaniel, C. & Gates, R. 2000.

9   Alan S. Kay, 2000.

10 Alan S. Kay, 2000.

11 McDaniel, C. & Gates, R. 2002.

12 Castells, M. 1996. *The Information Age: Economy, Society and Culture* (pp. 30–1). Blackwell: Malden, MA.

PART 1

Trends in Global Market Research

INTRODUCTION

A number of trends, both external and internal, are converging to affect market research firms, particularly those involved in global efforts. External to the research industry, market research firms are being confronted by:

- the ubiquity of the Internet;
- the globalization of end-clients;
- the appearance of new forms of competition.

Internal to the research industry, four trends lie behind a fundamental restructuring of the initiation, management, and delivery of research services:

- the consolidation of market research providers;
- the mainstreaming of online market research;
- the emergence of global access panels;
- the deployment of enterprise software for market research.

The combined effects of these internal and external forces are reaching every level of the market research enterprise – from the boardroom to the cubicle.

Figure 1.1 Trends converging on the market research industry

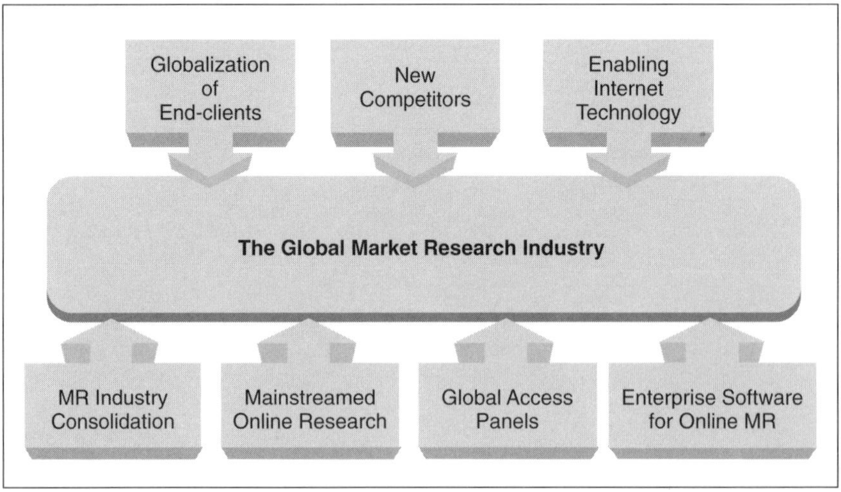

It is clear that clients today want, need, and expect marketing and advertising research solutions that incorporate the efficiency, interactivity, and speed of Internet technology. However, just moving traditional market research to an online approach to data-collection, data-delivery, and reporting is not enough. The market research industry is also being challenged to respond in many areas of contemporary business need, such as:

- customer relationship management (CRM) solutions that global companies, in particular, are striving to make work;
- Web and/or integrated audience, advertising, and marketing effectiveness measurement;
- marketing solutions capable of predicting, profiling, and segmenting at the level of "one-to-one;"
- decision support systems that streamline the process for making strategic decisions in less time, and with less risk;
- business intelligence tools that integrate online and offline consumer data for analytical and research purposes;
- diagnostic solutions for tracking customer satisfaction, customer loyalty, and return on investment (ROI) metrics;
- real-time, instantaneous reporting, and delivery of results directly to the corporate desktop;
- availability of an abundance of new kinds of raw information, including clickstream, wireless media consumption, and consumer transaction data.

A new competitive space is developing around the convergence of multiple players competing for a share of what has been termed the "customer intelligence" or "consumer insight" market. The primary objective is to better identify and understand customers in order to acquire and retain them through concerted communication, marketing, and relationship-building efforts enabled by technology.

A complex mixture of challenge and opportunity exists today for the market research industry. Market research executives are increasingly called to chart and steer a difficult course. With one hand, they must steer the firm to accommodate emerging global-level business requirements. With the other, they must plan and provide for a growing technology-oriented business presence or risk losing relevance with key clients. On top of this, they must somehow meet the appearance of savvy new technology-driven competitors trotting confidently onto market research's traditional turf. There will be casualties, both large and small.

A BLUEPRINT FOR ACTION: GLOBAL MARKET RESEARCH AND ENABLING TECHNOLOGIES MUST COME TOGETHER

A marked, but unbalanced, split exists today within the market research industry. Our interview research indicates that global market research firms' leaders and executives are quite responsive to the enormous competitive storm clouds looming very near to the industry. They are aware of and understand, in varying degrees, that technology is here to stay and that the use of enabling technology will only increase. Looking through their eyes, one can sense a realization emerging that CRM, databases, new media, and other technology-based solutions are encroaching on market researcher's historical domain. But, as the results of our practitioners' survey support, the bulk of working professionals still identify with the traditional market research model, although they do see enabling technology infusing their work in the very near future.

A dilemma arises as industry executives ponder how to take the best features of what market research has to offer and balance it with the need for continued investments in technology. CRM competitors, perhaps the most formidable force to unseat much of what could be termed "the business of market research," are generally not concerned or thinking about the value market research can bring to the table. That view is changing, however, as former market research industry executives are appearing in key roles at some CRM companies.

On the flip side, except for a few advanced thinkers, the market research industry as a whole appears to be blissfully unaware of CRM and integrating technology strategies, advances, and developments. Thus, these two substantial global industries are passing each other with nary a glance. Unfortunately, one of them is probably headed "in harm's way," and very likely the losing party will be the more personnel-intensive market research firms.

Although the authors hold a broad and integrative view of the potential and use of technology-based solutions and initiatives – based on careful study and contact with numerous firms within and without the general market research industry – we sense that we reflect the visionary views of only a very few in the market research industry at this point. It is evident that the converging forces and trends we have identified and attempted to correlate are indeed real. Work being done currently by the ESOMAR/ARF RELEAS team championed by Jim Spaeth[1] and recent presentations at ESOMAR events (see Rex Briggs' and Laurent Flores' excellent presentation,[2] a portion of which can be found in this book) support the emerging view that an all-encompassing review of the industry's direction is vital to its future.

Our research suggests, however, an even more urgent agenda. Leading global market research firms should be even more aggressive in studying and understanding the emerging competitive space, in promoting the strongest values that market research can deliver, in investing in technology-enabling initiatives, and in seeking out logical and robust partnerships and joint ventures with tech-savvy companies. Based on our discussions with leading executives, however, we sense only a narrow window of opportunity, as CRM, consulting integrators, and other tech-savvy professionals are already on the path toward improving customer experience, capturing the consumer voice, measuring increased ROI, and in creating or finding solutions that can advance their cause.

What is also clear is that the CRM industry is generally not looking to the market research industry for solutions. And the market research industry is not sure what the CRM industry is up to. So the situation that emerges is somewhat like viewing an impressionistic painting. The closer you are to it, the more difficult it is to make any sense of it. By pulling back and viewing it from a considerable distance, however, a structure, form, and essence emerge. This is what is occurring today in our industry. We may be too close to our problems, concerns, and issues to make any clear sense of them.

The Internet is about far more than web surveys. Soon, Internet-savvy CRM companies will be able to create and develop the very valuable solutions, insights, and deliverables market research firms already can offer. Traditional research firms stand challenged to redeploy their accumulated knowledge – industry, clients, and methodologies – in a way that fully leverages the enabling technologies made possible by the Internet. This is the surest path for market research firms to be not only relevant in the coming century, but at the core of a thriving business information and intelligence industry well into the future.

The three chapters that comprise Part 1 of this book begin to examine these realities: (1) the redefinition of the market research industry itself; (2) the dramatic change in business infrastructure occurring globally; and (3) the emergence of the Internet as an enabling technology for market research. Beginning with Chapter 1, we discuss the enormous pressure consolidation and competition are bringing to the market research industry as it attempts to redefine its place in the world of business.

Note

1   Jos Havermans. 2001. "RELEAS sends wake up call to industry." *Research World*, Vol. 9, No. 11. ESOMAR: Amsterdam.
2   Flores, L. & Briggs, R. 2001. *Beyond Data Gathering: Implications of CRM Systems to Market Research.* Presentation at the ESOMAR Annual Conference, Rome, September 21. ESOMAR: Amsterdam.

CHAPTER 1

The Market Research Framework is Redrawn

I n the emerging global economy, lines are being rapidly redrawn in order to allow market research firms to better serve global clients. This "mirror" strategy is based on a long-standing tendency of the market research industry to be client-driven; that is, aligning strategy to client requests and demands rather than being ahead of the market and educating the client. Market researchers still tend to follow clients rather than lead them, although this attitude is changing somewhat. Our exploration, however, revealed that a number of executive leaders in major global research organizations are attempting to bring new and innovative ideas and practices to clients' attention.

Two types of "battle lines" are being drawn. One is the evident trend toward consolidation many market research firms are pursuing. Already, substantial market research firms are either acquiring other firms to become even bigger or very large, or very specialized market research firms are being bought and incorporated into umbrella information services, marketing, advertising, and public relations conglomerates. Thus, two distinct models exist today: one, the large independent research conglomerate, and second, the "agency" approach, where the research firm is a specialized component equipped and encouraged to flexibly deliver solo or partnered research services to clients.

A second battle line is rapidly beginning to coalesce due to the emergence of competitors closely geared to the same or very similar activities that the market research industry has traditionally been engaged in: understanding consumers/customers to best serve, market, and sell to them. New entrants in this battle for "understanding the customer" are emerging from all directions: new media firms, "big five" consulting companies, and CRM software/solution providers. To wage battles on both fronts, market research firms are simultaneously extending their reach aggressively, using a variety of tactics, and seriously engaging in introspective exercises to define who and what they are and will be in the near future.

THE CONSOLIDATION OF MARKET RESEARCH PROVIDERS

A clear trend, visible to even the casual observer of the industry, is the race toward consolidation occurring today. Two definitive reports: (1) The Honomichl Report, issued by Jack Honomichl and disseminated through the American Marketing Association's Marketing News publication; and (2) an annual report completed by the European Society for Opinion and Marketing Research (ESOMAR), and published in its *Research World* journal, describes, in text and statistics, this growing phenomenon. In addition, others, such as Larry Gold of *Inside Research* and Robert Lederer of *RFL Communications* regularly report on aspects of this trend occurring in the industry. Phillip Kleinman, editor of *MR News*, is also known to add insider perspective on new and pending transactions.

A brief review of the findings shows that the top 25 largest marketing, advertising, and opinion research conglomerates produced revenues of US$8.96 billion in 2000, 56 percent of the worldwide total of around US$16 billion.[1] In addition, the top 25 in 2000 purchased 36 research firms. Honomichl notes that the acquisition "frenzy" continues into 2001 with 27 research firms acquired in the first half. Some of these acquisitions can be characterized as "huge": VNU's purchase of ACNielsen Corporation topped the billion-dollar mark. Similarly, NOP World's recent acquisition of one of the world's longest standing research firms, Roper Starch Worldwide, approached US$100 million. Clearly, the checkbooks are drawn, loaded, and ready for use.

The merger and consolidation activity of major market research firms also supports the trend toward globalization evident in business today. Figure 1.2 depicts the worldwide coverage that the top 10 global firms offer today.

Beyond the stimulus from obvious and larger overall business trends, what are the reasons for the market research industry's push to consolidate into increasingly larger global firms? Key comments from our interviews produced these points:

- **Market research firms must follow and respond to clients**: Heinrich Litzenroth, the Senior Director of the AdHoc/Custom Research Division at GfK, voiced what could be termed a traditional approach to business and business growth: "We build through acquisitions and in some cases partnerships and gradually grow services in response to client changes."[2] Others called this a "mirror approach," where market research companies

Figure 1.2 Top 10 global research organizations ranked by revenue (2000)

Organization	Parent Country	Number of Countries*
ACNielsen Corp.	US	80
IMS Health, Inc.	US	74
The Kantar Group	UK	59
Talyor Nelson Sofres Plc	UK	41
Information Resources Inc.	US	17
VNU Inc.	US	21
NFO WorldGroup Inc.	US	38
GFK Group	Germany	34
Ipsos Group SA	France	24
Westat Inc.[+]	US	1

* Countries with subsidiaries/branch offices
+Westat works exclusively with the US government

Source: Jack Honomichl, *Marketing News,* Aug. 2001

essentially "react" to changing client's needs and requests. This scenario does not preclude independent and advanced thinking or ideas, but it does move precisely as described: no major adjustments until client requests are clearly defined or they make known their needs and demands.

- **Consolidation is a natural evolution of any industry**: many executives said that consolidation is a normal pattern that occurs in maturing industries. Research supports this thinking – it is clear that consolidation has been widespread across many industries throughout the 1980s and 1990s.[3] Moreover, current thought leadership, by such firms as McKinsey and PricewaterhouseCoopers, has identified a further movement they call "business convergence." Although this exact term did not come up in our interviews, some executives we spoke to did mention the increased power of the end-customer or consumer, a key component of business convergence the consultants are promulgating.

- **The market research industry has no choice**: some felt, literally, that the whole consolidation and growth process was out of the control of the industry. Larger, umbrella organizations, such as Interpublic, VNU, Aegis, WPP, Omnicom, and so on, are intent on building conglomerates that include market research firms, including some formerly major names, in their mix of services for a variety of reasons. These huge organizations are driving consolidation to a new level. Thus, a certain sense of helplessness was evident in comments such as "market research has no choice." Some would characterize it as an acceptance of business reality. As David Jenkins of Kantar forcefully reminded us: "The market research industry is but one tiny component of the total business information industry."[4]

• **Getting bigger is sometimes viewed as the only way to compete**: many market research executives interviewed voiced the reality that the only way to compete effectively was to become larger. This, in effect, means that being competitive is based largely on a function of how many services, how broad a scope, and how much of the global needs a research firm can accommodate. The Holy Grail of a single vendor solution for a global multinational has proved more common in the accounting field, but somewhat elusive in the market research arena.

• **Consolidation is the only way to actually service the biggest clients**: reality dictates, once again, that the Global 2000 – who are the big customers for market research – desire and need broad, global services. As Simon Chadwick, CEO of NOP World, stated quite plainly: "The bottom line is that market research firms need global coverage as they increasingly are driven by client needs that are global."[5] Chadwick went on to point out the example of Nabisco, who recently went from considering 33 to three market research suppliers. Their reason? Only three were able to handle and manage their needs on a global basis.

One concern voiced a number of times by executives of major market research firms was that many firms in the middle range (US$20–80 million) of the industry may not survive in the near future. The lucky ones would be acquired. The rest may become history. Most saw the endgame as a startlingly bipolar industry: very large (US$200 million and up) global concerns doing perhaps as much as 80 percent of all business worldwide. The remainder of the business would consist of a coterie of numerous, but tiny, boutiques: cutting-edge, experimental firms that served to drive innovation, offered extremely specialized or local services, and could leverage the relationship and methodology knowledge of individuals, or groups of individuals, often affiliated in a professional service capacity. For example, Virtual Surveys, a successful UK-based market research firm, actually has but one employee. This model is further enhanced by the virtual nature of the Internet!

There are currently two major strategies to growth and a third minor one. The first remains growth through acquisition of smaller, desirable market research firms. Usually this focus is driven by a desire to either diversify or expand services globally, but also to remain an "independent" entity. Heinrich Litzenroth of Gfk voiced a concern that research firms embedded in advertising or marketing conglomerates become a "member of the family," raising serious concerns about objectivity. Thus, a strategy to grow but remain "objectively independent" was an important consideration.[6]

The second strategy is for market research firms to be merged into huge global conglomerates of communication, publishing, advertising, marketing, media, or PR firms. Proponents of this approach point out numerous advantages, not the least of which is the theoretical networking effect that occurs. Mark Berry, President of NFO Interactive, for example, cited two: "Efficiency gains across all components of business are enhanced ... intellectual capital across the organizations in the group is brought together in a variety of ways to stimulate learning, creative thinking, and shared knowledge."[7]

A third strategy, not as evident as the first two, involved smaller market research firms that wanted to become better and better at what they do. A drive to become "a recognized expert" is the primary focus and consolidation or being acquired is a by-product. Dynamic Logic, for example, is a New York City-based new media research firm that specializes in an innovative online ad-testing service. Nick Nyhan, CEO, has plainly stated that his objective is to "stay the course" and focus on building his specialization, rather than look to merge or consolidate to broaden out services.[8]

The effects, challenges, and pressures the consolidation trend brings are numerous. Elaine Riddel, CEO of NOP World Health, discussed at length the challenges of cultural integration that mergers and acquisitions bring. Making these various components understand each other and work together toward common goals is the key to success. But it is not easy, says Riddel: "For example, here at NOP World, due to our aggressive acquisition strategy, we work hard to build communication, to bring the strength of cultures together to form a new and better NOP culture. This involves team-building, uncovering and exploiting synergies that work, and time: the 18-month test, that's how long it takes to see if this is going to work."[9]

Consolidation in the market research industry, in whatever form it takes, is a prime response to the changes occurring in business today. Accompanying the strategic reasons for buying or not buying a firm is a desire to remain competitive and true to a company's core value propositions. However, the path after the acquisition is littered with challenges to "see if this is going to work." Thus, management imperatives and responsibilities are taxed in the realm of complex cultural and "people" adjustments. In the end, firms are required to call upon internal strengths that can support tasks to drive positive integration. The conclusion of *this* story – played out daily in individual companies around the world – while not reported as widely as the mergers and published trends, is really the key to successfully becoming or remaining a viable force in the industry.

THE APPEARANCE OF NEW TECHNOLOGY-DRIVEN COMPETITORS

Increasingly, the emergence of competitors equipped with new technology-driven approaches is influencing the industry. These competitors, coming from the new media and Internet, customer relationship management, and consulting industries – and even within the market research industry itself – are beginning to encroach on the activities and services traditionally associated with the market research industry.

If we look at the large picture facing businesses today, a universe of processes, procedures, and tools falling under the category of e-business and business information can be discerned. This can range from software, such as enterprise resource planning (ERP) and CRM solutions to syndicated research that companies buy off the shelf from firms such as Gartner, Forrester, and IDC. Deep in the mix can be found the activities and services of what we identify as the market research industry, a complex panoply of custom, specialized, and syndicated services, with a modicum of database, online, and technology-enabled efforts.

What sets the market research industry apart, we feel, is the ability of its "product," whether it is a report, a presentation, or raw data for further analysis, to deliver fresh insights regarding how customers/consumers think, feel, perceive, or intend to act. The objective, of course, is to enable marketing, advertising, and sales efforts to "meet the mark;" to better deliver to and serve the customers' needs, desires, and requests. What is occurring is that new competitors from the overall business information community are also, rightly or wrongly, saying the same thing (see Figure 1.3). Thus, new competition is arriving at every turn to test the mettle of the market research profession:

- **CRM providers and consulting integrators**: CRM itself, although fundamentally a technology-driven, software solution, is also an approach to serving customers to best retain, satisfy, and maintain profitable ongoing relationships. However, CRM analytic solutions – primarily advanced, automated approaches leveraging the collection of copious data on individuals – have arisen that seriously purport to inform advertising and marketing users of the CRM system about the customer: the who, when, where, and how to build profitable relationships. Consulting integrators, including the "big five," also have taken on the mantle of market research as a (sometimes minor) piece of what they offer to make CRM systems "work." The end-result is the CRM decision-maker – often the CTO, CIO, or even CEO – believes that these systems are essentially fulfilling the marketing research function as part of a "closed-loop" process. So, market research, its utility, and its function are potentially redundant.

- **Business intelligence and online analytical processing (OLAP) tools**: these tools are built off the data warehouse, data mart, or operational data store that a company erects for a variety of efficiency and effectiveness reasons. Originally a part of ERP solutions, they have migrated quite nicely to CRM software, and are sometimes embedded within them or can be purchased as a stand-alone package. What OLAP does, however, is not market research. OLAP tools are a way to get at, examine, and manipulate historical data about transactions (or in ERP solutions: financial, manufacturing, or inventory data). They do not tell a marketer or advertiser anything new about consumer attitudes, behaviors, or propensities.

- **New technology-driven audience management and measurement players**: generally, these are research solutions of value and use to marketing and advertising professionals that were built from the ground up to be technology-enabled or based. Almost without exception, they are involved with the online world of e-commerce, web traffic measurement, site statistics, online advertising and branding, and profiling or segmenting of online visitors. A number of large global market research firms, such as ACNielsen and their e-Ratings division, have entered this arena, building off successes and experience with traditional media. However, new players, most notably Jupiter Media Metrix (JMM), had built sizeable revenue streams (enough to propel JMM into the top 25 list in 2000). ACNielsen's purchase of Jupiter Media Metrix in October 2001 followed a consolidation trend that in this case secured what some fear may be a monopoly in the online audience measurement arena.

- **Pure play online firms**: this category originally included Harris Interactive and Greenfield Online, although Harris, with the recent purchase of Total Research, has modified its business approach as a result. The attempt here is to supplant, although today it is more to supplement, traditional market research techniques using extraordinarily sized "pseudo-panels" of respondents accessible online.[10] In one way, these efforts have been the "guinea pigs" for learning about the efficacy of this approach and for ways to work around various methodological deficits of the online sample universe.

- **Database and direct marketers**: although database and direct marketing companies are not strictly involved in market research, the analyses that these firms use to maximize the marketing effort are of interest and usefulness to both CRM and market research firms. In fact, prior to the Internet "revolution," shared practices and techniques were close to being perfected. Dennis Gonier, President and CEO, DMS, and Sr V-P, Member

Retention, AOL, affirms from experience that: "Prior to the Internet boom, database and direct marketers, along with savvy market researchers, were on the threshold of understanding and integrating powerful techniques, such as profiling, scoring, and segmenting of databases. What happened was that the Internet emerged overnight to catch our fancy and promise direct paths to money. So, that sort of work ground to a halt."[11] Interestingly, as the e-channel finds its natural place, the market research profession has resurrected concerns about the use of behavioral data in official industry policy statements that now focus on both direct marketing (transactional) databases and online data-collection.

- **"Big five" consultants**: while mentioned above, consultants also continue to infringe on market researcher's historical domain by incorporating forms of market research in myriad ways to their consulting arrangements. PricewaterhouseCoopers, for example, has developed a practice dedicated to data-warehousing and CRM analytics that uses aspects of the market research toolkit to enrich and amplify CRM-integration solutions.[12]
- **Syndicated research and expert analyst firms**: while primarily evident in the IT sector, certain syndicated products have become *de rigueur* for marketing departments to automatically purchase. Here, once again, the line is blurring as firms like Forrester provide essential services (such as technographics) that are remarkably close to what market research firms provide.
- **Global conglomerates**: these large umbrella organizations, mentioned in the context of other trends, also have bits and pieces within the agency stable that increasingly are "doing" market research. It is not a given that a market research firm within the larger organization will necessarily be called upon to do research. Many of the advertising, marketing, communications, and direct marketing firms have their own in-house researchers, and more frequently these are being linked up (via technology, the web, and intranets) to further extend and keep the research function in-house and away from market research "outsiders."
- **"Anyone" can do online research**: in taking advantage of the particular nature of the Internet structure, numerous services (some free) abound for people to do their "own" research. While not a significant trend, the perception of "do it yourself, easy, cheap, and fast" is still evident in a number of situations.

Space precludes a major discussion of the strengths and weaknesses of each competitor. What is evident is that the very fabric of what the market research industry is about is being challenged on multiple fronts. While it

Figure 1.3 A new competitive space

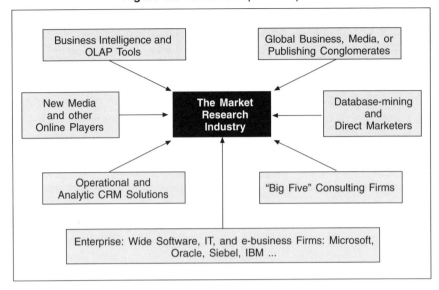

would be comforting to assume that long-lasting business and client relationships will remain permanent, common sense says that this is not a given in today's rapidly changing business scene (see Case study 1).

Case Study 1

Hearing and Understanding the Consumer Voice: Beyond the Province of the Market Research Industry?

The general failure of expensive operational CRM systems, coupled with the recent downturn in the global economy, have companies, analysts, and business gurus scrambling to capture the essence of the next "evolution" of CRM practice. Among the latest predictions is that CRM will evolve into "CVM" – or customer voice management.

Ironically what consultants and analysts are describing as the "silver bullet" for CRM fulfillment sounds suspiciously like market research. For example, according to Braun Consulting, CVM will be driven by "customer-shaping" activities, "such as understanding customer value drivers, focusing on the value contributions of different customer segments, and applying this knowledge to change the value equation for customers."

Aberdeen Consulting recently released an in-depth report on the subject, entitled "What's Next in CRM?" Among the conclusions is the revelation that, so far, customer preference has not been the focus of CRM, at least among the current field of industry competitors. However, as new vendors explore this particular niche, Aberdeen is forecasting the emergence of a whole new category in CRM, termed "customer voice management," or CVM.

Driving this improved method is the ability to track attitudes, stated preferences, and opinions – something operational CRM does not support. However, this is clearly one of market researcher's core practices. In the long run, the consulting firm concluded, successful CVM vendors will have to develop solutions or partnerships with vendors of related applications for collaborative product development. We might add that the market research industry, with its tradition and heritage in hearing and understanding the consumer, should step forward to take the lead.

Source: Erika Morphy, "After the Fall: The Future of CRM" (3 parts), November 9, 2001, CRMDaily.com.

The major issues that were identified in our interviews coalesced around the observation that the market research industry is in a precarious position today. Numerous executives voiced an understanding of the CRM movement, what the weaknesses were, and what the strengths of market research are. Some even identified tentative movements to enter the CRM fray or explore partnerships to test this. Simon Chadwick, CEO of NOP World, had this compelling commentary: "We have the opportunity to advise, based on our experience with the human customer and consumer, to build brand equity, to take data analytics to its proper level – as an intermediary that filters access to and makes sense of CRM data, even effectively delivering it directly to the corporate desktop in a form that can actually be used at multiple levels for decision-making. The big question is: can we rise to the challenge as an industry?"[13]

The potential threat is that we, as an industry, will neglect to answer the challenge put forth by Chadwick. In that case, the market research industry could well be relegated to a tiny corner of the business information industry. Yet, the fact remains that the solution is within our reach to understand, explore, and act upon: nearly all of the market research executives interviewed mentioned initiatives and investments in technology as a key step in remaining competitive and relevant to global clients.

As with any new business technology, fundamental business principles are often not changed, but business processes modified to some extent. Hal Varian, in "Information Rules," forcefully reminds us, "Technology changes.

Economic laws do not."[14] Many have blamed the dot com crash and resulting death of the "new economy" on a rabid belief that fundamental business principles had been radically altered. The market research industry, to a lesser extent, suffered some of this fallout in exaggerated claims and questionable business models that may have damaged the initial opportunity for online research to take hold. However, few are abandoning the online research channel. Larry Gold, Editor and Publisher of *Inside Research*, projects that, "all Top 25 firms will be providing online research within the next few years."[15] Indeed, key business principles specifically related to Web-based technology are gaining credence and acceptance.[16] Both clients and suppliers of market research are dealing with the subtle changes in a variety of ways.

Internet-based technology has affected key business principles for market research firms in the following ways:[17]

- **Competitive advantages**: these are more difficult to attain and even more difficult to sustain. Competitors with resources and capabilities to react can swiftly replicate solutions driven by emerging Internet technologies.
- **Strategic planning**: emerging changes in the economy will require market research companies to shift from purely strategic planning to holistic dynamic planning.
- **Relationship strategies**: in order to be competitive, market research companies cannot be completely isolated, but must consider forming a constellation of relationships. A company's ability to bring together the players needed and to form relationships will give it a distinct advantage.
- **Focus on key value drivers**: smart market research companies will focus Internet technology initiatives along their core competencies and key value delivery drivers.

In the fast-moving world of technology, change occurs quickly. Often, however, it is the human element that drags down full utilization of the opportunities inherent in this rapidly evolving environment. Thus, while competitors can replicate technical solutions more easily, it is in the human implementation (change processes, education and training, and people management) where advantages live or die. Ironically, the many, failed CRM implementations reported in the business press to date have universally been blamed on the failure to recognize the human element and need to adjust to change that is required. This first hurdle is significant. Then, companies must adjust to new ideas in planning and partnership. As listed above and highlighted in numerous real-world examples (the Time Warner/AOL merger being the supreme example of this century), the ability to build a multifaceted organization, capable of evolving into a business that can serve the needs of customers is vital. The actual strategy – whether merger, acquisition, alliance, or partnership – appears to be less important than the ability to form this "constellation" of relationships and remain competitive.

As we have seen, the market research industry is part and parcel of this whole trend and is living and, in some cases, suffering through it. Perhaps the most compelling take-away from the list of technology-driven principles is that market research firms, particularly those in, or planning to be in, the global arena, must align Internet technology initiatives to support their core competencies and key value drivers. Many executives, when asked what their clients most valued from them, said it was the delivery of actionable, insightful recommendations and informed suggestions that could help the client make decisions. For example, in a joint interview with Caroline Eichmann of ibm.com and Giorgio Licastro of Eurisko, both reinforced the long-term viability of the full-service model of bundling data-collection, methodology expertise, and analytic mastery.[18]

So, most agree that, yes, the Internet is affecting their business; however, the core value propositions will not be abandoned. Instead, a concerted effort to determine and utilize the online research channel as an integrated piece of what the firm can offer and has successfully delivered to clients and customers is the key.

However, one final observation remains. In the case of online enabling technology, such a massive opportunity to improve the infrastructure of research delivery, deployment, collection, and management exists, but we cannot overlook the forest for the trees. No serious company operating today is ignoring the online channel. The market research industry and related academic community can, and should, continue the debate on the methodological, technical, and procedural challenges or issues the online channel holds. However, the ability to enable technology and attendant web-based approaches to bring efficiency, management, and integration of an extremely wide variety of data that will be key to the future success of market research firms should not be overlooked. Compelling challenges in the form of new competitors and client needs will demand an industry that is at the forefront of turning enabling technology to best competitive advantage in the race to understand the consumer, deliver high value services, and remain a viable force.

Notes

1   Honomichl, J. 2001. "2001 Report on the Global Research Industry." *Marketing News,* August 13. American Marketing Association: Chicago, IL.

2   Heinrich Litzenroth, GfK Group, personal interview, August 2001.

3   PricewaterhouseCoopers   Research.   2001.   *Executive   Perspectives.*
    www.pwcglobal.com.
4   David Jenkins, Kantar Group, personal interview, July 2001.
5   Simon Chadwick, NOP World, personal interview, July 2001.
6   Heinrich Litzenroth, GfK Group, personal interview, August 2001.
7   Mark Berry, NFO Interactive, personal interview, July 2001.
8   Nick Nyhan, Dynamic Logic, personal interview, September 2001.
9   Elaine Riddel, NOP World, personal interview, July, 2001.
10 Göritz, A.S., Reinhold, N. & Batinic, B. 2000. *Marketforschung mit Online Panels:
    State of the Art.* Planung & Analyse, 3, 62–7.
11 Dennis Gonier, AOL, personal interview, October, 2001.
12 Bill Schlegel, MarketTools, personal interview, September 2001.
13 Simon Chadwick, NOP World, personal interview, July, 2001.
14 Shapiro, C. & Varian, H. 1999. *Information Rules: A Strategic Guide to the Network
    Economy.* Boston, MA: HSB Press.
15 Gold, L. 2001. "Industry News." *Research World, Vol. 9, #11.* ESOMAR:
    Amsterdam.
16 Ware, G., Hartman, A. & Roldan, M. 1998. *The Search for Digital Excellence.*
    McGraw-Hill: New York, NY.
17 Ware, G., Hartman & Roldan 1998.
18 Caroline Eichmann, ibm.com & Giorgio Licastro, Eurisko; personal interview,
    September 2001.

CHAPTER 2

The Internet as a Unifying Force

The Internet has become a pervasive force in business and has enabled the globalization of commerce and industry to flourish. It has made itself felt by its ubiquity and its impact on process – or the way we do things.[1] The "enabling" effect of Internet technology has opened the door for market research firms to vastly improve efficiency. However, the most visible response to the globalization of end-clients has been for major market research firms to pursue similar globalization schemes: consolidations, alliances, and partnership strategies. Less visible have been efforts to optimize the closed-loop, real-time process unifying research suppliers, consumers, and decision-makers. The trends driving this process are the:

- ubiquity of the Internet and its enabling power;
- continuing globalization of end-clients;
- emergence of global access panels for market research.

The three strands woven together in this chapter depict a fundamental shift that is strongly impacting the market research industry. In today's business and commercial world, consumers and customers are inexorably linked around the globe with the companies who are providing an expanding array of goods and services. Not only do manufacturers, retailers, and service firms need to be connected with consumers, they need to be able to continually reach and understand them. This, in turn, drives market researchers to offer research processes and techniques that can perform on a global basis, and also afford global comparisons. Thus, global access panels become increasingly important as an essential research tool. These panels, in effect, are linked – via the expertise, mediation, and management skill market research firms provide – to the end-client to provide a ready source of reliable and robust marketing measures and consumer insights. The "glue" holding this whole apparatus together is the Internet, which becomes the infrastructure and conduit that allows this powerful linkage to occur.

THE UBIQUITY OF THE INTERNET AND ITS ENABLING POWER

The effects of the Internet on global market research are both obvious and subtle. New and creative uses of technology seem to appear overnight and at increasing speed. In fact, the speed of new developments often masks the subtle, fundamental changes the Internet brings. For example, the 2000–2001 "bust" and the subsequent slow-down in the world economy provide strong evidence that a deep interconnectedness exists between the information technology (IT) industry and the rest of the economy. Manuel Castells, a noted University of California, Berkeley sociologist, has traced the diffusion paths of other technologies over the past century and has noted a subtle evolutionary process of integration into work practices that occurs. The authors of the Pew Internet and American Life Project term the Internet a diffusing technology that has become a significant part of everyday life and work.[2]

Without a doubt, the swift rise of the e-channel as a viable commercial force has embedded it inextricably with other traditional marketing channels; thus, as Gian Fulgoni, CEO and Founder of Comscore Networks, states: "A disturbance in it results in a ripple effect felt throughout the economy."[3] This can be seen visibly in the outbreak of computer viruses. It could also be seen in the September 11, 2001 attack on the World Trade Center in New York, which disrupted numerous major data networks that pass through lower Manhattan.

Case Study 2
A Short History of the Internet

One of the concerns that lingered after the end of World War II and into the 1950s and 1960s in the United States was the threat of nuclear war. Thus, the concept of a non-centralized communications network designed to survive (for example, nuclear war) and function when other parts of the network were destroyed emerged in the 1960s as a project of the Department of Defense of the United States. What we now know as the Internet began life as the Advanced Research Projects Agency Network (ARPANet), created by the Pentagon's Advanced Research Projects Agency. Established in 1969, the ARPANet project's main objective was to develop a secure and survivable communications network for organizations engaged in defense-related research.

The first implementation of the Net occurred in 1969, hooking the University of California at Los Angeles to the Stanford Research Institute. Over the next five years, many of the procedures still in use on today's Internet were developed. These included e-mail and the @ symbol in addresses (1971), remote accessing of computers through telnet (1972), multi-person chat sessions (1973), and the downloading of files through "file transport protocols," known as ftp (1973). In order to extend the network globally, a standard protocol was developed. IP, or Internet Protocol, technology defined how electronic messages were "packetized," addressed, and sent over the network. This standard protocol was invented in 1977 and was called TCP/IP (Transmission Control Protocol/Internet Protocol). TCP/IP allowed users to link various branches of other complex networks directly to the ARPANet, which soon was called the Internet.

In 1985, the National Science Foundation (NSF) began a program to establish Internet access across the United States. A communications backbone was developed, called the NSFNET, which extended the burgeoning network to all educational facilities, academic researchers, government agencies, and international research organizations. Soon thereafter, ARPANet was shut down by the Defense Communications Agency due to limited funding and support from the military.

By the 1990s the Internet experienced explosive growth and led to its emergence as a commercial force. By mid-1994, and the dawn of the commercial use of the Internet, an estimated 2 million computers, in more than 100 countries, serving some 23 million users, were connected. By the end of 2001, the current Internet universe was estimated to be around 175–180 million users, with consumer e-commerce and e-retail sales in the billions of dollars.

The Internet as a pervasive force affects four basic dimensions of our lives:

1. **Structural**: that is, the technology itself and how it supports and enables change in our lives.
2. **Economic**: how the Internet has impacted and enabled new businesses and markets to emerge.
3. **Social and cultural**: the emergence of a new form of communication, creative, media, and information-sharing mechanism via the web.
4. **Political and regulatory**: the debate about Internet taxes, online currency, and security and privacy issues.

Figure 2.1 Trends converging on the market research industry

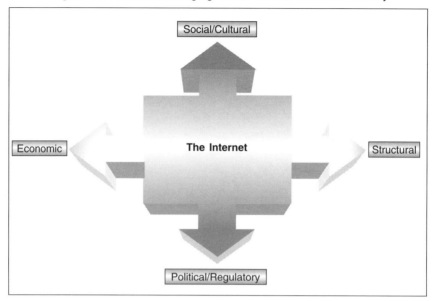

The Structural Frame

The concepts behind the Internet and web-based systems are fairly well understood today. The Internet is basically a "network of networks" that consists of a number of components that work together to promote fast, interactive, and efficient communication (literally movement of data in the form of electronic bits). Beginning with hardware, such things as routers and remote access concentrators link and enable communication between servers. Connectivity to servers is provided by web hosts, while software, in the form of browsers, enables individual computer access to the network. Access services (or Internet service providers), such as AOL, are a "doorway" to the Internet.

Once online, destinations for the web-user can be content providers, who create and serve up content for online visitors, portals, or sites that gather or provide access to existing content that is purposefully compiled (for example, Yahoo!), and search services that allow desired locations to be found quickly. In addition, online communities provide opportunities for feedback, chat, or posting – usually organized around a common interest. Finally, different flavors of online commerce (both business-to-business and business-to-consumer) and auctions, such as eBay,[4] have become very popular.

For the marketer, advertiser, and business, the Internet opens extraordinary doors to connect, communicate, and deliver goods, information, or services to customers anywhere in the world. The structural frame of the Internet is exemplified by virtual offices, networked corporations, and wireless communication.

The Economic Frame

The Internet allows for the first time a worldwide communication system that is instantaneous, interactive, and ubiquitous. The interactive and communication aspects of the Internet have allowed for creative use of the medium to advertise and sell, and to collect original data in a variety of ways.

For market researchers, the ability to collect, store, and manipulate data at numerous places along the system has resulted in an unprecedented wealth of detailed information on the behavior of individuals while they are online. The result is that when looking strictly at the online channel, it is entirely possible to track individuals' behavior closely and accurately. The inherent promise here is that marketing, advertising, and even product or service delivery, can be individualized. While the original thrust of the dot com boom, as embodied in the concept of a "new economy" totally driven by the Internet channel, has not materialized, it is still the case that the e-channel has arrived to take its place among the other marketing and sales channels that exist today. The subtle effect that is nonetheless evident is that in the economic sense, the Internet has raised the bar on the amount, type, and quality of data that marketers and advertisers can use to derive campaigns, services, and products; build brands; and assess the effectiveness of their efforts.

For the marketer, advertiser, and business, the Internet supports new and creative ways to capture people's attention, to build global brands, and to gather detailed data on transactions and shopping behavior. The economic frame is exemplified by such activities as shopping at online retail stores, participating in online auctions, responding to online advertisements, and purchasing through secure online payment channels.

The Social and Cultural Frame

The Internet has the potential to modify and reshape the basic foundation of the social and cultural frame. The Internet affords web-based, virtual places for community, dialogue, and interest groups to develop that are not strictly commercial. The social impact of information-sharing and dissemination, media images and brands, entertainment and the arts delivered online, and e-mail communications are all evident in this sphere. While traditional business practices, sales, advertising, and marketing channels have always had social and cultural elements embedded in them, the Internet brings the dissemination of online media and information-sharing to new heights. As the Internet, TV, telephone, and radio begin to merge into a single system, the underlying cultural assumptions and deep, hidden cultural bedrock of individual societies will be affected.

For the marketer, advertiser, and business manager the Internet breaks down individual cultural assumptions and promotes the development of new means for interaction between individuals. The social and cultural frame is exemplified by chat rooms, e-mail, online games, Napster, eBay, newsgroups, ICQ, Internet Telephony, and a variety of other means for information sharing.

The Political/Regulatory Frame

The political/regulatory frame revolves around the laws and regulations considered necessary to control and direct the activities engendered by the Internet medium for the best use of society. All laws and regulations grow from a felt need to codify practices that will protect and ensure the rights and survival of the society and the individual. The Internet space is no different. As the web becomes even more embedded in the economic, social, and cultural frames of people's lives, the more likely it is that political and regulatory issues will be raised, addressed, and resolved. The issue at hand is that laws and regulations move at a very slow pace, whereas the Internet is a rapidly evolving medium. One of the only ways to "stop" the Internet long enough to exercise the control that laws and regulations bring is to target serious accusations that garner public attention and alarm. Thus, Doubleclick's infamous problem with online privacy was undoubtedly made worse by the need to make a big issue to highlight the seriousness of an "offense" that could actually slow the company down enough to address it. One has only to glance at the news to pick out the issues: online security, privacy, copyright infringement, and to a lesser extent, taxation and currency. These topics are sufficiently serious to put the brakes on the Internet medium long enough for laws and regulations to catch up and deal with them.

For the marketer, advertiser, and business manager, the Internet stimulates issues and topics of a lawful nature that must be addressed and overcome so that free-flowing commercial activity and economic growth can continue. The challenges within this frame are further exemplified by the failure of any online currency system other than credit cards, which are adequate to the task, but also lack the option of maintaining anonymity. Despite the slow adoption of CyberCash, some online payment methods have achieved cross-border adoption, notably PayPal. The political/regulatory frame is exemplified in the following areas: how to protect Internet privacy and ensure security, e-commerce taxation, and the ongoing discussion and debate over an online currency system.

21st Century Marketing and Technology

When we focus the lens of our exploration more finely on how the Internet has affected marketing and marketing research, two primary features stand out. The first revolves around information. The Internet facilitates the following:

- the **creation** and recreation of information of all types: text, pictures, sound, symbols, artistic, video, and so on;
- the rapid **transmission** of information between and across this network;
- the instantaneous **replication** of information;
- the **customization** of information both purposefully and willingly.

These characteristics are evident in some form or another in nearly every marketing communication, marketing research effort, and commercial action that occurs online.

Second, the Internet, and particularly web-based technology, is enabling. Why do we say that the Internet is an "enabling technology?" The Internet brings an infrastructure and flexibility to the practice of marketing, selling, and research that has the potential to reshape the global market research industry. These characteristics of the Internet, taken together, are the building blocks driving a revolution in the way that market research will be accomplished in the near future. The seven characteristics inherent in web-based technology include:

1. **Interactivity**: the Internet is interactive, it enables effortless communication and intense collaboration. It drives such things as online entertainment, user engagement in communities of interest, while also allowing the precise capture of customer behavior and knowledge.
2. **Immediacy**: information (in the broadest sense) can be shared, collected, integrated, and distributed quickly.
3. **Connectivity**: the Internet is fast; information flows swiftly between computers located great distances from each other. This creates a unique and useful space for community, commerce, and collaboration.
4. **Interoperability**: from a marketing and advertising perspective, direct and seamless communication with customers and consumers is achieved.
5. **Media richness**: as Internet bandwidth grows, all forms of communication are enabled and enhanced. Thus, online users can leverage this situation to customize products and services, for example, in a way not possible in the offline world.
6. **Ease of use**: utilizing the online space translates into empowerment for the user. As Jim McDowell, Vice-President of Marketing for BMW of North America, shared: "Our customers are fast-track achievers. Their time is precious. They are looking for the 24/7 availability and convenience that the online channel affords."[5]

7. **Internet technology is facilitative**: it enables the retrieval, storage, and processing of all information. Ultimately, it broadens and extends the capacity to apply intelligence, both human and machine, to extract value from the Internet data space.

The Pervasiveness of the Internet Affects All Trends to Some Degree

What is the cumulative effect of the Internet on marketing today? If we look at such aspects as product, market size, competitive tools, and key success measures we would say that the impact of the web, including the ability to utilize e-mail, is profound. Products and services can be developed and sold anywhere in the world. Market sizes can range from global to an individual. Competitive tools revolve around the ease of use, speed, and interactivity of the medium, but also include new branding and customization possibilities. Finally, key success measures extend to not only market share or brand equity, but also more discrete and precise brand awareness, customer lifetime value, and return on investment (ROI) metrics.

The pervasive effect of the Internet touches nearly all aspects of our lives and is linked and woven between the frames that define many of our activities. Thus, it is not surprising that the Internet has become a force that underlies many of the challenges, opportunities, and issues facing the market research industry today. The remaining trends we will discuss are all affected in some way by the enabling effect of Internet technology and its pervasiveness in business, commerce, and industry.

The Global End-client

A second major trend affecting the market research industry is **globalization**. Globalization is no longer an option but a strategic necessity for all but the most specialized or localized firms. Global mergers and acquisitions, international profit centers, worldwide marketing, global branding, and cross-border business models have put increasing demands on the market research profession to provide new and effective solutions. This globalization of the client sector has challenged the market research industry to follow a path already well worn by other professional services providers.

In the past 20 years the pace of globalization has been accelerated by the growth of the Internet infrastructure and the rise of networked communications. Economic boundaries are blurring. The rules are changing. Increasingly, firms are expanding globally as opportunities abound to:

- reach more customers;
- increase economies of scale;

- adjust, control, shorten, or lengthen product life-cycles;
- make use of less restrictive sourcing policies;
- redeploy work to markets with lower operating costs;
- take advantage of worldwide consumer demand for greater varieties of products at lower prices.

To realize these potential opportunities, however, requires infrastructure for communication, management, marketing, and research that enables global coverage, but also allows local involvement. While it is tempting to rely on software and technology to achieve this, for the market research industry the road to gathering *customer knowledge* and delivering insights to clients is still a combined effort of tried and true market research techniques and creative use of new tools and processes. The key to useful and actionable research lies in combining the proper use of appropriate data-collection methods and thoughtful, high-quality analytics. Instead of embracing online-only research without question, clients should seek out research suppliers with the ability to blend technology with traditional research, including the ability to mix modes of research; for example, telephone recruitment coupled with self-administered online interviewing.

Without question, the Internet has opened the door to entirely new ways to gather, analyze, and deliver data. Researchers can now offer research using a platform designed and based on online technologies. In the vast majority of cases, particularly in the emerging CRM analytics space, this serves to enrich the overall market research process, shorten delivery times, and add needed value and business intelligence at key customer touch points along the market research value chain. For the global end-client, this is nothing less than the proverbial success formula known as "faster, cheaper, better."

Why go global?

Students of globalization will know the familiar arguments for why companies go global. For the non-initiated, there are five main reasons why the need to become global has ceased to be an option in most industries and has become a requirement for most medium-sized to large corporations.

1 **Pursuit of growth**: in the quest for continued growth, many companies have no choice but to look abroad. Developed country markets are increasingly saturated within mature product and service sectors. Thus, growth requires a continuous effort to locate fresh opportunities in emerging markets, as well as rapidly expanding the global distribution of new products. As a result, the term "global market share" is increasingly present in modern business vocabulary.

2 **Cost reduction**: a company with global presence will have an advantage over a company that cannot leverage the relatively large differences in labor costs between world economies. Consider that a Canadian call center with access to multilingual staff can reasonably cover prime time (5–9 p.m.) in all of Western Europe, the United States and Canada from a single global location. Utilization of fixed assets is significantly enhanced vis-à-vis a domestically focused competitor. Similar models exist in data processing; for example, the use of Indian or Eastern European data-processing centers to serve the United States and Western Europe.

3 **Market responsiveness**: when a company expands to other countries, it must often adapt at least some features of its products and/or processes to the local environment. This adaptation requires generating local knowledge. Some of this research may in turn be irrelevant outside the local market. Local market understanding on a global scale provides the basis for making targeted changes that can add value. For example, most consumer product companies will confirm that Japanese consumers have highly discriminating tastes and can be exceedingly articulate in communicating their unmet needs to researchers who ask using anonymous methods such as self-administered interviews (online or offline).

4 **Globalization of customers**: the phrase "globalization of customers" can actually refer to both "clients" (who are worldwide businesses) as well as "customers": people who are internationally mobile, such as executives served by credit card companies or serviced by hotels around the world. Three main reasons dictate why a company may seek to serve individual global customers. First, customers may strongly prefer worldwide consistency and coordination in products and services. Second, for the sake of efficiency, customers may favor dealing with a smaller number of partners or service providers on a regular basis. Third, allowing a customer to deal with different suppliers in other countries brings the risk that the customer may choose that competitor at home as well.

5 **Competitive response**: if competitors start to globalize, they can use their global presence to advantage against domestically focused firms. Initially, global companies can leverage this advantage by capturing new markets while pursuing efficiencies on a global scale. Soon, they can profit from knowledge exchange and development, and begin to provide a coordinated source of supply to global customers. Finally, they can use multi-market presence to subsidize and wage a focused attack in a competitor's home market. As a result, in today's world, it is dangerous to be a late-mover to a global strategy.[6]

Globalization, characterized by mega-mergers and foreign direct investment, is an accelerating trend. Even the current worldwide economic slow-down will not reverse this inclination (see Figure 2.2):

Figure 2.2 Foreign direct investment (since 1982)

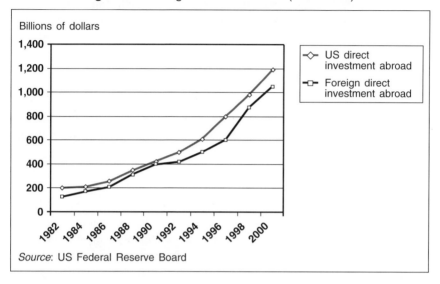

Source: US Federal Reserve Board

Within the market research industry, the 2001 Honomichl Report confirmed that the pace of global consolidation continues unabated, with approximately 60 percent of the industry represented by the top 25 firms based on revenues.[7] It is quite apparent that the global consolidation trend that has played out in other professional service sectors – notably accounting, advertising, consulting and legal services – is also taking place in market research. This global consolidation is occurring to some degree as a sub-component of the large media conglomerates such as VNU, WPP, IPG, and Omnicon. It is also happening among the more focused business intelligence firms such as IMS, TNS, IPSOS, GfK, ORC, and Intage, nearly all of whom are global in their view.

Global Market Research Equips Itself

Global market research traditionally has required considerable specialized attention. Methodology, questionnaire design, the length of time for respondents to complete surveys, the definition of target groups, and the provision of adequate geographic coverage each present unique problems and characteristics that must be addressed when approaching a global effort.[8] Using traditional market research techniques – phone, mail, and personal interview – this has been an expensive, difficult, and often unwieldy process. But with the rise of web-based enabling technologies built on a global Internet framework, an integrated, efficient, and effective worldwide system is achievable. Thus, while not minimizing the inherent challenges in producing high-quality global research results, an integrated web-based data management and collection approach can minimize the difficulties associated with key logistical aspects of gaining the proper data.

Challenges to Globalizing Market Research

A key driver of globalization is undeniably the pervasiveness of the Internet as an affordable means of communicating and gathering data over long distances. This has also created the framework for using the Internet, and particularly web-based enabling technologies, to do, among other things, surveys among consumers across the world.

Following on the heels of the acceptance of online surveying in highly industrialized countries, there has been an increasing trend toward managing the entire research process using the Internet as the enabling platform. Although the difficulties of carrying out cross-border surveys are well known to the market research profession, a compelling need still exists for an integrated centrally managed system for planning projects of this nature, executing them, and delivering results to the global client.

In fact, the first steps toward meeting this need are emerging in the form of web-enabled systems that use Internet technologies to construct an integrated global market research infrastructure. Companies are moving rapidly to develop these enabling systems for use by market research companies. These solutions allow the development, deployment, collection, analysis, and dissemination of a broad spectrum of research across the enterprise and around the world.

Solutions for Globalizing Market Research

Given the demand on market research to deliver a single real-time view of global research data, the fundamental model for data aggregation must change. The historical model is inadequate for the demands of the end-client who must make global decisions in less time than ever before. Consider the following comparison:

Table 2.1 Comparison of traditional and Net-centric market research work processes

	Traditional Model	New Model
Geographic focus	Local/single country	Multi-country
Primary sample source	Ad hoc recruited	Sourced from profiled panels
Project management	Offline tools	Online using web-based
Data-collection	Batch process	Real-time process
Data delivery	Batch data files and paper	Online
Reporting frequency	Upon request/upon completion of fieldwork	Continuous/real-time
Data-archiving	Non-mineable flat files	Scalable SQL/OLAP databases

The difference in work processes can be illustrated in the following comparison:

- **Traditional model**: the traditional model is based on batch collection often collating data from a variety of data formats, and perhaps using a variety of different data-collection vendors. The results are long lead-times and higher risk of errors due to batch data-processing. Data delivery is managed entirely in batch, usually in non-electronic forms such as printed or faxed tabulation reports. Analysis beyond the basics requires the additional step of a skilled quantitative researcher and possibly another loop back to the graphics department to turn results and recommendations into a report.
- **Updated Net-centric model**: the updated model leverages Internet-centric technologies while working with traditional web survey engines. Data are centrally collected into scalable relational databases that can be managed in real-time using web-based tools, and which can be accessed securely by clients using online portals. Data access/reports can be continuous, filtered through analytic experts, or published online and delivered directly to the client's desktop. Thus, elements of insight-generating collaboration and interaction exist here that are not possible in the traditional model.

The Issue of Pace and Timing for Global Expansion

Having commenced the journey of globalization, a market research company must still address the issue in building a global presence: how fast to expand globally? Research firms that aim to operate in the $100 million ranks have very little choice other than to pursue globalization.

Rapid global expansion, however, can emaciate managerial, organizational, and financial resources. The risk of this rapid execution is that the company may be unable to profit from the global presence it too hastily created.

Figure 2.3 Traditional global data collection process

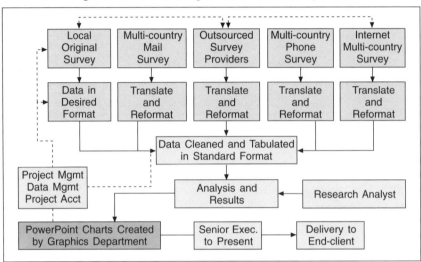

Figure 2.4 Internet-enabled global data-collection process

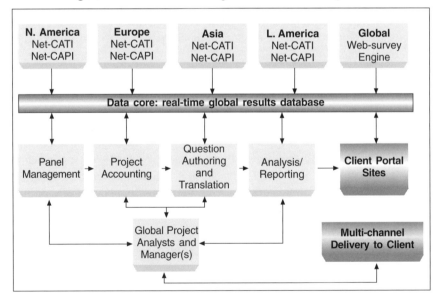

Taking into account the pros and cons, determining an appropriate pace for global expansion is dependent on the following conditions:

- **When it is easy for competitors to replicate your recipe for success**: the rapid globalization of companies like Microsoft reflects their determination to prevent replication and/or pirating of their product concepts in worldwide markets. Market research, as a sophisticated and involved service, by necessity will take longer to expand, since complex cultural, local, and business factors need to be carefully thought through and well planned.
- **When economies of scale are extremely important**: compelling economies of scale often give the early and rapid mover massive advantages while handicapping the slower ones for long periods of time. Here, the global acquisition strategy of many of the top 25 market research players makes sense. However, if any sort of global integration of research products and services is planned, it may be more prudent to wait and watch rather than blindly rushing in first.
- **When management's capacity to manage (or learn how to manage) global operations is high**: aside from the ability to manage global operations, the speed of globalization also depends on the company's ability to leverage its experience from one market to another. The faster a firm can duplicate its knowledge about market entry and market development from one country to another, the lower the risk of spreading managerial and organizational capacity too thinly. Thoughtful market research firms with global ambitions take great pains to build programs and processes that cultivate and train the managers and professionals necessary for successful and coherent expansion.

Becoming global is never exclusively the result of a grand blueprint. At the same time, it would be naive to view it as little more than a sequence of incremental, opportunistic, and indiscriminate steps. The wisest approach for a complex service industry is one of directed opportunism: an approach that supports opportunity and flexibility within a broad and systematic framework. ACNielsen's recent acquisition of Jupiter Media Metrix is a textbook example of moving at the right time to essentially corner the market on web traffic measurement around the world. Bill Pulver, President of ACNielsen's E-Ratings, who will head the much larger and expansive group, now faces the challenges of integrating and reshaping the organization into worldwide fighting shape.

Market research firms with global ambitions face formidable challenges. The globalization of business is redefining what a client wants and expects from their efforts. Challenges notwithstanding, at a fundamental level, global clients want:

- to be able to compare results between countries using consistent methods and assumptions;
- to achieve enterprise-wide understanding of geographically dispersed consumers;
- to develop work processes that enable faster global innovation.

To meet the speed, efficiency, and factors needed for global success, web-based systems are vital. Online research, and particularly the development of global access panels for research, can greatly enhance a firm's ability to learn and leverage its marketing intelligence and consumer insights across borders and around the world.

THE EMERGENCE OF GLOBAL ACCESS PANELS

For delivering in-depth, focused results and delivering insightful information to clients, *panels* of consumers, executives, or businesses have long been a staple of market research. Panels afford the market research firm a powerful tool for tapping into the attitudes, perceptions, and feelings of people on a variety of issues important to clients. Market research firms have built substantial expertise in developing and maintaining many kinds of panels that reliably can support the requirements, both practical and statistical, to answer important business questions.

Gathering information from panels today is still dependent on traditional telephone, mail, or in-person techniques; however, online panels, representative of the population of interest, are rapidly being built and deployed.[9] These panels are not limited to local or national panels, either. Increasingly, online global access panels are being developed and used. The demand for global access panels is driven by the same issues, benefits, and key principles driving consideration of online research in general, and traditional panels in particular. These factors include:

- **Customer (end-client) demand for speed and efficiency**: demand for high-speed data-collection and dissemination is becoming a reality. Panel-based research can be predictably completed in days, and sometimes hours.
- **Research cost-effectiveness and time efficiency**: the mantra appears to be "save time, save money, capture hard-to-reach targets, and leverage information quickly."
- **Superior way to reach respondents/customers**: online panels are equipped to gather market input quickly through an online database readily available for research, as well as to allow interaction with customers in the easy and convenient way they prefer.
- **Enhanced survey experience**: respondents "see" questions and answers,

unlike the telephone, thus quality and integrity of surveys is preserved; pictures, sounds, and video can be incorporated into surveys; questionnaires can incorporate complex logic.

- **Enhanced corporate image**: some[10] feel that an unsung perk of online panels is the enhanced corporate image that is projected by using advanced interactive technology.
- **Privacy accommodations**: the Safe Harbor Act. This agreement allows the uninterrupted flow of personal information from the European Union to the United States, based on firmly established Fair Information Principles (see Case study 3).

Many and varied uses of online panels are beginning to emerge in the market research industry. As an example, Vinodh Swaminathan, Principal Consultant for Technology, CRM, and Marketing at ABT Associates, said: "For certain types of projects, such as feature-testing in the design phase of autos, or to do marketing tests in the pharmaceutical area that require a quick response or have a short feedback cycle, an online panel and online research channel makes the most sense."[11]

Online panels require following many of the fundamental principles used in building traditional panels in order to be effective instruments for research. The basics, well known to market researchers, entail:

- determining the size of the panel (so as not to over-survey, and to be able to access at the appropriate depth and coverage required by the client's business need);
- determining the desired target characteristics of panel;
- developing a panel website or entry portal;
- promoting the panel to populate it;
- conducting a sign-up survey to gather important demographic, psychographic, and cognographic information;
- offering an incentives program;
- honoring privacy and personal preferences.

Case Study 3
Background on the Safe Harbor Agreement

The European Commission issued the Directive on Data Protection to protect the privacy of European Union (EU) citizens. The directive states that for those countries outside the EU whose privacy practices are not deemed "adequate," transfers of personal information from Europe to those countries would be stopped. To ensure that personal data flows to the

United States are not interrupted, the US Department of Commerce (under the Clinton administration) and the European Commission developed a "safe harbor" framework that allows US organizations to satisfy the European Directive's requirements.

US organizations that decide to participate in the Safe Harbor Agreement must comply with its requirements and publicly declare that they do so by signing up with the US Department of Commerce. Although the decision by US organizations to participate is voluntary, organizations that transfer data from the EU to the United States and do not sign up by July 1 may be subject to enforcement actions in Europe.

The Fair Information Principles

The Safe Harbor Agreement inherently involves a dedication to the Fair Information Principles of Notice, Choice, Access, Security, and Enforcement. It also adds the compliance principles of onward transfer and data integrity. For Global Market Insite (GMI) and other companies to comply with the Safe Harbor implementation of the Fair Information Principles, the following criteria must be met:

- **Notice**: involves informing online and offline users, in a clear and conspicuous manner, about the purpose(s) for which information about them is collected and used; the choice mechanism(s) available for limiting use and transfer; the types of third parties to which data are transferred; and how to contact the organization for inquiries or complaints.
- **Choice**: involves offering users a clear and conspicuous opt-out mechanism for any secondary uses of data and for disclosures to third parties. Opt-in choice must be available for sensitive information such as medical or health conditions, race or ethnic origins, political opinions, or religious or philosophical beliefs.
- **Access**: involves ensuring that individuals can obtain reasonable access to personal information about them held by the organization. With some exceptions, organizations must provide consumers with the ability to correct, amend, or delete information that is inaccurate.
- **Security**: ensures that an organization takes reasonable precautions to protect personal information from loss, misuse, unauthorized access, unauthorized disclosure, unauthorized alteration, and unauthorized destruction. This involves technologies such as encryption, access controls, and physical security of the data.
- **Enforcement**: this mechanism requires the existence of a readily available and affordable independent recourse for individuals, as well

as consequences for the organization when the principles are not followed.

- **Onward transfer**: dictates that an organization disclosing personal data to a third party must adhere to the Notice and Choice principles, unless the third party is acting as an agent of the company; and either the third party specifies, by way of a contract, that it provides at least the same level of protection as is required by the relevant principles, or the third party subscribes to the Safe Harbor Principles or is subject to the EU directive or another adequacy finding by the EU.
- **Data integrity**: personal information collected must be relevant to the purposes stated in the notice, and that reasonable steps should be taken to ensure that the data are reliable, accurate, complete, and current.

The US Department of Commerce is responsible for implementing the Safe Harbor Agreement for companies based in the United States.

Global panel management systems are a fairly new development that utilizes the power of enabling and Internet technology to automate and streamline the management of global panels. Fully equipped to scale to the size necessary to handle multiple panels, languages, incentives, and data, these systems are a key component of an enterprise approach to market research not possible in the past. They support and enable the logistics of global market research by assuming many of the onerous tasks required to make global research projects work. Thus, they free up and open up more time for the important skills of analysis, insight generation, and reporting to coalesce as key deliverables that global clients demand.

The representativeness of online panels continues to be a key issue. In some areas, an online choice is clearly superior. Our interviews indicated that IT professionals, business-to-business, and business/executive management panels were obviously served best by the online framework. For consumer online panels, continual recruitment is required to refine and grow the panel over time. On a global scale, some countries or regions will be "better" represented online than others. Even at this level, some, such as Pete Comley, CEO of Virtual Surveys, raise the question of "who" is signing up? Current estimates say one in 1,000 sign up for online panels. Another less-talked-about issue is "professional respondents."[12] Whether this is a valid concern has not yet been determined.

Current techniques for online panel recruitment make use of the full range of methods to access potential respondents. These include:

- random digit dial (RDD) calling and invitation to best secure a theoretically statistically representative sample of a population;
- banner advertisements using web partners;
- direct mail invitation;
- "viral" (word of mouth) methods;
- print advertisements;
- general publicity announcements.

A nagging question about online panels, which is relevant to our discussion of building and developing global access panels, is the cost of such efforts. While benefits of online panels are often not disputed – usually it is methodological concerns driven from within the research community that emerge – the true costs are not yet amenable to precise analysis. Are online panels "money losers?" Are the acquisition costs too high to justify them? If attrition rates are so high – McKinsey estimates a 50 percent turnover per annum – can online panels effectively be maintained?

Our interviews indicated that to some extent building and maintaining online panels is prohibitively expensive. Gian Fulgoni, however, conveyed this opinion: "It is to the point now where the benefits of the technology far outweigh the disadvantages."[13] That is, enabling technology can be the key to efficiently and effectively building, maintaining, and managing what is rapidly becoming a critical resource of the global market research industry. Interestingly, many of the problems associated with global panels, such as global coverage, management of survey projects and data-collection/ analysis, and administering survey instruments – aspects of global panels that are accomplished with great difficulty and expense on the traditional side – are reconciled by the establishment of online global access panels. These panels are and can be built to the same stringent standards using the expertise that market researchers have developed over the years in professional practice. The difference is in the ease and integration of the global panel management process afforded by enabling Internet technologies. In addition, costs can be better controlled, analyzed, and adjusted with the global online-enabled system. Finally, the key benefit of using a panel is that panelists can be deeply profiled allowing precise targeting of eligible respondents.

Enabling technology greatly enhances the feasibility and management of global panels. While online representativeness is growing worldwide, a viable alternative that integrates mixed mode panels, managed online, has emerged. It is possible today to build and manage online, telephone, mail, and face-to-face panels in one integrated system. While the method of data-collection obviously differs, the use of a centralized database can ensure that the results go into a common place for ease of management, analysis, and reporting. Internet-enabled CATI systems afford interviewers the means to populate, in real-time, the same databases that are capturing results from self-administered web interviews. Thus, a CATI interviewer can work from anywhere and record results directly into the database that has collected the online survey results. Similarly, the online system can be used for both online quantitative and online qualitative collection of panel results.

Thought leaders, such as Swaminathan at ABT Associates, argue that although there may be credibility concerns based on the composition of some well-known online panels available today – and a bias toward panel members being "techno-savvy" – this will iron out in the future. Without a doubt, most executives we interviewed agreed that *global access panels* will be a valuable resource for the market research industry. Consensus has been reached and confirmed through interviews and research that the following types of market research are best deployed online to access panels, either national or global:

- rapid and consistent gathering of customer profiles and purchasing attitudes, perceptions, and feelings;
- tests of advertising – both online and offline ads (print or video streamed and played as part of an online survey) – using a variety of standard statistical group tests and measures;
- marketing tests, particularly when quick feedback cycles are required;
- ratings of customer satisfaction for key or target segments;
- rating or evaluating new product offerings that don't require physical product manipulation, although, even here, 3-D rendering can allow a respondent to "manipulate" an object in space. For example, BMW's website allows site visitors to build a virtual "BMW," thus engaging them in the BMW brand and, in essence, educating themselves about the car's features, appearance, and attractiveness.

Much has been discussed in the market research community about the avoidance of infringing on the "individual" in research efforts. In fact, one criticism of direct marketing – that the market research industry has dwelt on considerably in large part to be distinct and clear about privacy concerns – is that direct marketing gets too close to the "personal identifying information" of the people it targets. Market research is built on an "aggregate" approach, with a long scientific history and foundation, and is extremely sensitive to the privacy issue on at least two levels: scientifically and personally.

As CRM analytics continue to drive the integration of direct marketing, behavioral, transactional, third-party, and primary market research data, a privacy backlash could erupt. Opt-in/opt-out privacy laws, already strict in

Figure 2.5 Online global access panel

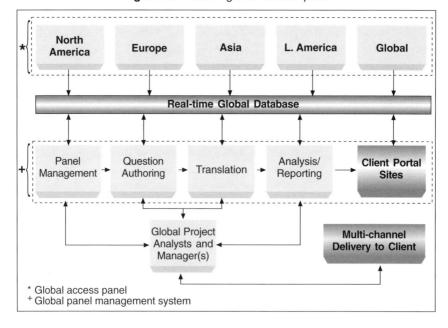

Europe, may preclude both CRM and direct marketers from assuming or leveraging a global analytical position. Online global access panels may become the only way to do proper customer research, segmentation, and profiling procedures. Thus, the global access panel managed and deployed using an integrated and efficient online system, may provide the solution that global clients will need to be successful.

Notes

1   Coltman, T., Devinney, T.M., Latukefu, A. & Midgeley, D.F. 2000. "E-Business: Revolution, Evolution, or Hype." Australian Research Council: Sydney, AU.

2   Howard, P.E.N., Rainie, L. & Jones, S. 2001. "Days and Nights on the Internet: The Impact of a Diffusing Technology." *American Behavioral Scientist*, Vol. 45, Summer 2001.

3   Gian Fulgoni, Comscore Networks, personal interview, July 2001.

4   Kessler, S.H. 2001. "Consumer Services and the Internet." Standard & Poors Industry Surveys: New York, NY.

5   James McDowell, BMW NA, personal interview, September 2001.

6   Govindarajan, V. & Gupta, A. 2001. *The Quest for Global Dominance: Transforming Global Presence into Global Competitive Advantage.* Jossey-Bass: San Francisco, CA.

7   Jack Honomichl 2001. "2001 Report on the Global Research Industry." *Marketing News*, August 13. American Marketing Association: Chicago, IL.

8   Gunilla Broadbent, BAI Global, personal interview, October 2001.
9   Göritz, A.S., Reinhold, N. & Batinic, B. 2000. *Marketforschung mit Online Panels: State of the Art*. Planung & Analyse, 3, 62–7.
10   MacElroy, W. 2000. "International Growth of Web Survey Activity." *Quirk's Market Research Review*, Article no. 0629, www.quirks.com.
11   Vinodh Swaminathan, ABT Associates, personal interview, September 2001.
12   Pete Comley 2001. "Internet Panels – Are They Another Dot.con?" http://www.virtualsurveys.com/news/mar2001news/int_pan.htm.Virtual Surveys, Ltd: Hampshire, UK.
13   Gian Fulgoni, Comscore Networks, personal interview, July 2001.

CHAPTER 3

Net-centric Market Research Emerges

A s external forces are buffeting the market research industry, they are also generating internal changes within organizations in response to these demands. These are trends that are affecting the internal workings of market research organizations as they seek to equip themselves to come to grips with technology changes, global demands, and new competition. They are forcing a degree of introspection and exploration unprecedented in the industry and great consequences are riding on the outcomes of these decisions.

Business practices and processes that utilize the Internet and enabling technology are being mainstreamed into the market research industry in a number of ways:

- to manage the flow and collection of data within the modern research organization;
- to deploy research and collect and manage the results for clients using the online channel;
- to enable the ability to create and offer multi-mode research (a variety of types of online research), as well as multi-method research (a mixture of online and offline techniques);
- to enrich and extend CRM analytics;
- to deliver the results of (raw) data-collection directly to clients via their web browser;
- to deliver completed reports directly to the client's desktop;
- to develop and deliver a partial or complete "business information" package (that includes original, syndicated, and other forms of business intelligence and knowledge needed to reach decisions) directly to the desktop; that is, Enterprise (or Client) Knowledge Portals.

Remembering that the market research function is but "one small part of the total business information requirement,"[1] market research firms are stepping back and carefully weighing the investment needed to build a suitable IT infrastructure that will best enable them to deliver their highest quality skills and expertise to clients. For most, the decision is clear: in order to keep up with client need and development, the investment is an absolute necessity.

Two major trends drive this third aspect of change affecting the market research industry today: (1) the mainstreaming of online research techniques, processes, and methods; and (2) the deployment of enterprise-strength software to collect market research data, manage market research processes and methods, and deliver research data and results to the end-client.

THE MAINSTREAMING OF ONLINE RESEARCH AND THE DELIVERY OF RESULTS

While doing research online is not the major activity of most of the top 25 global market research firms, it is evident in all of them. The appearance of online research efforts and plans to develop this channel by all major providers is an indication that online research is taking its proper place within the industry's delivery mix. Another indicator, pointed out by Jack Honomichl in his latest report on the global market research industry[2] is that two firms, Harris Interactive and Jupiter Media Metrix, both made the Honomichl top 25 in 2000 based on total yearly revenues. The existence of two companies, one focused exclusively on researching the Internet channel and measuring Internet audiences, and the other, a kind of "traditional" market research firm deployed online, offers evidence that the online research business has reached the mainstream of the industry. In fact, the recent acquisition of Jupiter Media Metrix by ACNielsen brings the Internet channel squarely into the mainstream and on a par with all other forms of media research.

While the short history of online research already includes a range of techniques from "do-it yourself" to highly automated approaches, the real value – as judged by the debate and discussion going on within market research firms today – clearly lies in an integrated and managed approach. Descriptions of the fragmented variety of online research offerings, mostly in the form of "fast, easy, cheap" online survey services, have given way to thoughtful exploration of ways to manage, collect, store, integrate, and analyze data collected online. As Gian Fulgoni, CEO of Comscore Networks, recently declared: "There are too many things of value that can be accomplished online for it to be ignored any longer."[3]

The mainstreaming of online market research is the inevitable outgrowth of an attempt to deal with multiple external forces, but also to optimize the best that market research has to offer through the use of enabling technology. Careful and measured adoption of online research techniques, *where appropriate for the client and the business problem*, characterize the actions of most of today's top 25 global firms. While response to client request is still a factor in the decision to use online research, more often than not, market research firms are willing to offer advice and counsel on the best use of the techniques, where they make the most sense, and which ones can drive an added-value delivery to the solution. This underlying theme of engaging in "thought leadership" as a key high-value deliverable from market research firms has been voiced by executives at ABT Associates, ORC, NOP World, Gfk, Intage, and many others. Understanding the forces that are driving the need for a mainstreamed online research system is vital for market researchers.

Four forces in the business world have combined to drive home the importance and viability of investing in building a web-based, technology-enabled research and delivery channel (see Figure 3.1).

Figure 3.1 Four forces driving the adoption of a web-based technology-enabled Internet research channel

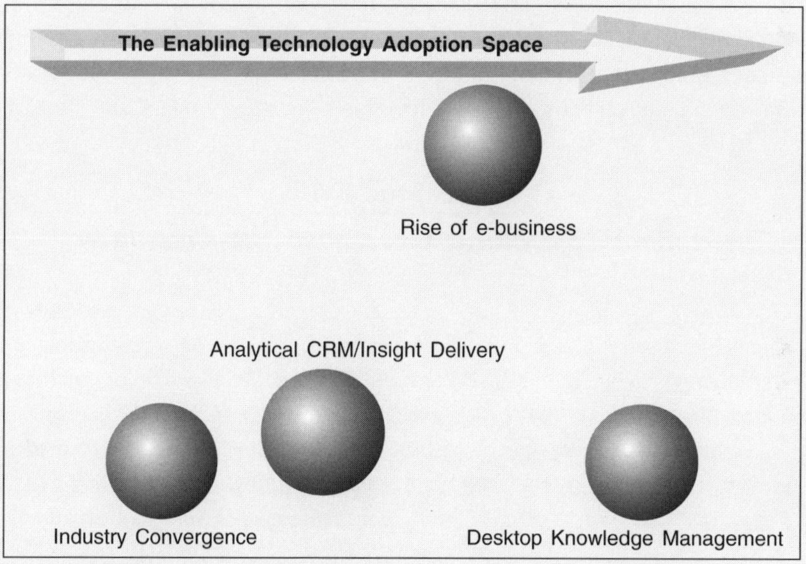

Source: Adapted from PriceWaterhouseCoopers Research

Beyond Consolidation – Convergence

Consolidation was the watchword of the 1980s and early 1990s, and is just now being played out seriously in the market research industry. In some industries, however, consolidation has given way to convergence, which is the dissolution of boundaries between consumers and businesses, and within businesses themselves. The establishment of direct links to customers has accelerated research client's needs for timely deployment and reporting of results via a mainstreamed infrastructure. In addition, the ability to flexibly collaborate and interact in the search for insight and actionable information becomes essential.

Customers drive convergence, empowered by technology. Today, the Internet brings sales and communication channels into many households around the world. This not only enables businesses to reach far more customers than ever before, it also allows customers to express their views, wants, and needs immediately through e-mail communications and more formal customer satisfaction or loyalty surveys. Their participation is driving and accelerating convergence by directly influencing businesses to respond with better products and services and new offerings.

The Internet offers great opportunity to companies that can effectively understand and respond to customers. The web's expanded channels enables sellers to reach buyers and gain their attention – but it also lets buyers search with ease for the products and services they want at prices they are willing to pay. Therefore, successful companies are seizing the opportunity to know and understand the customer. Although this appears to be a simple idea, very few companies have yet to fully exploit this opportunity (see Case study 4).

Case Study 4
BuzzBack: Speaking Directly to the Consumer

One innovative firm that is leveraging the power of convergence for key clients, such as Coca Cola, Stonyfield Farms, and Kraft, is BuzzBack. Profiled recently in a *BusinessWeek* article titled "Friendly Spies on the Web" (July 9, 2001), BuzzBack exemplifies this new approach.

Carolyn Fitzgerald, CEO, and a veteran of the CPG industry and qualitative research arena, reports on her company – living proof that clients still hold direct communication with consumers in very high esteem:

Increasing pressure to innovate and differentiate in a global marketplace demands new kinds of tools – tools that connect companies quickly and efficiently with their customers and consumers. Consumers are the ultimate source of insights leading to ideas and innovation. Naturally the Internet offers one solution for faster access to them. However, not all online research is faster and cheaper. Many online tools are clunky and don't offer the speed, depth, and breadth required for effective decision-making.

BuzzBack is an innovative way to effectively balance quantitative data with in-depth qualitative insights. Harnessing the Internet as a powerful communications tool, BuzzBack bridges two traditionally separate research methodologies: rich qualitative insights that augment quantitative results. Further, respondents provide compelling, personal stories that reveal deeper issues. And the most relevant and articulate respondents are identified and selected for in-depth follow-up sessions.

Within hours after the QuickBuzz session begins, consumer insights begin to unfold. From the first phase, BuzzBack re-contacts the most relevant and articulate participants for in-depth follow-up and probing. Clients can react to learnings unveiled in the QuickBuzz session, plus develop more questions to gain additional understanding about topics or targets. And unlike other online methods, BuzzBack provides a personal glimpse of the consumer/customer target that adds personality and brings insights to life.

For example, in addition to a purchase intent score, clients hear why *Mary, Homemaker, 21, Asian from CA* would use a new product idea several times a week – or why *Joanna, Medical Professional, 35, African-American from IL* thinks your new packaging is not eye-catching. We never reveal an individual's identity or violate personal privacy. In fact, TRUSTe, the leading Internet privacy advocate, endorses BuzzBack.

Fast and Immediate Reporting

As soon as a BuzzBack session begins, clients can log-in from their desktops to view results unfolding immediately in a protected environment. A complete BuzzBack study, including final report, can be fielded and completed in as little as five or six days. The final report summarizes key quantitative findings with charts and tables, plus clusters, and distills ideas and themes. This unique combination of quantitative data and in-depth insights provides more actionable results to streamline and guide decision-making and product development.

Follow-up Probing For Greater Depth

To probe even further into respondents' personal experiences, BuzzBack follow-up sessions can be arranged that may include live chats, a consumer-driven online message board, telephone interviews or even in-person interviews. All of which enable clients to continue the dialogue with BuzzBack participants for deeper understanding. Our research team works with clients to develop the most appropriate approach.

Clearly, a unique convergence of research and communication directly with respondents/consumers is providing a compelling breadth and depth of information that today's global corporate clients find valuable.

Source: Carolyn Fitzgerald, BuzzBack, personal interview, August 2001.

The Rise of E-business

E-business is reshaping the business world by:

- redefining business processes and functions;
- influencing conventional concepts and rules about strategic alliances, outsourcing, competition, industry specialization, and customer relationships;
- creating detailed information about customers, enabling businesses to anticipate and satisfy customer needs with improved precision.

How does this affect the market researcher? The migration to an e-business model is occurring in stages. Some companies have already moved well beyond the first stage – establishing an Internet presence or channel – and they are now actively integrating and connecting the buying and selling processes of their websites using ERP and CRM systems. It is here that a technology-enabled online research system becomes a key component for the market research professional to deliver the insights and information that can answer client needs and questions.

In the next stage, web capabilities are actively integrated throughout the value chain. Here, customers and suppliers work together to build online value chains that improve service and reduce costs. In the business-to-business environment, market research's online presence is rapidly becoming mandatory. The overwhelming cost efficiencies and speed of information delivery and dissemination require the research provider to be "up to speed," or be left in the dust.

In the near future, businesses will converge electronically to combine their expertise and provide services. They will use their current e-business capabilities to transform their strategies, organizations, processes, and systems so that they can best meet the needs of their customers. At this point, a robust, flexible, and multi-varied online infrastructure for market research becomes a requirement. The ability to both collaborate with others within and without the organization, and to interact with information to glean insight will become a key factor for nearly all people in the corporation.

Case Study 5
Siebel Systems: Every Corporate Knowledge Worker is an Analyst

Dan Lackner, V-P and GM of Marketing and Analytic Products at Siebel Systems, the market leader in CRM software, is an experienced veteran from the market research industry. Dan spent a number of years at Information Resources, Inc. (IRI) during their formative and innovative early years, under Gian Fulgoni, now CEO of Comscore.

Lackner's mission at Siebel is clear: to lead efforts that break down the data silos that plague a corporation's ability to gain a complete view of its customers. Siebel has identified the fact that CRM analytic solutions only comprise a minute portion of CRM installations. Yet, the emerging reality is that nearly every corporate employee will be a knowledge worker, and the vast proportion of them will be doing analytic work. Thus, Lackner's quest is to unearth, uncover, create, or obtain the most compelling solutions to advance analytics that are available today. This has led Siebel, among other things, to the purchase of a company named NQuire that will become a key component of the Siebel Analytic strategy.

Lackner has also revisited Gian Fulgoni at Comscore to discuss efforts to incorporate the Comscore network into the Siebel effort. Realizing that CRM analytic data is primarily behavioral in nature, Lackner knows that the Comscore panel can provide the context for analytic results, as well as provide answers that can guide marketing programs.

Under Lackner's leadership, Siebel is leveraging the robust experience and value that market research can offer and combining it with leading-edge, technology-driven components that will advance the Siebel vision.

Source: Dan Lackner, Siebel Systems, personal interview, October 2001.

The Importance of Knowledge Management

Business is about products and services, and about generating a reasonable profit while delivering those products and services to customers. But this definition overlooks the importance that knowledge plays, and says nothing about the fact that knowledge management is rapidly becoming a highly valued business asset.

The global economy is gradually shifting away from traditional assets toward intellectual assets. It is estimated that intellectual resources account for about 75 percent of the world's corporate market value. Executives are only now learning to identify the types of knowledge that, taken together, represent a positive asset and an organizational priority.

Improved technology has enabled the creation of pathways of communication among people within and without an organization. For knowledge to be shared quickly, thoroughly, and productively a connection between all levels of the organization is needed. This has also revealed a potential for market research firms to establish themselves as facilitators and filterers of key informed insights, recommendations, and guidance through a technology-enabled link.

Today, many enterprises are implementing formal knowledge management (KM) initiatives, such as enterprise portals and intranets for sharing knowledge internally, and extranets for sharing knowledge directly with clients and other external stakeholders. Yet, marshalling knowledge resources across an enterprise is no easy task. A complex mix of focus, planning, development, technology, and – especially – education, is required. The market research industry can contribute powerfully to this process while exploiting established networks and new technology channels to enhance their position as advisors to corporate knowledge management initiatives, as well as to traditional marketing and sales clients.

Market research's role must be linked within this system to specific business levels, issues, or strategies. As more corporate employees become knowledge workers and move to developing analytic skills, the value of market research can be transmitted via training and implementation protocols designed to enhance collaboration and interaction. Only then can ongoing programs be sustained in which full value is created, harvested, shared, and continually refined and refreshed via the market research professional's contributions.

Analytical CRM and Insight Delivery

As companies amass customer data, they seek technologies that allow them to use this data to, among other things, uncover additional revenue opportunities and interpret consumer spending patterns. Analytical CRM and the delivery of results to the corporate desktop promise sophisticated and up-to-date customer information and analysis to guide these objectives.

Due to the presence of CRM technologies across the business landscape, an increasing amount of information about the customer has accumulated, such as account information, transaction history, service requests, satisfaction surveys, and channel purchase preference. Companies believe that by exploiting this mass of data there may be a significant opportunity to increase revenues and enhance customer satisfaction. Further, companies that can effectively manage and analyze this data should be able to develop important and actionable insights into customer behavior. What is missing, however, is the leadership a market research firm can provide in turning data into insight into profit.

The evolution of CRM analytics[4]

Online analytical processing (OLAP) tools first appeared in the early 1990s. These systems analyzed data from a variety of sources within organizations, and generally did not focus on customer data. OLAP applications, found primarily in ERP software solutions, were most commonly used for financial/sales reporting and analysis, budgeting, and planning. Most of these applications required aggregated data housed in data warehouses or data marts in order to facilitate reasonable and timely access. Thus, they were limited to the analysis of "past" or historical data. This limitation frustrated marketers since their real need resided in answering seemingly simple predictive questions, such as: "Which customer is likely to buy our new product?"

Also, in the 1990s a new class of heavy-duty data-mining applications was rapidly evolving. Like OLAP, these tools were designed to analyze data from a variety of data sources. In addition, they were explicitly designed to handle the enormous volume of data stored within operational and transactional databases. These tools were initially touted for their ability to answer predictive questions and guide and deliver complex classification, segmentation, and profiling schemes. Unfortunately, the new data-mining tools required sophisticated and complex statistical and analytical skills, and fairly expensive analysts to deliver the detailed insights that corporate users were looking for. And often the analysts, though skilled in the data-mining function, could not translate results into marketing terms.

Today, a new form of analytic technology has emerged that attempts to blend the best characteristics of OLAP with the insight afforded by data-mining tools: Analytical CRM. The development and delivery of easy-to-use, insight-generating mechanisms to understand customers and enable improved relationships has become a key objective of most CRM vendors. While approaches vary greatly in their potential, feasibility, and usefulness, the CRM industry is convinced about Analytical CRM's benefits: the ability to place, in the hands of those closest to the customer, tools to generate actionable information that will guide and inform an improved understanding of customers and how best to serve them; thus improving customer relationships, and driving increased satisfaction and, ultimately, profitability.

The (Near) Future: Real-time Analytics and Reporting

As companies continue exploration and development of Analytical CRM solutions, with counsel and guidance from market research professionals, and reap incremental benefits, the next step will be away from periodic reporting and analysis to executing real-time analysis. The next wave of Analytical CRM is already being discussed and is based on real-time analysis. This has the potential to allow companies to intelligently and expeditiously interact with their customers across all channels.

The ability for Analytic CRM applications to drive process improvements in operational systems is substantial. As a result, the mainstreaming of online market research is a vital component for exploiting and mediating:

- multichannel data integration: call center, sales force, wireless, and the web;
- delivery of market researcher's core values: insight, recommendations, and counsel;
- collaboration and interaction between researcher and client;
- an optimized environment for delivering directly to the corporate desktop;
- tight synchronization between analysis, insight, and execution;
- the ability for companies to be equipped to react and refine in real-time, via a robust data-delivery system filtered and monitored by the market research partner.

Coupled closely with the mainstreaming effect is the trend toward deploying the widest variety of research techniques possible using an online infrastructure and system. Together these two trends combine to impact and extend the potential for global market research organizations to truly deliver in step with the clients they seek to serve.

THE DEPLOYMENT OF ENTERPRISE SOFTWARE FOR MARKET RESEARCH

As consolidation and globalization continue for both client and supplier, it will be imperative to have software capable of performing across the enterprise. Building on the natural advantages the Internet network holds, the customization of research, online data-collection and storage, the widespread communication of results and data, and the flexibility of open source solutions, can combine to create an integrated research network we refer to as: *Enterprise Software for Market Research*. This system delivers across the entire work process: project management, respondent management, data-collection, analysis, and reporting. These combine to allow the full range of market research processes to be completed anywhere at anytime.

The online enterprise market research system gives the market research supplier the ability to manage and deliver the complete continuum of research. All aspects of research coverage can be achieved in an integrated manner: from qualitative research to branding studies, to online surveys, to varying types and degrees of access panels, to data-mining, and business intelligence exploration. This full range of services can be managed, deployed, and utilized in one integrated system.

Business organizations of all shapes and sizes are rapidly embracing Internet technology for many reasons. At the very least, the explosion of web use on both the consumer and business level has promoted new ways to advertise, market, sell, and communicate. One of the primary by-products of this has been the generation of massive amounts of data – and the need to collect, explore, and make sense of this information.

While it is tempting to rely on software and technology shortcuts to handle this overload of information, for the market research industry the road to gathering customer knowledge and delivering insights to clients is still a combined effort of tried and true market research techniques and creative use of new tools and processes. The key to useful and actionable research still lies in the proper use of appropriate data-collection methods and thoughtful, high-quality analytics. Instead of embracing online research without question or in a fragmented way, clients benefit most from market researcher's control and integration of new technology and traditional research.

However, the Internet and related ways of collecting data have also opened the door to new information-gathering, analytic, and delivery possibilities. Researchers can now offer customized research approaches based on data-mining techniques and/or the integration of market research, CRM analytics, and database technology. In the vast majority of cases, especially in the CRM space, this serves to enrich the overall market research process and add needed value and business intelligence at key customer touch points.

E-research and Business

E-research is a practice concerned with all approaches to market research, both qualitative and quantitative. From focus groups to standard research instruments to advanced data-mining approaches, techniques are utilized to make sense of market research, business data, and information. The key component, however, is that the management, deployment, collection, and access of data is integrated and carried out using enabling Internet technologies.

Business is enhanced by an integrated e-research approach, since not only is the full range of research available to attack problems and assist in informing solutions, but lower cost and efficiency are built into the system. By utilizing the e-research approach, enabling technology opens the doorway to an integrated system of data-collection and delivery not possible in the past. However, and this is key, none of the value-added analysis and insightful delivery of recommendations and guidance need be sacrificed. Quite the opposite is true. E-research lends itself particularly well to being embedded into intimate client-delivery platforms. Thus, in combination with original custom research results, new features, such as searches, libraries, and related syndicated reports, can be delivered directly to the client desktop. The range of information can include raw data for additional, ad hoc desktop analysis to fully completed and polished reports, as well as tracking, both syndicated and proprietary, that complement the whole package.

The Five Components of e-research[5]

The five components of e-research support a thorough approach to the informed business intelligence needs of clients. They trace the following research path:

- website, marketing, and advertising assessment protocols;
- positioning, strategy, and branding studies;
- online market research surveys;
- online advisory, business, or consumer access panels;
- business intelligence tools, and data- and web-mining.

Website and related assessment protocols inform *about* the sales and marketing channels and the impact/perception of advertising/marketing campaigns. They sharpen business focus and assist in fine-tuning both online and offline messages. In addition, they can begin to address branding and positioning issues in the total marketplace the consumer inhabits. Without a doubt, this step is one the most important to business success, but unfortunately one easily overlooked or passed by in the rush to "get to market" or "expand globally."

Positioning, strategy, and branding studies follow closely from assessments. These studies identify and explore competitor's strengths and weaknesses, help businesses devise and test creative strategies, and examine the power, perception, and awareness that branding can bring to the mix.

Online market research surveys are deployed to allow businesses to get to know customers: a key step in CRM. With online surveys, just as with

Figure 3.2 The five components of e-research

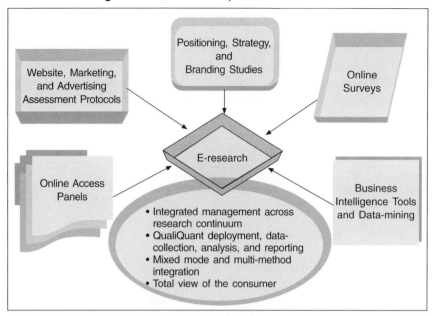

traditional market research surveys, actionable business information can be gathered toward improving service by better meeting the needs of customers. Custom surveys form the basis for best understanding people's perceptions, attitudes, feelings, and intent.

Online advisory, business, or consumer access panels are key ways to regularly and effectively track critical business issues/trends, customer perceptions, and changes in attitude and satisfaction toward product, service, or industry. In addition, the nature of online panels and the online environment affords quick collection and assembly of research data. As the consumer privacy issue rages, and more and more restrictions to data-collection appear, access panels, particularly of a global nature, may be the only legitimate way to approach and reach people for marketing and advertising research purposes. Enabling technology is critical here as well, since the better integrated and managed this key resource, the more likely it will yield valuable results that can be delivered to clients.

Business intelligence (BI) and data-/web-mining techniques are coming of age quickly. These highly sophisticated tools allow exploration of warehoused data in real-time, segmenting and profiling of customers (including integration with corporate or third-party databases), and the construction of predictive models. Increasingly, these tools are incorporated in CRM or eCRM software solutions. However, they currently represent only a small portion of assessment and are often the most complicated solutions available. In addition, attempts to "template" them for ease of use is a sure-fire recipe for disaster. While not typically thought of as tools within the market researcher's toolbox, the enterprise market research system does bring the capability to use BI and data-/web-mining tools within the market researcher's domain. Precisely since analytical CRM is notably weak at the moment and CRM firms generally do not carry the sort of expertise needed to carry out a high-quality market research function, this is a key area for competitive consideration that market research firms are currently exploring.

Website and Marketing/Advertising Assessment

Many web efforts suffer from a lack of attention to the user. Recent research has shown that most sites fail basic reliability and consistency tests. Web usability and navigability, although deemed important by experts in web design, is often neglected. Finally, too many e-business websites suffer from a "lack of identity." Advertising and marketing efforts are making valiant attempts to build online brand and awareness. However, without a thoughtful study and understanding of basic business fundamentals, no "idea" – no matter how compelling – can flourish for long.

The first stage of "need" in building business insight often resides in the exploration of basic business issues through the use of focus groups. Additional sessions can range from the truly scientific (for example, the tracking and measurement of eye movements) to "softer" assessments, such as group critiques and explorations of a variety of website designs, advertising creative, and positioning issues. This is often followed by website design that is assessed and studied through usability and navigability tests.

The insights, results, and observations made in focus groups, both online and offline provide the grist for the next step, which is to creatively and deeply explore positioning, strategy, and branding issues; that is, to begin to enter the realm of customer knowledge: the who, why, what, where, and when of your business.

Positioning, Strategy, and Branding Studies

A variety of methods are available to construct the legs on which a business stands. All require an inordinate sense of the competitive set, practical experience within an industry or market, and extreme creativity to enable the development of new and exciting ideas. All *customer knowledge* begins by understanding what your brand says to people, how and where it is said, who sees it, and why it makes them respond. All advertising should be an outgrowth of how research and analysis help you determine position and strategy within your brand's effect.

Positioning studies make use of competitive market analysis, critical looks at what constitutes the strengths, weaknesses, and uniqueness of your business proposition, and how to best "place yourself" for success.

Strategic studies are similar, but are often done to test the success or failure of a "position" you have devised, or to explore multiple ways of achieving strategic success.

Finally, branding and brand perception studies bring a qualitative, often "hard-to-measure" property into play. The key in studies of this nature is to have a robust research plan that can adequately measure perceptual and attributional changes. This often requires a creative combination of research and statistical methodologies to achieve useful and actionable results.

Online Surveys

Once an advertising or marketing plan has been adequately tested and developed – and positioning, strategy, and branding have been addressed – businesses need to continuously learn about their customers, visitors, and prospects. This is the essence of CRM: constantly making the best use of customer interactions and data to improve communications, message, and service.

While web-mining tools exist that "automatically" track and report on information found in web log files, they are limited – and do not constitute the whole picture by far. Just as valuable, and usually more useful, is the deployment of online surveys that gather important information which businesses need to enhance their customer "relationship": satisfaction, awareness, usage, attitudes, behavior, and the like.

Deployment of online surveys can be accomplished in a number of ways: by e-mail invitation, by website "pop up," and by formal invitation through letter or phone. Online surveys can be timed to appear at a certain place in a website, or to capture every "n^{th}" visitor. Results can be merged with stored data from website registration forms or data on databases in a corporate warehouse or data mart.

Since the collection of data and feedback is so rapid in the online environment, such deliverables as real-time reporting, tracking reports delivered directly to the desktop, and online report publishing, provide valuable and actionable business intelligence in a familiar form to marketing, sales, and executive divisions.[6]

Advisory, Business, and Consumer Access Panels

An access panel is a dedicated group of specific users, clients, or advisors who agree to provide substantive feedback on a regular basis. Access panels are no different from traditional advisory, executive, business, or consumer panels that provide business leaders and strategists with useful and critical research information.

Developing an access panel can require an extensive evaluation and search process to best reflect the population of interest. They can also be expensive to maintain and manage. Once created, however, access panels can be housed in an attractive password-protected website that serves as "home base" for the administration of timely or mission critical surveys of great value to research clients. Access panel management and maintenance assured a continuous supply of opinions, attitudes, and information that can be assessed to address business issues, perceptions, and concerns. In addition, access panels are valuable as devices to track important metrics over time.

On the buy/sell side, access panels can be used to test products, concepts, and positioning strategies. With the advent of online focus group technology, participants can be chosen from the panel, and group results can be immediately analyzed or mapped to other information about the panel member. Thus, synergistic and valuable qualitative/quantitative potential is built into the system.

Business Intelligence and Data-/Web-mining

Web-mining is more than the automatic counting of web clicks, or even when/where someone "clicks off" on a website. Data-mining is more than building automatic cross-sell models to deploy against a database list. While valuable, these approaches tell us little about the "who, what, where, why, and how" questions that need to be effectively answered to drive the customer relationship-building process. Relying on "the numbers," while ignoring important attributes and information contained in "knowing about your customer" can be extremely misleading.

Web- and data-mining tools handle extremely large quantities of data – too large for a human analyst to consider – and search for patterns, associations, and relationships. Data-mining enhances traditional and advanced market research approaches by employing a bottom-up approach. Data-mining tools can measure individual customer/visitor-level behavior and help to make sense of a vast assortment of variables. In addition, web-mining incorporates data collected from log files, online surveys, information contained in corporate or third-party databases, and can supplement software solutions such as online analytical processing tools.

Increasingly, data- and web-mining are being integrated into a larger process termed "knowledge discovery in databases." While many variations of the model exist, it is essentially an effort to tie the entire business process together into a coherent whole *built around the customer*. The net effect is efficiency and effectiveness in communicating and building customer relationships, and forms the essence of the "one-to-one" business revolution. The elements consist of:

- data-warehousing and data marts;
- target data selection: getting at the data you require;
- cleaning;
- preprocessing;
- transforming and reducing data;
- data-mining;
- selecting models;
- evaluating and interpreting models;
- consolidating and using models.

Data gathered as a by-product of web activity and behavior, consciously collected, used, and mined, is another potent facet in the overall picture. These solutions show great promise, but currently are extremely complicated to structure and implement. In addition, the relationship to original survey data is often difficult to ascertain. They remain, however, a potential area for extending customer analytics that is viable and possible within an integrated data-collection system.[7]

Coda

The five components of e-research constitute a framework for approaching the continuing and necessary research necessary to drive business success. Businesses can enter the research protocol at any step. Market research suppliers can and do offer some or all of the services described. Increasingly, however, it is clear that this continuum of research services can be delivered most effectively, creatively, and efficiently via an integrated online channel.

What are the challenges and opportunities facing the global market research industry? We find out in Part 2 straight from voices in the industry. Original research and personal interviews capture a rich story of success, vision, and perspectives from a wide-ranging sample of business executives and practitioners.

Notes

1   David Jenkins, Kantar Group, personal interview, July 2001.
2   Jack Honomichl 2001. "2001 Report on the Global Research Industry." *Marketing News*, August 13. American Marketing Association: Chicago, IL.
3   Gian Fulgoni, Comscore Networks, personal interview, September, 2001.
4   Dan Lackner. "The Evolution of CRM Analytics." www.crmdaily.com, 2001.
5   Raymond Pettit. "5 Steps to eBusiness Success." www.crm-forum.com, 2000.
6   Hanson, W. 2000. *Principles of Internet Marketing*. South-Western College Publishing: Cincinnati, OH.
7   Mena, J. 2001. *WebMining for Profit: e-Business Optimization*. Digital Press: Boston, MA.

PART 2

Global Market Research:
Challenges and Opportunities

INTRODUCTION

The trends facing the global market research industry are complex and daunting. Part 2 of our book explores how practitioners and executives – scattered across the market research, CRM, business and customer intelligence landscape – perceive these issues, challenges, and opportunities. The questions range from the practical to the theoretical, gauging attitudes and feelings, as well as actual current usage of Net-centric tools. Our interviewees were given wide latitude to discuss the current state and vision of a technology-enabled industry, or to describe where they felt the industry was headed in the next five years.

Chapter 4 presents the results of an online survey of marketing and market research practitioners recently completed by the authors. The objective of the survey was to gain a snapshot of the views and perspectives of working professionals around the world concerning the use of Net-centric research techniques. Chapter 5 offers the distillation of many hours of interviews and in-depth personal discussions with key leaders in global market research, CRM, new media, consulting, and on the client side.

CHAPTER 4

Results from the Field

THE STUDY: PERCEPTION, USAGE, AND ATTITUDES TOWARD ONLINE MARKET RESEARCH TOOLS AND TECHNOLOGIES

The survey was launched on November 19 and closed on December 4, 2001. A random sample of approximately 4,500 e-mail contacts was extracted from professional organization lists and other sources that included practitioners and professionals from all regions of the world. A modest incentive was offered.

The questionnaire consisted of 24 questions, including open ends, and covered:

- trends affecting you today;
- aspects of work involving Internet or web-based tools/techniques;
- important success factors related to Internet or web-based tools/techniques;
- perceived competitors.

The entire survey process was handled using Net-MR, online survey software provided by Global Market Insite. This afforded integrated and collaborative management of the whole project.

Results

An examination of the breakdown of the responding group (see Figure 4.1) shows, as expected, a preponderance of market research suppliers (91 percent) versus buyers (9 percent).

Figure 4.1 Report graphic 1 – breakdown of respondent sample

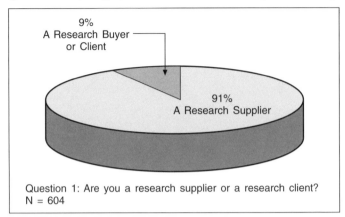

9%
A Research Buyer
or Client

91%
A Research Supplier

Question 1: Are you a research supplier or a research client?
N = 604

Trends

Six influential trends, from a list of 18 provided, emerged from the voice of the global practitioner (see Figure 4.2). The following were rated "high impact" by 30 percent or more of respondents:

- declining cooperation rates for telephone interviewing: **39%**;
- clients more eager to know influential and important factors that affect their business: **38%**;
- demand for rapid turnaround of data-collection and results via online portals: **38%**;
- pervasiveness of the Internet: **36%**;
- the trend toward globalization of business: **35%**;
- online research becoming more important/requested by clients: **33%**.

The growing difficulty of completing phone research appears to be a problem that is not going away. The increasingly tech-driven environment and rapid pace of business today is reflected in the impact rankings. Clients want insight delivery and decision-guidance – hallmarks of market research strengths – but they want it fast.

The highest rated "moderate impact" trends revolved around the emergence of a single-source online research solution and an awareness of client needs. At a fundamental level, clients are eager to gain decision guidance and a total, integrated view of the customer via the use of market research. This finding resonates closely with comments that emerged from our interviews with research clients (see Chapter 5).

"Low-impact" trends are areas of awareness that practitioners most likely are not interested in or evaluating at their level of involvement in the nitty-gritty of serving customer needs. Such aspects as the client's use of CRM software and BI tools and the pervasive use of, or usefulness of, syndicated

Figure 4.2 Report graphic 2 – high-impact trends

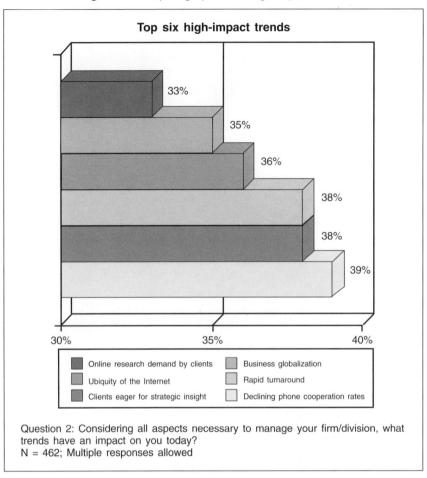

Top six high-impact trends

- 33%
- 35%
- 36%
- 38%
- 38%
- 39%

30%   35%   40%

Legend:
- Online research demand by clients
- Ubiquity of the Internet
- Clients eager for strategic insight
- Business globalization
- Rapid turnaround
- Declining phone cooperation rates

Question 2: Considering all aspects necessary to manage your firm/division, what trends have an impact on you today?
N = 462; Multiple responses allowed

research logically would fall outside their purview. This is in direct contrast to market research executives' perception of the relatively serious threat that these competitors represent.

Use of Internet and web-based tools

Figure 4.4 presents the breakdown of ways that practitioners report they are using Internet market research. These fall into four rough categories:

- online surveys and data delivery: **65–70%**;
- reporting or publishing via the Internet: **46%**;
- a mix of traditional techniques supported and enabled by technology, including online focus groups, panels, CAPI, and CATI: **23–32%**;
- Net-enabled data-mining and discussion boards: **14–18%**.

Figure 4.3 Report graphic 3 – trends: moderate and low impact

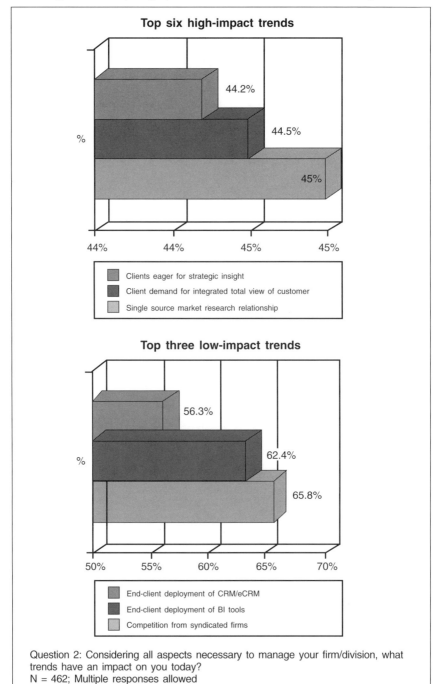

Question 2: Considering all aspects necessary to manage your firm/division, what trends have an impact on you today?
N = 462; Multiple responses allowed

Note, only 11 percent indicated no usage of Internet techniques, which is a *de facto* indication of the pervasiveness of the medium.

Figure 4.4 Report graphic 4 – current use of Internet techniques

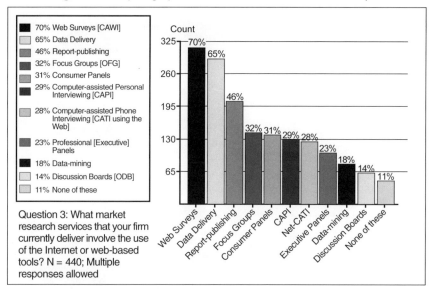

The pervasiveness of the Internet and the combined trends it affects are evident in the response to this question. Internet-based techniques and tools are infusing the industry and rapidly becoming embedded in daily work processes. The usage of CRM and other software solutions within corporations is not a mitigating, but a supporting facet of this phenomenon.

Growth in use of Internet and mixed-mode techniques

Survey participants were asked to indicate the change they expect to see in the use of Internet techniques and mixed-mode (online/offline) projects in the next five years (see Figure 4.5 and Figure 4.6).

Practitioners expect to see the use of Internet techniques and mixed-mode projects more than double in the 25–50 percent and 50 percent categories in the next five years. This supports the observation and identification of a growing technological pervasiveness recognized at a practical and utilitarian level by practitioners around the world, as well as the perception that an overlap between traditional methods and new technologies will reshape practice in an evolutionary way, rather than a lock-step replacement manner.

Figure 4.5 Report graphic 5 – % of projects completed online now and in five years

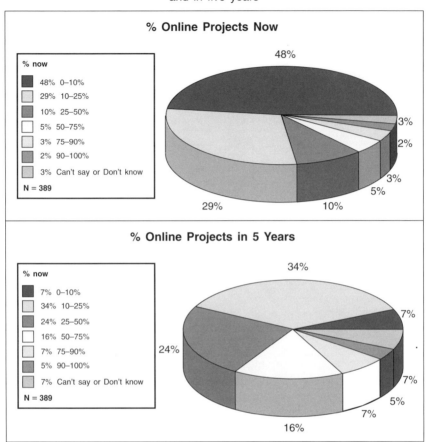

Importance and effectiveness of online tools and techniques

Slightly different rankings of the importance and effectiveness rankings of online tools and techniques appeared. Figure 4.6 presents the ranking of factors considered "very important" by respondents. Overall, the practical utility of real-time analysis, and reporting and delivery of results to the desktop drove the perceived importance ranking.

To the practitioner in the trenches, speed of fieldwork is paramount and online's greatest strength. While reducing cost and increasing productivity are important, the actual ability for Net-centric tools and techniques to deliver is supported by the effectiveness ratings. In the workaday reality, this is what they do best:

- improve speed of fieldwork: **54%**;
- reduce research costs: **49%**;

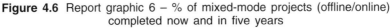

Figure 4.6 Report graphic 6 – % of mixed-mode projects (offline/online) completed now and in five years

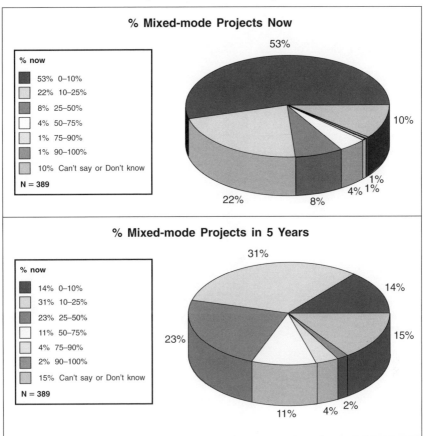

- increase research productivity: **43%**;
- enable delivery of results directly to corporate desktop: **42%**;
- real-time analysis and reporting capabilities: **37%**;
- deploy and manage multi-mode research: **32%**;
- integrate data from multiple data-collection sources: **30%**;
- contribute to adding insights and added value of research to research results: **27%**;
- ability to do data-mining: **15%**.

Awareness of online firms

From a global perspective, SPSS emerges at the top of the awareness list regarding firms that do market research. SPSS's strong brand as a primary statistical tool used by marketers and researchers around the world is evident here. At the next level of perception, CFMC, Global Market Insite, and

NIPO – all fully equipped online research or data-collection software-enabling tools – appear. Finally, the remaining companies (mostly regional players) – MarketTools, PTT, Mercator, and FIRM – are identified.

Figure 4.7 Report graphic 8 – awareness of online market research firms

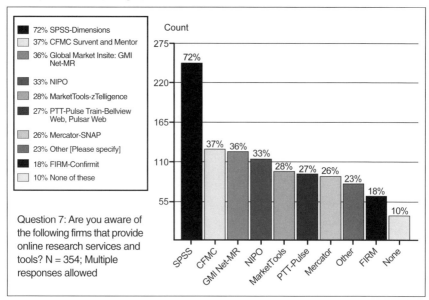

Question 7: Are you aware of the following firms that provide online research services and tools? N = 354; Multiple responses allowed

Profile of respondent activities

Respondents exhibited an expected conservative profile here by identifying mostly with traditional market research firms (see Figure 4.9). Below the 20 percent level, online, consulting, and syndicated firms appeared on the radar screen. Perhaps tellingly, the more cutting-edge CRM analytic, new media, and BI identification were less likely to be chosen, which suggests that these activities are not generally part of the market research practitioner's responsibility set to date.

Online research staffing

Most practitioners (66 percent) reported that a full-time division or staff devoted to online research was not evident in their organizations. However, 54 percent indicated that research is embedded throughout their organization in some fashion. Open-end comments suggested that in many cases online research is outsourced, or the partial responsibility of a single person within a division (for example, our "resident online research person").

Figure 4.8 Report graphic 9 – profile of participating respondents

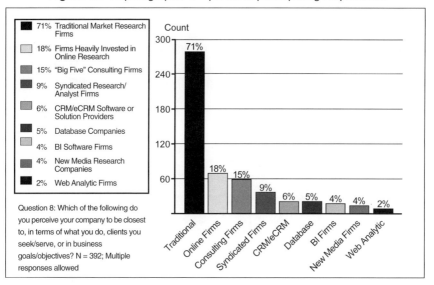

Figure 4.9 Report graphic 10 – Online research staffing

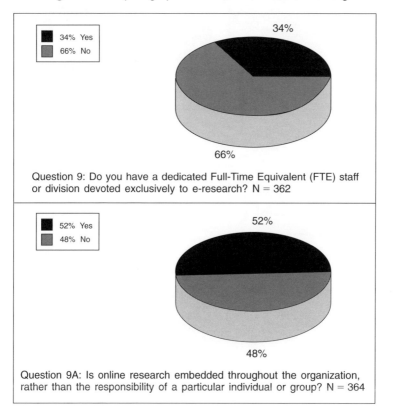

Online data-collection

Respondents indicated that nearly half of online data-collection is not outsourced, which aligns with the 54 percent figure reporting that online research is being infused within their company in some way. What is not clear is the breadth and extent of the online tool's capabilities. The open-end comments alluded to, "we do it all in-house" and "we do all online surveys in-house," are two different things. As we have noted throughout this book, online market research is more than web surveys.

Figure 4.10 Report graphic 11 – Data-collection

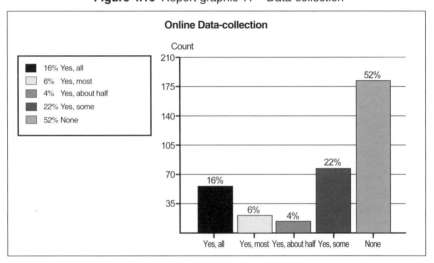

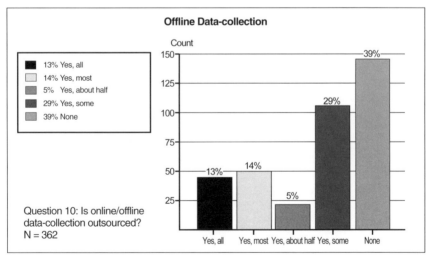

OBSERVATIONS AND CONCLUSIONS

The market research industry, whether it is explored in depth or informally, continues to see itself as a traditional industry. While this is not in itself bad, it also suggests an inertia that may be difficult to reposition against emerging technology demands and tech-savvy competitors. Since many of these software companies are aligned with corporate executives at the upper levels of decision-making authority, often at the CTO, CIO, or CMO level, a failure to understand and counteract this could result in the blindsiding of the market research industry. While industry executives may see the light, they have to convince the general organization to follow it with them; and that may be a significant challenge.

Our research suggests that a snapshot of global marketing and research practitioners still yields a familiar picture. As will be presented in the next chapter, industry leaders and executives generally are aware of and understand, in varying degrees, that technology is here to stay and the use of enabling technology will only increase. And as the survey of practitioners indicates, they do see enabling technology increasingly a part of their work in the very near future. However, the bulk of working professionals still identify strongly with the traditional market research model.

A dilemma arises as industry executives ponder how to take the best features of what market research has to offer and balance it with obviously needed investments in technology. A fine line needs to be respected in upholding and championing the expertise and skills of existing professionals and in meeting the challenges that new technology presents. All the while, the impact of the Internet is inexorably growing. Practitioners are intensely involved in the daily struggle, and are seeing first hand the effects. As our survey's open-end comments revealed, they are bombarded on all sides by client pressures, methodological quandaries, and immature or poorly designed technological tools. It is no wonder that they are unconcerned about, or perhaps uninterested in, CRM and new media developments. For the most part, they are working to adapt, adjust, and prepare for changes, instigated by client and technological pressure, seemingly out of their control.

Our research suggests an urgent need is at hand that may not be reflected in the perception of the working body of the industry. In our opinion, leading global market research firms should be more aggressive in studying and understanding the emerging competitive space, in promoting the strongest values that market research can deliver, in investing in technology-enabling initiatives, and in seeking out logical and robust partnerships and joint ventures with tech-savvy companies. However, the challenge requires organization, mobilization, and planning at primary organizational levels to avoid a haphazard metamorphosis based on unrelated, discrete, and tiny adjustments to technology trends, overhyped "cures," and client demands.

CHAPTER 5

Perspectives of Leading Executives and Practitioners

INTRODUCTION

Between July and September 2001, 50 companies agreed to participate in in-depth interviews for this book. Interviews were conducted by telephone and in person with executives and practitioners around the world who are responsible for market research, data analytics, market measurement, and consumer insight (details of companies, participants, and the complete interview guide can be found in the Appendices A and B). These professionals are deeply involved in negotiating the converging trends described in Part 1 of this book. They come from many settings and all parts of the globe:

- top 25 global market research firms;
- CRM software companies;
- new media companies;
- advertising agencies;
- pure-play online research firms;
- "big five" consulting firms;
- web analytics firms;
- data-mining companies;
- syndicated research firms;
- Global 2000 clients of market research.

What is evident at a fundamental level in many, if not all, of the discussions is a deep conviction that the better understanding of consumers and of being able to leverage insights, draw conclusions, and provide actionable decision support to improve marketing, advertising, and sales activities are the most important outcomes of a research function in business. Whether this is called market research, customer intelligence, a CRM analytic solution, or knowledge discovery through data-mining is very much a semantic point. What is relevant is that the key strengths inherent in the market research function – assets that we know and value in the industry – are indeed essential to the health, viability, and ongoing growth of businesses. From this basic starting point, the path opens up onto a superhighway of global client needs, new technological impacts and challenges, and innumerable competitive situations. But the basic premise is solid: market research is important.

The impression one has is that the market research industry is just now easing onto the business superhighway, loaded with traditional and new ideas, practices, processes, and lots of value. Our destination is the business and corporate desktops, to become the primary provider of their entire customer information and intelligence needs – a vast array of solid and useful offerings. Unfortunately, we are a little late to hit the road. Shinier, faster, and turbo-charged competitors are ahead of us. And sometimes traffic jams lurk around the bend. As a result, we face a terrific challenge and realize the need to pull out all the stops if we want to arrive at the client's desktop before the corporate portal is closed.

Our strategies vary: some try and do more of the same, but on a bigger and bigger scale. Others hitch a ride on a massive conglomeration of advertising, marketing, business information, and public relations firms, hoping to take advantage of an extended network that can reach, literally, around the world. Still, others are trying to incorporate new tools and technologies to go faster, become more efficient, and run ahead of client needs in anticipation of the future. In some locations, unique solutions, products, and services are evolving that best meet the needs found in that region of the world. No one strategy is foolproof. We go with our best instincts, analyses, and feelings. But our objectives are essentially the same: to be the primary and favored provider of consumer insight and business knowledge to the clients we wish to serve.

Many, many bright and intelligent people are involved in the scenario described above. It is encouraging that we, as an industry, are generally on the right track, albeit with a number of different strategies in operation. However, there is really no time to sit back complacently – all of the executives spoken to displayed an urgency, energy, and enthusiasm for the future that we sincerely hope will prevail.

TOP LINE PERSPECTIVES ON THE CHALLENGES, ISSUES, OPPORTUNITIES, AND THE FUTURE OF THE MARKET RESEARCH INDUSTRY

Interview questions were structured in an open-ended discussion format. An interview guide outline was offered before the actual interview to allow preparation. Interview participants were all executives who fell into one of five groups:

- top 25 global market research firms;
- new media/online market research providers;
- CRM/business intelligence tool/service providers;
- Global 2000 clients of market research;
- market research or "big five" consultants.

Five major insights were distilled from the more than 80 hours of interviews and discussions:

1   **A unique differentiation of viewpoints emerged concerning the trends, challenges, and opportunities being faced today:**
    - **Top 25 market research executives** generally had the broadest views on this question, evidenced by a concern for and thinking about a wide array of issues: industry consolidation and business globalization, online research and technology, business intelligence and how best to deliver it, defining where the industries greatest strengths lie, and competition.
    - **New media** leaders were more apt to talk about online research and technological innovation, analytics, and the cost/time benefits of tech-driven research.
    - **CRM** executives were clearly focused on software solutions, enterprise-wide initiatives, and the need for better data analytics and result delivery. Some evidence appeared that demonstrating implementation effectiveness via ROI was a serious preoccupation at the highest levels.
    - **Clients**, in general, were mostly interested in the effectiveness and efficiency of solutions, the quality of supplier relationships and the depth of insight and guidance that could be delivered, and the ability of the supplier to incorporate multiple views of the customer in research.
    - **Consultants'** views fluctuated between expounding upon issues very specific to their focused practices, and, in some cases, offering quite broad-reaching and innovative analyses of the current situation.

2 **When viewed through a global lens, the US/EURO focus on trends and current issues was quite similar, whereas Asian and Latin America's were distinctive.** In terms of market research, Asia is still a highly fragmented conglomeration of many small competing companies. The Japanese firm **Intage**, a member of the global top 25, expressed a unique stance that more closely resembled the CRM approach. As can be expected, the business model it described "looked like" a CRM company: an extraordinary focus on technology and business intelligence. But there was also a key concern for high-level, high-touch insight delivery and a client service relationship not found in the typical CRM business model. Likewise, in Latin America, **IBOPE**, another major firm in the top 25, evidenced a strong, concerted focus on new media convergence and the use of online research tools. Interestingly, the impression from both of these firms was that global expansion was not necessarily of prime importance. Rather, they expressed the desire to be the leader in their respective regions who more or less were the focal point for primary and leading-edge market research activities that may or may not come from other places around the world.

3 **A dichotomy exists when gauging the future:**
  - **Global market research executives** appeared to be more concerned about the future of the industry. A number of predictions had to do with the polarization of the industry, the attempts to "fit into" the larger business information industry, and the clear picture of an increasingly technology-driven future. A major focus was on describing scenarios where market research could be the central figure in the collection, delivery, and dissemination of data and ideas.
  - **New media, CRM executives** and, to a lesser extent, consultants had much more difficulty describing a future. The sense is that, in a way, they are creating the future now. This tended to inhibit their discussion beyond fairly urgent deficiencies in current approaches that needed to be rectified. What is clear is that, particularly in the CRM industry, solutions are being actively sought that can be integrated with CRM software or a technology-driven model. It just so happens that the current need is most accurately reflected by the sorts of things that the market industry can provide: analytical expertise, customer insights, profiling/segmenting of consumers, and so forth.

4 **Online and offline data-integration must be realized.** Across all interview segments, the driving importance in the future centered on the ability to collect, store, inspect, analyze, and disseminate information quickly and efficiently. Each segment then had distinctive touches they added to the mix. The market research viewpoint added the component

of traditional value and expertise they can bring when being a guide to consumer insights for clients. The CRM/BI stance was in bringing intelligence to the tech-driven relationship or in the customer experience management solutions they offer. New media folks appeared to strive for a bit of both in their play to drive the future of business enhancement and solutions.

5   **A broadened and much larger business information industry may be forming and is now only in its embryonic stages.** To establish this view, one must step very far back and look at the underlying driving forces suggested by the interviews. From one side is the traditional media, publishing, marketing, advertising, and PR organization. Also included here is the traditional market research industry. In essence, it represents content, or information, that people consume or use, and have used for quite a while. The fringes here stretch into the training industry, traditional communications, and government/educational establishment. On the other hand is the technology industry, driven primarily by the Internet, under the rubric of e-business. Their main goal is to leverage all of the content more efficiently and effectively, mostly through complex, global, and enterprise-wide technological systems. Running through all of this as a unifying stream, but not yet a fully fledged river, is the Internet. For all intents and purposes, the Internet appears to be the future conduit that will allow the extended BI industry to do what it does best: provide information in its many forms. Thus, rather than a future where CRM "takes over" market research, or vice versa, what may be occurring is an evolving BI technology industry that merges all under one roof.

DISCUSSION OF MAJOR INTERVIEW QUESTIONS[1]

Extracting the essence from the many insightful answers provided in the interviews was a challenge at best. It is difficult to capture the nuance, flavor, and importance of all of the interviews; however, the approach we have chosen is to use verbatim quotes where possible that best illustrate a theme or stream of thought. The discussions that revolved around the following interview questions are explored:

- What are the major trends (short and long term) affecting your firm today?
- What do you feel are the most important aspects of your value proposition? What are the factors that are most important to your clients?
- What do you see the future of global market research, or customer intelligence gathering, to be in 2005?

PART 1: WHAT ARE THE MAJOR TRENDS AFFECTING YOUR FIRM TODAY? WHAT DO YOU FEEL ARE THE MOST IMPORTANT ASPECTS OF YOUR VALUE PROPOSITION? WHAT ARE THE FACTORS THAT ARE MOST IMPORTANT TO YOUR CLIENTS?

The global market research perspective: The global market research contingent clearly had the most to say in answer to this question. Issues of consolidation (of supplier and client), globalization challenges, and the unique footprint that the market research industry should possess were paramount. **Heinrich Litzenroth of GfK Group** (Germany) had perhaps the broadest view when discussing globalization and consolidation trends affecting both clients and research companies. Global branding, exemplified by such worldwide giants as Unilever, has brought both far-reaching and larger contracts and projects to the table. Along with this opportunity comes the challenge to deliver on such a broad spectrum. And, "of course," said Litzenroth, "we must follow our clients, wherever they go." He went on to expand upon the deficiencies of CRM, the importance of custom research work, and the rise of outsourcing of market research. In essence, said Litzenroth, "we should like to tell our clients: we will be your market research department."

Jeffrey Resnick, President of Opinion Research Corporation's International Division (US), energetically proposed that top global market research firms take the lead in adopting a consultative approach, rather than sticking so firmly to the traditional data-collection and "tab house" model. The paradigm is simple and direct: "clients value direct feedback and guidance from consulting experts who use information and expertise to recommend effective business strategies. Market research's value is in providing thought leadership built on primary, research-based feedback." Executives at Intage (Japan), NOP World (UK), ABT Associates (US), Ipsos Reid (CA), GfK (Germany) and TNS (UK) echoed this view.

Simon Chadwick, CEO of NOP World, provided a thoughtful analysis of the CRM space, and the market research industry's competitive response. Chadwick was not alone in this concern, although he was perhaps the most eloquent in his formulation. Case study 6 depicts in detail Chadwick's take on the rapidly evolving competitor – CRM – in a presentation he delivered in May 2001.

Case Study 6
Two Potential Futures for the Market Research Industry

In 1997, Simon Chadwick was already starting to think about CRM and its potential as a threat to the market research industry. Upon close analysis, he noted that the things CRM purported to be doing were suspiciously close to what market researchers actually do. When he first spoke of this "threat" in public presentations to other industry professionals, he had two personal reactions: (1) fear for his life and (2) fear of being totally ignored. By 1999–2000, however, clients of research were starting to come by with new and unusual requests that were, essentially, CRM-type projects. By 2001, Chadwick believed, the realization was just starting to dawn on the market research industry that CRM is a serious competitive threat. "To our favor," he added, "CRM implementations have been dismal." Plus, he saw a non-alignment in the CRM industry with US CRM firms more technically oriented and European firms more "people" oriented. This lack of focus affords our industry a tiny window of opportunity.

Chadwick strongly asserted that the global market research industry has extraordinary expertise in both quantitative and qualitative research that can transform CRM into a "complete" global solution. As an industry we have the opportunity to advise, based on our experience with the human customer and consumer, in numerous and vital areas. For example, we can consult on how best to build brand equity, how to take data analysis (analytics) to its proper level, and act as an intermediary that filters access to – and makes sense of – CRM data, even delivering it directly to the corporate desktop in a form that can actually be used effectively for decision-making. The big question is: can we rise to the challenge as an industry?

Chadwick defines CRM as the management of an interface between a company and its customers. It represents a growth industry larger than the total research industry. As well, it is serving to refocus corporate interest back to the customer. Finally, it harbors a unique repository of data, both behavioral and attitudinal. Thus, opportunities abound for market researchers to assume the following roles:

- foundational precursors to CRM solutions;
- scorekeepers of CRM effectiveness;
- purveyors of CRM solutions.

Chadwick depicted two futures for the market research industry. In the first, the industry is doomed to assume a negligible role in the total process of understanding the consumer. In the second, market research is poised at the center, as the primary mediating, processing, and filtering authority in the BI scene. Chadwick, by putting his strong intellect and analytic skills to work, has truly defined a contemporary challenge with enormous implications for the future of the market research industry.

Source: Simon Chadwick, CEO, NOP World, Presentation at SumIT01, Portugal, May 2001.

Intage

Intage is one of the leading market research firms serving the Japanese market. The comments of **Norio Taori, President and CEO of Intage**, expressed most clearly a business approach for his firm that was akin to what most in the United States and Europe would characterize as CRM. After discussing the various trends from the Japanese perspective through the 1990s, Taori described a current approach where, "We bring business intelligence by bringing together the data from client, data from market research, and investing our expertise." Thus, Taori described data-integration, as well as the integration of the technical and "people" side. Taori stated:

This is a challenge involving client business model development, a challenge that calls on systems development including business process re-engineering (BPR). Across a wide range of industries there are needs to run businesses effectively and efficiently, both by incorporating improved data-collection steps into the business process, and by integrating the feedback from analytical results into the process. Development of new business models, utilizing BPR, demands not only literal "information technology" itself, but also data-collection skills based on research know-how, data-handling capabilities, analytical skills, and a deep understanding of marketing. Intage has secured the resources that major players in the field are required to be successful.

However, Taori went one step further, by clarifying the close-consulting bond Intage aims for in serving the client: "Market research firms have to educate the client: how to use data, integrate it, make it actionable. Our expertise in key areas – consumer panels, transactional data, online panel data, and our interpretation and expertise in planning areas – drive system solutions." The take away from this discussion is that Intage is most near to doing what analytical CRM firms are trying to do in the United States and Europe. It is, however, driven from the perspective and focus of a market research firm taking the initiative to foster and encourage traditional service, care, and insight to clients, while also tackling the stickier technical problems that may plague them. Surely this model is worthy of thoughtful consideration if the market research industry is to attempt to tackle the technology-driven CRM competitor.

Online Research

A number of executives spoke of online research, the importance of global access panels, and enterprise-wide technology solutions for market research. Of those that did, additional stress was placed on delivery of data, results, and information directly to the corporate desktop via corporate information portals. Attention was divided equally between delivering reports and analytic access to the client, and with providing continuous "streams" of tracking, trending, or syndicated data/reports. **Mark Berry, President of NFO Interactive**, described a number of converging influences that centered on efficiency gains via the use of online research techniques. At TNS, **Arno Hummerston, Director of TNSi**, is in charge of innovating online products and services for that global giant's clients. He spoke also of client's rapid and emerging acceptance of the online channel.

IBOPE

The story in Latin America is an intriguing one. Three executives from **IBOPE (Brazil), Paulo Pinheiro, Pedro Donda, and Tolis Vossos** spoke at length about the importance of media convergence and its measurement. Case study 7 presents this unique Latin perspective and why it makes sense for IBOPE. IBOPE executives were quite frank about the issue of expanding globally. Just like Intage in Japan, the Brazilians are more comfortable in becoming the premier clearinghouse in the region, controlling input and output, and being recognized as the Latin American authority. This view diverges sharply from the general concern in the industry about expanding through consolidation, merger, or acquisition to best serve clients at a global level.

Case Study 7
IBOPE Interview

A major trend that IBOPE has identified is the rise of new media; specifically, new media measurement. It is a complex task, Pedro Donda said, and difficult to pull off. It is fragmented, interactive, and personalized – thus very different from traditional research. But it is vital and a direction Ibope wants to pursue vigorously. The objective is to be the leader in media convergence measurement for the Latin American region. Ibope's long-range projection is that within five years television and the Internet will be "one," so it will be in a position to be in the forefront of that trend. Thus, it looks both to partner, where appropriate, and to develop its own new technologies as needed. For example, Donda described a real-time television audience-reporting tool IBOPE is working on.

Use of Internet Tools and Technologies
Vital to achieving a new media vision is the ability to do mixed-mode online projects. Although acknowledging some of the problems with Online Surveys (such as sampling, understanding probabilities, representativeness, and so on), they generally agreed these were not insurmountable obstacles and radiated a good positive feeling about the techniques. They were also excited about ways to deliver real-time results, seeing solid potential here to reach directly to the client. Finally, a recognition that online and offline research can complement each other, and that clients could save money by doing what was appropriate and feasible to do online, was advanced.

IBOPE's Most Important Value Proposition
IBOPE's focus is on providing "information for decision-making." If a client is just curious about something, IBOPE is not particularly interested – the company prefers real problems and in providing information to reduce risk. With clients IBOPE focuses on strategy and on stressing the value it brings. Paulo Pinheiro stated that reducing risk and solving business problems are difficult without proper information. The return on the risk has great potential to be negligible.

IBOPE is often called on to be the "experts" in Latin America, a role it relishes. Often a worldwide study or one with a global focus will be handled better in a New York or London office – and it will even encourage that, acknowledging a very clear sense of its special expertise and domain. They would prefer to "represent" Latin America as the premier, high-quality research source and is content with fulfilling that role.

Global Mindset

IBOPE, however, is not averse to global work, if the projects are Internet-related. As stated by Donda, "there are no frontiers on the Internet." In traditional matters, IBOPE is content to be the Latin American experts. However, in Internet projects, IBOPE can compete by preserving the context in the same way as anyone else; that is, it can serve global clients as easily and as well as local ones.

How Does IBOPE Perceive Itself in the Industry?

Right now it sees itself as having a broad and deep footprint in Latin America. It is, however, a very broad offering in a limited territory: consumer panels, public opinion, and e-ratings with a strong Latin American focus. As it looks to the future, it will examine its portfolio of clients and ask, "Are there any areas where we can provide something unique and special?" If not, it will do nothing. If so, it will go hard after that. For instance, what if IBOPE had the capabilities to do online surveys in Portuguese, Spanish, and English? What would stop it from trying to get clients in Spain and Portugal, and (with English) anywhere? The bottom line is that it is thoughtfully searching, looking for that "special" contribution it can make that no one else can offer.

Source: Paulo Pinheiro de Andrade, IBOPE Media Information – Chairman, Pedro Donda, IBOPE.Com – CEO, Tolis Vossos, IBOPE eRatings.com – CEO; July 31, 2001.

Riddel stresses organizational change

Regarding the changes wrought by global mergers and acquisitions, **Elaine Riddel, CEO of NOP World Health, a Division of NOP World**, touched on a unique, and important, facet of the discussion not raised by anyone else. Given the state of rapid change in the industry, Riddel spoke at length about the challenges of integrating organizational cultures when mergers and acquisitions occur. As Riddel clearly stated, the real work often begins after the merger, when the new organization must work hard to take the potential and opportunity inherent in the new situation to the next level of performance. It is not an easy task and it is often a component of business not given the time and respect it deserves. However, if the merger and acquisition mania continues in the industry, it is a task that assumes critical importance for success.

The New Media Perspective

In contrast to the executives from large global market research firms, new media leaders showed a propensity to dwell on online research benefits and technological innovations. This most often included the cost savings and speed of delivery, but also lengthier discussions on analytics, establishing access panels, and database issues. **Gian Fulgoni of Comscore**, for example, stressed, "It is important to be able to integrate online and offline data. Since most business is still offline, there is an enormous pressure to access and integrate this data with the newer online data collected." Clearly, Fulgoni, who established and built **Information Resources, Inc.** (IRI) into a behavioral data powerhouse, understands that all forms of data on consumers are potentially important. This is the essence of the "360-degree view of the customer" concept that runs throughout marketing, CRM, and business intelligence conversations. With a bit of frustration, however, Fulgoni noted, "Online has proven it is a targeted, interactive, and powerful new addition to the sales/marketing mix, but it still has to prove ROI; whereas, more traditional channels do not."

Proving the worth of online techniques

This same sense of having to "prove" the value and worth of online techniques also emerged from discussions with **Doug Knopper, Managing Director of Diameter, DoubleClick's Research Division, and Dave Morgan, CEO of True Audience** (now Tacoda Systems). Knopper identified that the continuing weak economy has strengthened pessimism and skepticism regarding the online channel. However, the fact is that it has endured, prompting his comment, "I feel that skepticism is changing to: 'Okay, it's here to stay, now how is it going to work?'"

Much of Knopper's work will be spent in enlisting DoubleClick's massive ad network, creating new products and solutions, and building research partnerships to assist in proving the worth of online data-collection, research, and analysis.

Dave Morgan was formerly CEO of **RealMedia**, and like Knopper, realizes that a big part of his job will be in demonstrating that his True Audience online "audience management system" can truly deliver value to online advertisers, marketers, and content providers. If anyone can do it, Morgan can. He started RealMedia and built it into one of the top three ad-serving networks in the world and into a key competitor of DoubleClick. However, his new effort is different: "Then, we were creating technology. Now we have the technology and can put it together in new and unique ways."

Morgan noted the same shift to a customer focus in the online media environment evident in most industries today, "Marketers now want (and want to know) prospects and customers. True Audience provides the plumbing to do this. It's all about audience management, although analytics, business intelligence tools, and market research are parts of this. Sites have traffic: our system provides a phased plan and ongoing effort to build a richer and richer database of online visitors and consumers, then to improve advertising and marketing efforts." Suffice to say, Morgan's solution is highly technology-driven, complex, expansive, and ambitious. It indicates a direction that is revolutionary in the sense that it is attempting to synergize new methods and new technology in one package.

Knowledge Networks
Knowledge Networks of Palo Alto, CA, has garnered attention, from the market research industry, in particular, due to the participation of some stellar names in its development, launch, and growth. **Norman Nie, Doug Rivers, Lynd Bacon, and Doss Struse** are but a few of the highly regarded market research professionals involved in this effort. From the starting gate, this brilliant crew has labored to make it clear that they value and hold to traditional and rigid statistical standards, while employing new technology to drive their efforts. **Doss Struse, Senior V-P**, who has had a rich and varied career in the research industry, spoke about technology: "The advantage technology brings is connection. It allows us then to analyze thinking and feeling in the context of marketing actions taken, [to ask] who were the people exposed to that ad, how did they process it, and connect it back to buying things. The linkage is there. Ultimately, you can tie it back to ROI – did they buy, how much, etc. The key is to capture as much information as possible over time. This allows businesses to come back with highly targeted marketing efforts."

As most in the industry know, Knowledge Networks has chosen that most ubiquitous form of communication, television, to establish a panel research platform. Using a web-television interface, they are the high-tech version of a traditional mail/phone-based panel – and are connected to a sizeable research panel via the Internet.

Connecting to consumers to hear their voice
The concept of connection – and communication – has become a key factor in another new media effort that is attempting to exploit the trend powered by the Internet. **BuzzBack**, a firm based in New York City, has merged basic qualitative and quantitative market research techniques, compressed the time needed to deploy them via online techniques, and extended their research model by, literally, creating a dialogue with the respondent/consumer. As most in the market research world would attest, the clients BuzzBack serves

hold the "consumer voice" in very high esteem. It is likely that more marketing and advertising decisions have been made based on comments from focus groups than from sophisticated statistical analyses. Be that as it may, **Carolyn Fitzgerald, CEO of BuzzBack**, said, "We do a very quick and focused quantitative snapshot for the client. Then, we take a small segment from the survey and form focus groups (online or offline) to build up richer, deeper insights. In fact, we may have multiple sessions over time – almost like an ad hoc panel – to get reactions, information, additional feedback, and so on, on products and ads, whatever clients want to probe." In essence, through BuzzBack, clients are getting a level of connection directly to the people they are trying to understand and sell to that is unprecedented in the traditional research world.

Dennis Gonier, now a V-P at AOL, understood the "connection" possibilities very early on when he approached AOL to support his online research effort, **Digital Marketing Services**. Gonier saw clearly that the Internet, and the vast coverage AOL could provide, afforded a sampling frame that more closely resembled a "river," or stream, of potential respondents who could be surveyed and queried for marketing purposes. The alternative approach, more familiar to market research, is the "pond," or panel, that is devised to represent the "river," or true population. While not exactly airtight in the statistical sense, the reality that AOL reaches so many people, coupled with the fact that the Internet provides such a rich communication medium, and that Gonier and his team have been relentless in testing the efficacy of the new medium, is compelling. And, as an Internet connection becomes globally pervasive, the discussion about representativeness will necessarily die down (as it did from mail to phone). What is important, and what many of the new media leaders have understood, is that market research doesn't necessarily end with dissemination, collection, and distribution. It involves – can involve – elements of ongoing communication, connection, and insight-generation over time that should be readily and freely shared with clients, rather than locked away in a completed project drawer.

The CRM/BI Perspective

In a certain sense, the CRM/BI perspective is the farthest removed from the concerns voiced by the global market research industry. Yet, they also have the potential to become the industry's most formidable competitor. The CRM software industry, and the tag-along BI tool sector, is blithely forging ahead, looking for global, enterprise-wide opportunities where they can, essentially, to install a very expensive technology-based system that integrates the corporate front and back offices for efficiency and, ultimately, cost savings. The realization that there are other vital components to the CRM process also has them scrambling to build "analytical" CRM solutions to provide the brains behind these all-encompassing systems. Thus, the colossus market research industry and the slightly smaller CRM provider group appear to be passing each other by with nary a glance. One of them, however, is headed "in harm's way."

If you were to study 50 different operational/analytical CRM models in existence today, not one would mention or include "market research" as a function of the system. Either CRM thinkers or developers aren't aware of the importance of the market research function, or they don't think it's a real necessity. But they are aware that some sort of analytic "guidance system" is necessary to drive the success of installations in actually establishing more profitable customer relations. Naturally, the CRM brethren turned first to their BI cousins from the enterprise resource planning (ERP) era. Increasingly, however, they are generating, creating, or developing analytical solutions that mimic many of the things that market research provides: customer intelligence, consumer insight, segmenting/profiling of customers, customer satisfaction protocols built into the CRM system, and so on.

What is uncanny in the discussions with some of the CRM/BI leaders is their relative lack of awareness of market research firms, beyond a general notion that market research provides some sort of traditional – perhaps outdated – support and guidance to sales and marketing personnel scattered throughout the corporate structure. Yet, others involved have actually come out of the market research industry and are quickly and quietly starting to exert the influence necessary to bring some of the more common, valuable, and useful market research activities into the picture. The bottom line, however, appears to be that the solutions must be technology-driven. And it is here where the market research industry, as a whole, may be left holding the bag.

SAS stakes a claim
Donna Callahan, Director of CRM and Marketing Partnerships at SAS, noted that, "The key to useful and actionable research still lies in combining the proper use of appropriate data-collection methods and high-quality analytics." Speaking about a recent partnership effort with **MarketTools** (an online market research company), she added, "One of the differentiators of our partnership is the fact that customers will have the ability to include their online research with traditional customer research information stored in a data warehouse. The first phase of the partnership was being able to download the web survey information (meta data and survey data) into a SAS data warehouse, then building a data bridge that takes the information from MarketTools, analyzes it and passes the information back, enabling a

closed loop intelligent survey process. The third phase was to have a powered-by-SAS or SAS analytics embedded into the MarketTools application." It is clear that a strong technological undercurrent is at work here that may or may not align with global market research firms today. But it is a reality they must confront.

Siebel: The knowledge worker as analyst

Are analytics effective in CRM projects? **Dan Lackner, V-P and GM of Marketing and Analytics at Siebel Systems**, would say they have to be. "Operational CRM is not true CRM. It has limited scope, delivers limited efficiency benefits. A rich mix of customer intelligence (analytics) is the real key to ROI. A recent survey by Cap Gemini Ernst & Young found European executives believe CRM is a critical component of their business strategies: 67 percent of respondents' companies have launched a CRM initiative in the last two years compared to 74 percent in the United States. Seventy-nine percent believe a successful CRM strategy requires changes to traditional business models, processes, and culture." Sung Lee, **CEO of TheResearch**, a CRM consulting firm that handles both Asian and North American clients, said that Korean CRM companies, such as UniBoss, are focusing heavily on the analytic side of the CRM equation. Intage, as discussed earlier, also appears to be creating a unique convergence of CRM analytic and market research services to serve the Japanese market.

Siebel, according to Lackner, is exploring multiple avenues to analytic success. In addition to partnering with, or in some cases buying, clever technology-driven solutions that can help CRM systems turn toward the elusive ROI they promise, Siebel is also exploring solutions such as the Comscore Panel to provide context for marketing decisions; that is, the ability to hear the consumer voice through surveys and other forms of traditional market research. Lackner, formerly from IRI, understands the value of traditional market research practices. The key will be in integrating them into the Siebel system and enabling the Siebel vision of an analytic-driven enterprise to emerge.

Analytical CRM

One substantial CRM company, e.Piphany, burst on the scene from the analytic direction. Originally a data-mining and personalization company, they expanded quickly into a major enterprise software solutions company. **Paul Rodwick, V-P of Marketing Development & Strategy at e.Piphany**, strongly supports the analytic CRM line, "With analytical CRM, CEOs gain competitive advantages with customer intelligence strategies, including multichannel communications (analyzing information from all channels), acting on that intelligence through segmentation management (more effective marketing strategies), predictive analytics, and event-triggered marketing." The bottom line, according to Rodwick, "is to take maximum advantage of customer knowledge."

Mike Christian, Sr V-P of Analytics at WebSideStory, takes the CRM analytic story to another level. He believes the trend will be to outsource CRM analytics, much as traditional market research has been outsourced in the past. The difference here is that WebSideStory will be continuously linked to its clients, since it hosts the data that is used for all analysis. A hosted solution avoids the huge expenses of software/database integration, building of middleware connections, and potential failures. In addition, clients reap the benefits of automatic upgrades and improvements, as well as continuing consulting services down the line.

WebSideStory also recently partnered with the Comscore Network to bring into the loop the "context" factor so desperately needed to make sense of vast amounts of behavioral data. CRM, as a process or business strategy, still needs to know the "why," and this is only available via a dialogue with people. This understanding is also driving the existence of firms such as Customersat.com and Netmetrix, which essentially are striving to include the "voice of the customer" into CRM solutions. Once again, these are all things that market research providers have done well in the past, but may be in danger of losing as the CRM machine marches on. To paraphrase a story about former US President Bill Clinton: "It's all about the technology."

Certain business intelligence tools, such as OLAP, are rapidly being retooled, according to SAS's Callahan, "Yes, query and real-time reporting are essential. Gathering and analyzing clean data are probably the first and most important steps necessary in [the] reporting of any kind, and storing the information gathered in a customer-centric warehouse is critical for all business needs, including web-reporting. The complete enterprise data management framework then prepares the data for fast analysis and delivery to the web." Thus, it is clear that in the minds of the CRM/BI folks the trend to take numerous aspects of the market research function and rapidly deploy them online has already emerged. The sense is that we will see more, rather than less, of this.

Data-mining

Usama Fayad, a former Microsoft executive in charge of directing its data-mining division, started **digiMine**, a highly successful hosted solution that focuses on data-mining. Fayad made a conscious choice not to become part of a larger CRM solution for similar reasons given by WebSideStory's Christian. Fayad carefully studied many of the emerging CRM companies and decided that the best way to provide advanced data-mining solutions was via a hosted solution. While not directly involved in providing market research assistance, Fayad is concentrated on the upper fringes of the analytic continuum where massive data sets need to be approached with advanced analytic techniques. Fayad stated, however, that some past Digimine projects did involve an overlay of market research results, and he can foresee that this sort of work could be prominent in the near future. Case study 8 describes the concepts and process involved in Digimine's successful development and practice.

Case Study 8
The digiMine Story

Usama Fayad started to think about founding what would eventually become digiMine in late 1999 and early 2000, while still employed at Microsoft. As venture capital was readily accessible, he would constantly get calls from venture capitalists saying that if he wanted to start a new company, funding would be instantaneous. Two major factors drove his final decision. On the personal side, he had reached a point where, despite massive academic and industry achievements, he lacked the "thrill of the hunt." The decision was made, and the capital materialized instantly. In less than a year, digiMine had grown from three cofounders to over 100 people.

As for the second factor, Fayad noted during his years at Microsoft how much companies were really struggling with data-warehousing and data-mining. They could not effectively run and maintain data warehouses; existing warehouses were overly complicated and expensive, and business users were not getting any value from the data. Consequently, running a data-mining application was essentially out of the question for most businesses. To run a data-mining application, Fayad saw that one had to embark on a multi-month data quest to prepare a viable foundation. So, he concluded that the only way to get data-mining to work was to solve the data-warehousing problem and to integrate business solutions simultaneously.

Key to Fayad's vision was running the data warehouse as a fully hosted, fully managed service for companies. Since the technology is so complex, a hosted model was the only way to make it work, to make it economical, and to assure that business users received the benefits. To readily assure benefits, digiMine now packages and builds business applications that utilize data-mining and the data from the warehouse that include real-time cross-sell, up-sell, predictive, and segmentation technologies. Fayad has found a tremendous market for this type of solution, as it cuts across many industries and companies of all sizes. The result has been a sizeable boost in business, particularly in the down economy, as companies look to save money. Clients are finding that Fayad's hosted solution does the trick.

Source: Usama Fayad. "Interview with Gregory Piatetsky-Shapiro in KDD Nuggets" www.kddnuggets.com, 2001.

The Client Perspective

Research clients in the corporate pressure cooker tend to be pragmatic and focused individuals. The substance of the interviews with this group fully supported that reality. The trends and issues that concerned them most focused on getting research done quickly and cheaply, with the maximum amount of decision guidance and insight that could be attached. All felt the online medium could deliver the former; however, they also indicated they were reluctant to let go of the traditional routines that afforded them the depth and reliability of insight that they have come to expect and depend on from favored research suppliers.

Some evidence of clients' desire to see a more complete picture of the customer/consumer was noted. But in the delicate balance, this was felt to be more an opportunity for market research to deliver, rather than something clients would demand. The bottom line prevails: clients want it quick, fast, and timely.

Jim McDowell, V-P of Marketing at BMW, NA, in suburban New Jersey obviously serves a highly affluent and educated market segment. Naturally, he saw the Internet as a core communications vehicle with his customers. In fact, just prior to our interview, McDowell had just finished a unique project that involved producing, filming, and running a short Hollywood-style movie to draw and engage BMW visitors to the site that turned out to be fabulously successful. In line with this, McDowell saw the ability to do online research as a "convenience" for his customers that fits into their active and hectic lifestyles. This "connection" perspective even spilled over into a trend McDowell saw for marketers to be more involved in the design of research studies and for the use of in-house analysts to displace research supplier's analysts. Thus, he noted a tendency back to collection and dissemination of data as the key role of the market research industry, with the higher valued front-end development and back-end analysis being done by the corporation and its knowledge workers.

Relationship marketing is not a new concept, but at **Tribal DDB, Deborah Korono, Director of Relationship Marketing**, has developed it into a key facet of the company's offering. Just like McDowell at BMW, the ability to communicate and engage customers is the key. One trend that Korono saw emerging to support this idea is the increased focus on integrating sales/marketing channels to better personalize or customize offerings. Thus, Tribal DDB offers a number of data, research, and consulting solutions to serve these emerging needs. **Louise Bahns, European Research Manager for Yahoo! Europe** in the United Kingdom, concurred. "Media convergence is a big trend: it drives cross-utilization and [finds] fertile new ways to reach the customer. We have to understand how the Internet fits in the consumer's perspective, how online and offline factors interact and affect each other. This allows tactical approaches."

Betsy Frank, EVP, Research & Planning, MTV Networks (US), further supported the notion of staying in close touch with what consumers were thinking. A challenging trend she noted was declining response rates for phone surveys, with the promise of online research to ameliorate this situation. She, and **Laura Wendt, Sr V-P, Research & Planning, Nickelodeon, Nick at Nite, and TVLand**, posed the conundrum of a desire to use multiple methodologies to get a more complete view of the consumer, but the prohibitive cost aspects abound. In their opinion, a cost-effective, robust online solution has not arrived yet. But the sense is that if it could be delivered, it would be an enhancement and a desired solution.

Finally, one executive had an intriguing notion about the way research fits together and how it may be deployed in the near future. **Jean Schmitt, CEO of SLPInfoware** (France) – now with **Sofinnova**, a Paris-based investment firm – has built a business by developing predictive modeling solutions that enhance call center operations. GemPlus, the world's largest supplier of Smart Cards, recently purchased his firm to provide predictive algorithms that can be embedded into the Smart Card. This fairly cutting-edge product led Schmitt to describe the "perfect" research model: "At the most basic level are what I call 'tracking' studies. These are regular, but well-spaced research protocols carried out to understand one's attitudes. At the next level are 'tracing' studies, where perceptions are followed in-between the attitude measures, and a correlation can be made. Finally, at the finest level, we have the 'monitor', which is a device that continuously reports activities, behaviors, spur-of-the-moment feelings, and so on. This could be deployed through an always-on wireless device equipped with the proper analytic device. *Voila!* With the three levels in progress, numerous reporting, measurements, correlations, and insights can be generated. One could track at the individual level, or aggregate as traditional market research has always done."

The Consultancy Perspective

Rex Briggs — A call to arms

Consultants from quite varied backgrounds offered compelling insights into the challenges and issues facing the market research industry today. **Rex Briggs, Principal of Marketing Evolution**, is an expert in online research and advertising. His recent paper, presented at the 2001 ESOMAR Annual Conference in Rome with colleague **Laurent Flores, CEO of CRMMetrix**, raises a battle cry to the market research industry. Case study 9 presents the introduction from that paper.

Briggs's work in both the MR and CRM space has equipped him with a keen understanding of the strengths and weaknesses of both industries. The major trend he saw affecting the research industry is that the combination of CRM solutions and "big five" consultants working together to integrate a "total" solution has the potential to push the market research industry right out of the picture. Briggs said that the industry has two problems it needs to confront and solve:

- The comfort level of doing the familiar and the routine. Market research firms have great experience with aggregate level analysis, which is built on a powerful base of statistical theory, sampling, and experience. However, there are now equally powerful data-mining and CRM analytic tools that can be used to generate insight from the ground-up, rather than the top-down, traditional approach.
- The industry "code of conduct": clients are desperate for, and CRM solutions can provide, individual level data. A way needs to be found to get around this potential sticking point to utilize that data to generate important insights and for the experts to deliver insightful solutions.

Essentially, Briggs stated that it comes down to whether a firm wants to provide information versus enabling relationships. Providers of information are merely information-gatherers, aggregators, and disseminators. This is certainly a viable, though not particularly high-value, business, and market researchers could find themselves there permanently, if not careful.

Companies that enable relationships (CRM, consultants, and so on) have high value-added services, are tech savvy, lead clients (rather than follow), and deliver a solution that both supports the client and allows understanding of the individual consumer to best build a profitable relationship.

Case Study 9
Beyond Data-gathering – Implications of CRM Systems to Market Research

Introduction

Over the last few years a new industry and "buzzword" have emerged. CRM or customer relationship management has an annual growth rate of over 30 percent, and, according to IDC, will reach up to $12.1 billion by 2001. The technology analyst firm Gartner is even more bullish and recently stated that the market will be $15 billion in 2001. Whatever the source, the projections show CRM surpassing the global revenue of the entire market research industry within the next five years. In our analysis, it becomes clear that a new multibillion industry has emerged, with the purpose of allowing companies to better measure, understand, and manage customers. Is this mission not at the core of market research?

Although market researchers are quite familiar with the notion of measuring, understanding, and managing customers and prospects, few, if any, stand as the vanguard of CRM. Talk to market research leaders and ask them who their competitors are and precious few mention CRM companies. The CRM industry is after all dominated by companies that have emerged from technology and Internet industries specifically to provide Fortune 500 companies with systems that allow tracking of all their customer points of contact. Names such as Siebel, e.Piphany, Kana, Atg Dynamo, and so on, aren't research companies are they? An aspect of the mission statement of these CRM companies is to transform data into insights. Sound like a familiar mission? CRM companies are now encroaching on what marketing research companies believe to be their turf. Many of the CRM companies initially built technology to track customer contact/correspondence and behavior. These CRM companies are integrating customer intelligence tools into their systems that will help their clients better measure, understand, and act on their customer knowledge base.

Meanwhile, as the CRM companies build analytic expertise, we fear that traditional research companies have been watching without moving, or even worse: the majority of them are not even aware of the implications of the emerging CRM industry to their long-term survival.

Are market research companies missing the CRM opportunity? We think so. We believe that the main reason for this is that market research companies did not fully appreciate and leverage the opportunity offered by Internet-related technology. Although the so-called online research industry is largely growing by replacing traditional data-collection means, such as telephone and face-to-face interviewing, we think that bigger value for marketers resides not only in the ability to better collect data, but most importantly in the ability to transform data into insights and distribute this knowledge in new ways through the Internet. As Tom Miller (2000) put it in a recent article, "most research companies should think about themselves as being in the information industry rather than in the marketing research industry." Or as Barbara Hisiger, CEO of Lightspeed, put it, *"There is a world of difference between a market research company that uses the Internet and an Internet company that does market research. It's been near impossible to the sleeping giants of the research industry to wake up to get the challenge."*

How can traditional market research companies leverage the Internet as a means to transform process and value creation? To provide more than data? To provide information when decision-makers need it, and to make it instantly available and insightful?

Source: Laurent Flores, founder and CEO of CRM Metrics, and Rex Briggs, Principal, Marketing Evolution: Beyond Data Gathering: Implications of CRM Systems to Market Research. From the presentation at the ESOMAR Annual Conference, Rome, September 21, 2001. ESOMAR: Amsterdam.

Michael Schroeck – An elegant technical approach to enabling e-business

Michael Schroeck, Director of the Global iAnalytics practice for PricewaterhouseCoopers, recently published an article in *DMReview* that succinctly describes an integrated CRM solution that uses customer analytics to drive value. This exceptional piece, grounded in the reality of integration work that Schroeck has experienced, should be required reading for the market research industry. Case study 10 presents Schroeck's description of the difference that customer analytics can bring to CRM success.

Case Study 10
Enabling E-business Through Customer Analytics

"Customer Analytics Making the Difference in CRM: Customer Analytics Amplify the Value of Integrated CRM Solutions"

Introduction

Given the current economic climate, companies are valuing the benefits associated with understanding the economic and behavioral features of both current and prospective customers. An important element of their corporate strategy has centered on CRM. To help support their CRM strategy, companies have invested in multiple customer-facing solutions, such as sales force automation, enhanced customer service centers, marketing automation, or business-to-consumer (B-2-C) websites.

While these applications help facilitate better service and drive more efficient interaction with customers, they have often been implemented as distinct, nonintegrated solutions. As a result, they have failed to secure two very important objectives:

- A single view of the customer, via multichannel integration, to accurately inform all customer interactions.
- Customer information that is consistent and reliable across the enterprise.

Without this integrated customer information, companies cannot apply the appropriate analytics necessary to understand consumers and drive real value from relationship management.

The Integration of CRM and Customer Analytics

A customer data warehouse (CDW) provides the most effective way to create an integrated CRM data environment. A CDW aggregates data from each customer touch point to enable analysis to proceed in a holistic manner. It is only through the effective application of customer analytics and research that companies can generate insight into the customer's needs, perception, and attitude. As well, analytics can be extended to ROI classification (for example, expected customer revenue associated with attracting, retaining, or cross-selling loyal customers) and prediction (for example, will this customer be profitable?). In fact, by blending in financial information, companies can also calculate and forecast the lifetime value of customers.

It is well known in the industry that techniques exist that will provide unique insights into customer behavior. These methods leverage past customer behavior, trends, psychographic, and demographic data to help identify, attract, and retain a company's most profitable customers. To accomplish this requires that people, processes, data, and technologies align in order to understand the customer better. Only then can an organization use these analytical results to measure, anticipate, and influence customer behavior.

When performed effectively, this information can be garnered to strategically influence customer relationships. In the CRM industry, this process is known as closed-loop relationship management, as it reflects information flowing to and from every customer interaction, no matter where the source.

The Goal: Shaping Customer Behavior

It follows that businesses that use customer analytics are better able to understand and respond to – as well as anticipate – what customers expect. This gives them the power to be proactive in taking steps that can positively influence customer relationships.

For example, when the organization continuously tests and adjusts their actions over time to each customer segment, they are also more likely to be able to define the optimal strategy for retaining customers. Such a strategy leads to the development of robust customer models that enable the company to accurately identify valued customer segments and the ability to design and introduce protocols that speak to each of these segments.

The future will bring more extensive use of the Internet as an important enabling component to support customer behavior shaping. The key to success will be a customer data warehouse that contains accurate, consistent customer information sourced from multiple systems. The results of advanced analytics will be delivered to a web-based access point that informs employees and ultimately benefits the customer. As the new customer-driven economy continues to grow, integrated CRM and customer analytics will be vital to success.

Michael J. Schroeck is a partner in PricewaterhouseCoopers' Global Data Warehousing and Customer Analytics Practices. He is also the global champion for the firm's iAnalytics Solution Set.

Source: Michael Schroeck 2001. "Customer Analytics – Making the Difference in CRM." *DMReview*, Vol. 11, No. 9. EC Media Group: NY.

Ashley Friedlan – A CRM primer

In one of the most enlightening presentations currently available on CRM **Ashley Friedlan, CEO of e-Consultantcy.com**, clearly defined and put forth the opportunity, bottom line, and business case for CRM. While not a purposeful intention of his presentation, he also "raises the lid" on numerous areas where market research fits in the successful CRM process.

Of particular interest to those in measurement is the extended discussion about customer value. Friedlan stated:

> In the real world you might aim to treat everyone you meet fairly and courteously, but this does not mean you want a "relationship." There has to be some value exchange for a relationship to occur in new ways, such that different forms of relationships can grow over time. However, the notion that a fruitful relationship is based on a mutually appreciated value exchange is no different. As in real life, there are likely to be those who you are happy to treat politely, but whom you are certainly not interested in developing a relationship.
>
> Clearly, a company needs to make value propositions to its customers. The more differentiated, the more targeted, the higher the perceived value of the proposition – the more likely it is to succeed in attracting and retaining customers. However, what about the other side of the value exchange – how does a company understand the value of its customers?[2]

The answer, of course, is measurement. Relevant customer value criteria include:

- recency, frequency, and monetary (RFM) transaction values;
- the length of a customer's relationship with a company;
- churn rates by customer segment;
- a customer's future value;
- relationship marketing costs;
- marketing expenditures;
- cross-sell ratios;
- sphere of influence.

Measures such as these assist in understanding customer segments and their value. This understanding can motivate strategies for migrating or retaining customers based on their relative worth and potential to the company. Further, within a CRM software system, these strategies can be mapped to customer touch points at the front end. McKinsey has even gone so far as to develop an e-performance scorecard to better track customer attraction, conversion, and retention (see Figure 5.1).

Figure 5.1 An e-performance scorecard

Inside the e-performance Scorecard: The Indicators

ATTRACTION	CONVERSION	RETENTION
• Visitor base	• Customer base	• Repeat customer base
• Visitor acquisition cost	• Customer acquisition cost	• Repeat customer acquisition
• Visitor advertising revenue	• Customer conversion rate	cost
	• Number of transactions per	• Repeat customer conversion
	customer	rate
	• Revenue per transaction	• Number of transactions per
	• Revenue per customer	repeat customer
	• Customer gross income	• Revenue per transaction of
	• Customer maintenance cost	repeat customer
	• Customer operating income	• Revenue per repeat customer
	• Customer churn rate	• Repeat customer churn rate
	• Customer operating income	

Source: "E-performance: The path to rational exuberance" *McKinsey Quarterly*, 2001, #1

To those in the market research industry still contemplating whether or not to dive into the CRM pool, Friedlan's four-stage strategic development framework for CRM (see Figure 5.2) readily acknowledges that few companies have reached advanced stages of customer insight, particularly when multiple channels are involved. Not only are the key levers of CRM untested and under-researched, but the primary approaches and techniques suggested for determining basic customer insight are heavily weighted to rather common market research procedures: focus groups, surveying (online/offline) to hear the "consumer voice," and basic segmentation studies. Why the market research industry has not fully realized the opportunity to exert a leadership role in such a high margin industry is puzzling.

PART 2: WHAT DO YOU SEE THE FUTURE OF GLOBAL MARKET RESEARCH, OR CUSTOMER/CONSUMER INTELLIGENCE-GATHERING, TO BE IN 2005?

The Global MR Perspective: TNSi Bets on Broadband

Arno Hummerston, Head of Interactive Solutions, Worldwide at TNS and an experienced analytical thinker, predicted a research convergence; that is, all the variety of ways that people communicate (Internet, wireless, telephone, and so on) will be tapped by market research so that data can be drawn together in a common storage and access place for analysis.

Figure 5.2 CRM strategic development framework

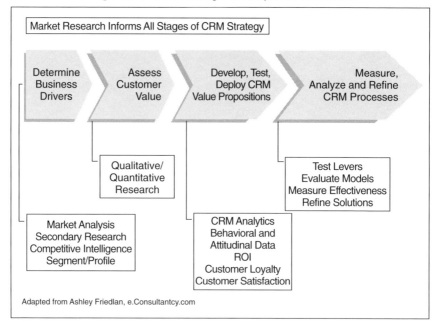

Broadband will enable "content and context richness" to emerge for researchers:

- analytics running in the background in real-time while people are in phone conversation or especially online;
- real-time interviews, online focus groups (OFGs), and discussion boards;
- "smart surveys" that adapt themselves to respondents' answers via a neural network analysis engine continually processing predictions;
- links between customer databases and surveys that will automatically populate and enrich results.

As Hummerston affirmed, however, the "sticky wicket" will occur over privacy concerns. Will people accept technology that links personal data to other information about them? This is a great unknown and fraught with complicated social, political, and legal issues.

Emerging markets: Is there an Internet?

Ipsos Reid's Gerry Grise, Sr V-P, is a specialist in researching emerging markets. From his vantage point, there is a "race toward getting solid national representative data in emerging markets," and the capabilities of the online medium are not necessarily useful in these locales. Theoretically, he can envision a truly global panel, but it must possess three characteristics:

(1) it must be representative of the country and the world; (2) it must be representative of these households; and (3) all respondents must be equally accessible. The penetration rate of Internet access and the ability to do this all online is quite a way down the road, in his opinion.

According to Grise, online research is feasible for most things Internet-related, For example, take "Internet behavior, pop-up surveys to capture 'at-the-moment' opinions, and website testing." These are obviously good applications. But what about the future? Grise envisioned six characteristics and changes in the industry we can expect to see in the next five years:

- traditional methods will gradually be replaced by newer, tech-driven ones;
- there will be a continuous and steady growth of online research with the result being that we will have the ability to correlate the growth of both the customer base and online users;
- panels will continue to be a problem due to two persistent sources of bias: (1) the Internet-user population as a subset will still be skewed; and (2) those that agree to be on a panel distinguish themselves from those that do not choose to be on a panel to an unknown degree;
- cheap and fast online research will fly in emerging markets, but has to be approached carefully. The Net bias issue will still be evident, and viable alternatives such as Net-CAPI and Net-CATI may need to be actively deployed;
- the market research industry, as a whole, will change:
  - most, if not all, medium-sized firms will be gone;
  - as mergers and acquisitions continue, the face of the industry will be made up of a handful of extremely large companies, and a layer of many smaller, specialized boutique firms;
  - market research in emerging markets will not be developed internally, but will be driven by outside interests;
- most clients will be looking for quick, reliable, and cost-efficient global information, including cross-border global snapshots. The challenge to the industry will be exacerbated in finding and developing new global skills in research personnel.

ACNielsen is squarely in the information industry

Bill Pulver, now **President** of the leading global online ratings and measurement company in existence (**ACNielsen's Net-Ratings**), is highly dedicated and focused on the ability of ACNielsen to fulfill with the online channel the same role it fulfills in other media-rating and measurement domains: as the dominant and undisputed leader. Pulver saw the Internet space clearly as evolving and maturing to allow enriched drilling deeper and deeper into available data, thus driving value-added insight to tracking and metrics delivery. The industry on a basic level will change via the correlation between the number of users online and the type of global consumers that will emerge. Thus, the economic viability of the Internet is still evolving. Finally, Pulver said that face-to-face and traditional methods will always have their place and will always be there, regardless of the ubiquity of the Internet infrastructure.

V-P of Marketing, Bob Tomei, focused on ACNielsen's strong attachment to the importance of seeing market research through the lens of the larger information industry. Information access, collection, dissemination, and analysis will drive the continued consolidation of companies into information-driven services companies that include capabilities in research, promotions, advertising, marketing services, and sales improvement. The continued growth of databases will result in both larger collections of accessible data, but also more differentiated ones. Thus, the whole spectrum of market research and a broad continuum of studies will be made possible.

As a result of the vital place information will play in the future, the role of market research will expand significantly. As an influencer and informer of business insights and decisions, the industry will be diverging into all sorts of report and support services for clients' sales, marketing, and executive needs. In fact, anyone who uses information to make decisions and execute against them will be a potential client of the new information-driven market research company.

David Jenkins sees a bigger picture

David Jenkins, CEO of Kantar Group, presides over a formidable array of research-related companies under the WPP umbrella. From his perspective, the market research industry is somewhat naive about the reality of its place in the larger business picture. As Jenkins noted, "Companies use market research as a relatively minor piece of their total information, dissemination, and analytic use." As Jenkins observed, the universe of business intelligence and business information is quite substantial. To believe that market research is the center of it borders on foolishness.

What then, is the place of market research in the future? Jenkins saw the convergence of data- and information-collection into one primary system – a fusing of databases – as a key area rife with potential. The opportunity, however, is for the "integrators," those who can go in and design solutions that pull data and information into one place, make it accessible, and enable component development that makes sense and is useful for business people. Currently, "big five" and second-tier consultants appear to have a handle on this. Could market researchers be more involved? Not without a substantial change in attitude, Jenkins declared.

Jenkins likened the future of the market research industry to the current automotive industry alignment: in the auto industry, consolidation, acquisitions, and mergers will continue unabated until only a few industry "giants" are left. At that point, or perhaps even before, even these behemoths could be swallowed up by even bigger technology companies, such as Microsoft, Oracle, and IBM. This would complete the cycle by making these "new" corporate entities a currently unimaginable conglomerate organized around information access, services, and delivery.

GfK group: An objective independent giant

Heinrich Litzenroth of GfK, like Jenkins at Kantar, agreed that increased consolidation in the industry is inevitable. From his perspective, however, this engenders a twinge of concern that the era of the objective, independent market research firm may well end. GfK's position is that the loss of objectivity would be harmful in the end to clients. According to Litzenroth, "Imagine if the only choices open to clients are to use market research services embedded in a 'family' of other sales, direct marketing, advertising, public relations, and planning members. How can that service be objective? Why would it not be biased toward the safety and health of its other divisions?" Obviously, GfK is determined to be one of the largest independent firms left standing, regardless of future consolidation trends.

Litzenroth felt that the strengths of the independent model would be bolstered by factors such as a growth in "implementation consulting." As business problems and research solutions become more complex, firms will be called on to find new and better ways to deliver decision support. Outsourcing will grow, as market research companies become, in some cases, de facto research divisions for large global clients. But the market research firm must bring its technology skills up to speed to succeed here, as the continued proliferation of data, the inevitable merging of databases (marketing and traditional market research data), and the ability to eventually integrate them will be a fundamental task of the market research industry. Indeed, it will be a prerequisite before any long-term serious value-added insight delivery can be managed in that new space.

NFO interactive: Efficiency rules

At NFO Interactive, now a part of the Interpublic Group of Companies, **President Mark Berry** lauded the umbrella model of organization as a great source of knowledge transfer and corporate learning that wouldn't exist if they were an independent company, rather than the arm of one of the larger global business conglomerates. To Berry, the future is entwined with raising marketing efficiency. Marketing is a terribly inefficient function, but the incredible reduction in the time it takes from the experience of a marketing event to a consumer response is stretching traditional capabilities of market research firms to the limit. Clients need research that a mature online research service company can deliver. Such a company needs:

- processes that uncover the highest value-creating customers and consumers;
- fresh thinking about the depth of consumer reactions, attitudes, and perceptions that are occurring;
- unique contributions, only achievable with an online system that will drive marketing efficiencies.

Thus, the future, according to Berry, is in "building bridges to insight" via the online channel.

ABT associates senses the power of online panels

Vinod Swaminathan, quoted earlier in this book, and his colleagues at ABT Associates – **Susan Windham-Bannister, Managing V-P Business Research, Consulting Division, and Richard Pace, V-P of Sales & Marketing** – saw the emerging role of the Internet in the future, especially as broadband becomes more accessible, to accelerate the capability to do more projects online. Swaminathan, in particular, is supportive of online panels in the future: "Online panels will increase the speed clients can access perceptions and attitudes in the marketplace. Designing group studies, representative panels, and global access panels will be the key. Online branding studies and direct-to-consumer studies in healthcare and the pharmaceutical industry will increase the value of market research, particularly our ability to advise clients with appropriate well-grounded information."

Mark Sievewright of TowerGroup: The outlook for financial services industry research

TowerGroup, operated via a joint venture with the Reuters Group, is a specialized, high-quality research firm with a focus on the financial services industry. **CEO Mark Sievewright** brings a well-rounded global and financial services background to the company as it works with Reuters toward global expansion. Sievewright, in developing an innovative 10-step plan that he is executing against for Tower, has had more than one occasion to mull over the future of the industry. Key for the future, in his mind, is the ability of market research firms to continue to add value that can be measurably demonstrated to clients. If they cannot, clients may decide to blend the market research function – using new tools and technologies that become available – into internal processes due to cost, speed, and control efficiencies.

The global perspective, already in sight for Sievewright, is extremely important. The ability to benchmark, compare, track, and trend financial services on a global basis is the key. Along with that, research firms will have to learn how to cope with and maximize the value of data in multiple forms. Citing the Onstar system found in some General Motors vehicles, Sievewright contended that this is valuable information that is being sent, stored, and is accessible somewhere right now. It functions indirectly as a tracking system for the customer. This holds enormous implications for the merging and analysis of structured, familiar forms of data and unstructured data not normally associated with consumer research. Yet, here it is – the future will bring more, not less, of this, according to Sievewright.

Opinion Research Corporation: Focusing at the cusp of consulting and high-tech delivery

Opinion Research Corporation, a high-end, high-quality marketing and opinion research company with a solid history, firmly believes in the value of accumulated wisdom. **Jeffrey Resnick, CEO, US Group, ORC International**, envisioned a future scenario where market research firms will open up the "hood" for clients to access valuable and insightful data that top research industry leaders have collected and stored in abundance. Noting that CRM solutions do not have such a repository of "accumulated wisdom" to share, Resnick stated that it is "all about accessing and sharing wisdom and knowledge directly and intimately with the client." Along with this concept, Resnick predicted that up to 70 percent of information which clients need to make business decisions will be delivered directly to the client's desktop under the control and guidance system of the market research provider. The focus will be on value and execution.

Regarding the future of the industry in general, Resnick said the emergence of a highly specialized, cutting-edge layer in research companies, just as the current middle layer in firms begins to disappear. This smaller, but potentially more creative and innovative, segment of the industry will become the testing ground for what works and doesn't work in the marketplace, and eventually the successful ones will join bigger and bigger firms as the forces of business consolidation continue to reign.

INTAGE

Norio Taori, the President and CEO of Intage, saw the future of market research as a provider of intelligence, closely aligned in today's terms with a combination of skills and services found in CRM, syndicated, database, and consulting companies. This unique blend allows the research firm to put a focus on the database and technology, and to turn it into useful information, literally turning that information into "intelligence." The final step is to take this useful data and the systems and make wise decisions for and with the client. Thus, in Taori's words, "We help them run their business better by assisting them in planning wisely."

The New Media Perspective

WebSideStory: ASPs

Michael Christian, Sr V-P of Analytics at WebSideStory, predicted that Application Service Providers (ASPs) for software services will prevail and flourish in the future. The compelling reason this will occur is because of the increasingly long software development cycles. While changes and developments in hardware, in the form of chips and memory, progresses quite regularly according to Moore's Law, software does not. Mission critical software is becoming so complex that development cycles threaten to make the final product obsolete by the time it is debugged, tested, and ready to use.

An ASP, or hosted solution, runs software development in tandem with running the software itself for the client. Thus, it eliminates that tedious cycle for the client, and instead offers upgrades instantaneously when they are completed. But there are other advantages, said Christian. In the near future, he predicted that the integration of online and offline data will be critical. WebSideStory is already exploring a "self-reliance" model, where it equips clients with the tools to take online data and integrate it with offline data. An alternate model, called the "push" model, does the reverse. It moves offline data directly in with online data. Thus, offline data can be fed into the real-time system, automatically enriching it, enabling fast analysis and reporting. Only with a hosted solution can this flexibility be delivered efficiently and effectively.

Knowledge Networks: Beyond the traditional household panel

Doss Struse of **Knowledge Networks** said the inconvenience of traditional marketing research techniques will become a major problem in the near future. Even as communications devices proliferate, and more avenues to collect data appear to open up, consumers seem more reluctant to interrupt activities to participate in surveys, for example. The cooperation rates in phone surveys is at near-record low levels, and legislation to outright ban unwanted phone calls will give citizens the power to tune out of market research surveys forever. So much for the random digit dialing (RDD) technique.

Knowledge Networks iTV panels are well known in the industry. What Struse predicted, however, goes well beyond just reinventing the household panel. The very technological advancements that have enabled rapid and widespread communications, mostly based on the Internet, can be harnessed by blending the access panel concept and new technology. In the near future, Struse believes that access panels will be leveraged into "CRM" research panels. Since participants agree to join an access panel, the research company can manage their trust, security, and privacy. Once a member, technological advancements will allow the panel company to embed multiple levels of data over the panelist's responses to surveys, online focus group discussions, or other forms of primary research. Thus, the melding of one-to-one research and traditional aggregate approaches can be accomplished to enrich results, increase precision, and open doors to new insights. Opt-in secures that personal data can be managed and used, third-party data can be appended (if needed), and fresh survey insights can be gathered. This approach also solves the puzzle faced by the market research industry regarding how best to handle personal, transactional level data and use it without violating industry standards and codes of conduct.

TrueAudience

Dave Morgan, CEO of **TrueAudience**, now TACODA Systems, described a future where all media will be interactive, highly segmented, and capable of being highly personalized. The marriage of online and offline data, and personalization and segmentation, will enable us to build a rich blend of personal media preference profiles to drive advertising, marketing, and sales efforts. By favoring behavioral segments over demographic ones, marketers and manufacturers can more precisely balance efficiency and customization. In the near future, said Morgan, the whole concept of media and advertising will be much broader, encompassing full digital, digital/analog mix, and full analog. By collecting and analyzing behavioral data, researchers can more precisely pinpoint where on the continuum segments lie, and predict with more accuracy how they will respond to marketing and advertising appeals. Morgan's TrueAudience AMS (audience management system) offers a phased approach to building the infrastructure to accommodate this vision of the future.

AOL/DMS

Digital Marketing Services is a wholly owned subsidiary of America Online, providing exclusive online survey research services to AOL Time Warner and its properties. **Dennis Gonier** anticipates the day when a ubiquitous broadband network opens up online personalization possibilities and the ability to extend online research effectively into qualitative arenas. With the broadband connection, online focus group (OFGs), for example, can more closely resemble a videoconference, a platform in widespread use throughout the corporate world. Gonier has an interesting take on the recent talk and attempts to marry online and offline data. He related that just before the Internet revolution broke open, certain folks in the direct and database marketing arena were just on the threshold of understanding how to integrate custom research and database data. Of course, in an era when "pigs could fly," said Gonier, everything was dropped to pursue the pot of gold at the end of the Internet rainbow. Interestingly, the Internet-enabled digital revolution has brought us back around again to the possibilities inherent in those nascent schemes and plans.

ResearchLab – A Scandinavian view

ResearchLab's CEO **Ulf Andersen** has mixed feelings about the staggering growth of wireless usage in his native Norway. While the fact that perhaps up to 10 percent of the nation's population only have and use a mobile phone, and they seem to represent a fairly specific segment of the population, it means that standard telephone RDD may become a thing of the past. However, it is exciting to be so close to the cutting edge of solutions and practices in this new era. Andersen believes that the use of the Internet will continue to grow, with portal delivery to clients of research becoming a ubiquitous standard. Other aspects he foresees are interactive research tools more and more in the hands of clients, the rise of "virtual MR" firms, and a desperate need by clients to move beyond traditional methods to creative new approaches that make best use of the digital channel. While much of the development of new techniques and practices may be the province of smaller firms scattered around the research marketplace, he envisioned the possibility of the development of coordinated networks, similar to "skunkworks" in the R&D industry, that operate at or near the cutting edge in development, solutions, and services. In fact, discussions in Scandinavia have already begun about ways to create virtual "market research and development centers" that mimic very successful standard industry ones already in place that employ a physical campus and join a network of academic, industrial, and business professionals in close proximity.

SAS – The CRM/BI Perspective

Donna Callahan of SAS sees the direction of market research-type activities moving toward the increased business value of real-time analytical CRM solutions in a multichannel environment. The opportunity here lies in the shift in business strategy from product sales and profits to customer profitability. Poor implementation of multichannel strategies is lowering customer satisfaction and loyalty and advancing CRM's critical importance. With increased customer expectations and demands for an exact fit to personal requirements, it is increasingly vital for businesses to understand the customer and act accordingly. Of all the customer touch points, marketing is tied the most closely to analytics. Multichannel marketing has increased the cost of campaigns that need to be justified with a higher ROI. Thus, companies will be looking for more robust and flexible analytical CRM solutions like those that SAS is in the business of providing.

Callahan believes that three types of analytics – market relationship, customer-centric, and historical – are required for a complete solution to emerge. In her opinion, it is most important to keep in mind that successful CRM requires analytical support. A sound business strategy, however, must also be in place that the whole enterprise embraces. Callahan posits that CRM is not a technology: it is an enterprise-wide strategy enabling organizations to optimize customer satisfaction, revenue, and profits, while increasing shareholder value through better understanding customers' needs.

A step in this direction has begun via a joint partnership between SAS and MarketTools, a hosted online market research software provider. Together, they are working to deliver all the customer information needed to maximize the returns on multichannel marketing investments. By enabling the client to build complete customer profiles by bringing together information about behaviors and attitudes from all touch points; collecting, consolidating, and analyzing this data to make informed predictions about customers; and providing analytic tools to segment and target the products/ services they are most likely to purchase, the SAS/MarketTools solution hopes to deliver the right information, in near real-time to make effective marketing strategy decisions.

Callahan sees three aspects driving near-future solutions:

- the capability to combine enterprise-wide analytical CRM with online customer survey information;
- the ability to effectively combine comprehensive market research information to offer a complete online and offline customer view;
- the quality and reliability of business intelligence software and enterprise-scalable survey technology, including data-mining and warehousing.

A CRM future?

Seeing the future is difficult for those involved in the CRM and tech-driven BI tools industry. In many ways, they feel as if they are creating the future now. This is at once CRM's strength and its soft spot.

Thus, **Usama Fayad** of **digiMine** spoke of the advantages of the hosted model for complex data-mining solutions. **Dan Lackner** and **Paul Rodwick** of competitors **Siebel** and **e.Piphany**, respectively, talked about consolidating data to inform completely about customers, and **Rex Briggs** predicted a future for the market research industry that well may be embedded in the future of the CRM industry. The future of CRM is clearly tied to technology and the ability to leverage technology via new systems that drive more effective and efficient business processes.

It is also clear that the missing piece in CRM today is its lack of a "brain." The Digital Nervous System cannot function without it. Thus, concerted efforts are underway to put together solutions that are most closely related to the activities, techniques, and processes of the market research industry. CRM executives, business developers, and analytic experts are scouring the global countryside looking for ways to integrate the customer voice, improve the customer experience, develop loyalty, and assess customer satisfaction in ways that improve the CRM proposition and solution.

The Client Perspective

Yahoo! Europe

Louise Bahns, European Research Manager, described the necessity of researchers on the client side becoming more involved at the decision level. The market researcher is the logical person to carry the "voice of the consumer" to important decision-makers. As Bahns said, this is "to make sure that consumer insights are present in every business decision."

The future for market research on the client side will be bleak, unless people inside companies are more proactive. In line with this, market research providers will have to become more comfortable drawing information from diverse sources; that is, data not traditionally dealt with currently in the industry. This could mean the use of new technology-based tools or in utilizing mixed-mode research techniques.

Market researchers will have to learn to better balance the technical/ analytic side (where they are most comfortable) and the business objectives and purposes side. The historical tendency for the industry still prevails: this is a preoccupation with detail, method, and process. This may or may not be the right approach in the rapidly emerging Internet-driven future.

Bahns also had the greatest future concern about respondents. She pondered, "What do we do if some day no-one decides to answer our questions?" The future of market research will be directly correlated with the trilogy of respect, privacy, and security.

Believers in traditional market research

Bob Herbold, former Chief Operating Officer of **Microsoft** and now retired, has a refreshing take on the future of market research. In placing his emphasis on the continuing evolution of companies paying more attention to customers, Herbold felt that both CRM and market research have their place. Market research is a science that will endure.

At **BMW NA, Jim McDowell** has the enviable task of getting to know a high-income segment that purchases expensive automobiles. To him, the Internet is a given for market research. It affords communication, customer service, customer relations, and allows an unprecedented focus on the BMW consumer. Thus, for McDowell, research is about consistently and regularly testing clients directly at all levels for ideas, perceptions, attitudes, and opinions.

Relationship marketing

Deborah Korono, the **Director of Relationship Marketing** at **Tribal DDB**, has distinct ideas about the future. She believes we will see more and more behavioral data, more true one-to-one marketing – which she defined as, "a detailed look at the individual to best market and sell" – and a growing focus on rapid delivery of consumer insight. One area that will grow more important is the concept of "fair exchange;" that is, the giving of something for getting personal information from consumers. The final future trend she noted had to do with the continued growth of word-of-mouth (viral) marketing in the online space. This concept of a "consumer influencer" is not new. What is emerging is the unique ability to track this sort of person (once identified) across the online landscape to assess and learn behaviors, attitudes, and demographics: in essence, "living research."

Coda

How can we best leverage Internet technology to improve market research? Part 3 of our book presents a detailed blueprint for action. This section presents and discusses the ways that market research can be supported across the qualitative-quantitative research continuum.

Notes

1   All comments and quotes in the remainder of this chapter are the result of personal interviews that took place from July 2001 till November 2001. The authors gratefully acknowledge the many professionals who took the time to discuss important industry and business issues with us.

2   Ashley Freidlan 2001."CRM meets eCRM: An Executive Briefing" Wheel and e.Consultantcy.com.

PART 3

Leveraging Internet Technology:
A Blueprint for Action

INTRODUCTION

Part 3 of our book discusses in detail the components of a complete online-enabling technology system for market research. Facets of such a system exist today and are available from a short list of vendors in the market research industry. The essence of the next six chapters is on the exploration and description of a broad all-encompassing market research framework that is scaleable, has the ability to extend across the enterprise and around the world, and that integrates all major research processes available and necessary to serve the global client.

CHAPTER 6

From Transaction to Tracking

The complex mixture of challenges and opportunities facing the market research industry today – as presented and described in Part 1 and Part 2 – are also motivating enabling solutions that can allow the industry to move forward. A two-part solution: (1) the ability to deploy multiple methods and types of market research within an integrated web-centric system; and (2) the delivery of data and/or results directly to the corporate desktop has emerged as the vehicle by which the market research industry can meet the challenges and optimize the opportunities afforded in the Internet Age.

For truly effective solutions, a proper plan or blueprint is devised. This chapter presents such a blueprint for managing and delivering global market research via a web-enabled system. We will explore the components of this system, the key logic and potential advantages gained by integrating data for analysis within such a system, and the major ways to leverage the technology as a potent tool for understanding consumers and customers.

MANAGING GLOBAL RESEARCH VIA THE INTERNET

Figure 6.1 depicts a comprehensive online market research system. This integrated infrastructure has six components:

1 **Project management**: delivers capabilities to manage a complete research project from initiation to deployment to delivery to payment.
2 **Panel management**: provides the ability to fully build and manage panels online, as well as manage other sources of ad hoc samples.
3 **Mixed-mode data-collection**: affords the capability to collect response data in multiple ways using the online system.

4 **Global data store**: a database integrating data collected in real-time from all data-collection components.

5 **Analysis and reporting**: supports familiar traditional and advanced market research analytic tools, as well as the delivery management of raw data, top lines, and fully completed reports directly to the end-client.

6 **Direct delivery to the end-client**: the capability to deliver customized and customizable data, reports, and analyses directly to various levels of the business hierarchy via a desktop corporate information portal.

Figure 6.1 Comprehensive online research system

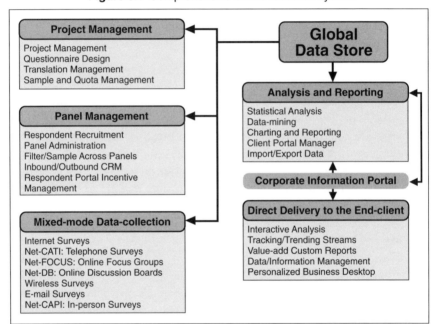

Key Characteristics of an Integrated Online Global Market Research System

An integrated online system for global market research has several characteristics that distinguish it from earlier processes and methods. The primary attributes differentiating this system include:

• **Technical**: the global market research system exploits the latest technologies available to improve processes, projects, and products. Most prominent here is a fully integrated infrastructure, utilizing a common data core, that can be accessed by multiple components configured to support the most common market research processes. In addition, the system is customizable for enhanced usability or specific needs.

- **Integration**: a key characteristic of the system is a robust and pervasive integration driven on the one hand by the capabilities of the Internet and web-based technologies, and on the other by fully understanding, designing, creating, and enhancing global market research processes and fulfillment on the technology platform.
- **Management**: a core characteristic is the ease and thoroughness for managing multiple processes and information workflows. The online global market research system centralizes, integrates, and tracks all of the management functions required to deliver market research insight.
- **Control**: in conjunction with management, greater control is exercised as a by-product of the centralized and integrated system. Tracking and accounting for billing, costs, and revenue are brought together under one controlling system for ease of administration.
- **Efficiency**: integrated management and greater control naturally result in efficiencies across many operations. These are not limited to cost efficiencies, but include time savings, personnel savings, and more efficient reporting and insight delivery.
- **Scalability**: a Net-based technology system is capable of essentially infinite scalability. What this means is that the system can grow to meet increased demands across the board without any major changes or retooling.
- **Languages**: critical for a global system is the ability to carry out language translations in the most efficient manner possible. Note that this is not a protocol to replace substantive knowledge about cultures and peoples, but a way to take the more mundane processes involved in the translation process, standardize them, and deliver a procedure for making the task as efficient as possible.
- **Effectiveness**: this characteristic is an outgrowth of the combined effects of the features listed above. Effectiveness is enhanced when numerous and time-consuming processes that can be automated, made more efficient, or improved are in place. Thus, multiple improvements can occur; for example, when increased time can be spent by the market research professional on delivering true higher value insights, recommendations, and decision actions; the wall is broken down for clients to effectively close the loop on information interactivity; and new and innovative ways to deliver multiple insights directly to the client desktop are achieved.

The five components of a comprehensive online market research system are tightly interwoven in delivering a complete global market research solution:

Component 1: Project management

Rationale: A web-based interface and system affords unprecedented control, efficiency, and monitoring of projects. This component is explored and described in Chapter 8: "Online market research project management."

Component 2: Panel management

Rationale: An online management system enhances the efficiency, development, administration, and use of global access panels, thus extending the market researcher's reach around the world. This component is described in Chapter 7: "Global access panels."

Component 3: Mixed-mode data-collection

Rationale: The ability to extend and enhance the broadest possible set of the professional market researcher's techniques, processes, and methods is a critical success factor. Technically, an enabling online system can host, store, and provide access to data-collection from virtually any source. The key point is not to replace existing, time-tested research methods, but to use the online system to enhance, extend, and make more efficient the processes that can be readily adapted over time. This component is examined and described in Chapter 9: "Mixed-mode data-collection," and Chapter 11: "Scaling the one-to-one experience."

Component 4: Analysis and reporting

Rationale: To fully exploit the technological capabilities that are available, demanded, and in use in many companies today new forms of analysis and reporting are needed. The global online market research system affords multiple delivery modes and channels. In fact, a well-formed, well-integrated online system can strongly support a key market research industry objective: to become the primary provider of intelligence, insight, and decision support to executives, managers, analysts, and knowledge workers across the enterprise and around the world. This component is examined and described in Chapter 10: "Analyzing data and reporting results."

Component 5: Direct delivery to the end-client

Rationale: The rapid rise in the use of corporate information portals on a stand-alone basis, or as part of a sophisticated CRM system, has already reached critical proportions in many Global 2000 companies. This represents an unprecedented opportunity for the core strengths of the market researcher's value to be delivered directly to the corporate desktop. While efforts are underway from numerous and converging points, the path to the desktop is clear. Chapter 10, "Analyzing data and reporting results," will examine this key component and its potential in the online market research delivery system.

INTEGRATING TRANSACTIONAL AND MARKET RESEARCH DATA

One key concept of an enhanced and technology-driven solution that has been attempted in a variety of database, data-warehouse, and CRM solutions is that of "database integration." Essentially, the architecture of this integrated system attempts to break down the "silos," as separate database collections are called, to afford a common source for data to be accessed. Figure 6.2 depicts the essence of such a system.

Note that multiple sources of data that make sense to combine for analysis, storage, or access can be accommodated. On the other side of the data-collection process are multiple access or "touch points" where a variety of research techniques can be applied. In Figure 6.2, market research can be deployed at key customer touch points via customizable or standard Application Program Interfaces (APIs) to access data for analysis and delivery. In effect, what this allows for is the potential to close the loop on understanding, tracking, or reporting on key customer characteristics or events. For example, a question concerning customer satisfaction and purchasing behavior: "what are people buying *and* how satisfied are they?" can be answered in this integrated system. As well, certain particulars about these results or implications can be delivered very quickly, or the client can gain access to run their own ad hoc queries similar to what is now done with online analytical processing (OLAP) tools used in the back office. In short, a highly flexible and powerful analytic and reporting system is in place that can readily evolve as needs change.

SEGMENTING CUSTOMERS FOR PREDICTIVE AND BEHAVIORAL KNOWLEDGE

An interesting conundrum exists today for the market researcher regarding the use of multiple forms of data that are collected. While systems exist – and some marketing disciplines promote the use of them – that can combine behavioral and attitudinal data for analysis, the market research industry in general has been careful in treading on what it feels is a potential landmine of personal privacy. This reluctance, coupled with the industry's strong scientific foundation (based on sampling theory and practice) and its tendency to rely on traditional deliverables and services, have tempered

Figure 6.2 Integrating transactional and market research data

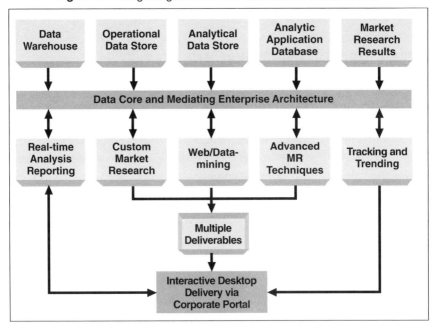

strong industry efforts to leverage multiple forms of data in building consumer insight. Figure 6.3 presents a broad picture of the essential components that the market research industry – utilizing a technology-driven and Net-centric system – can potentially draw on to extend the usefulness and breadth of its analytic expertise and to knowledgeably inform marketing strategies, responses, and actions.

Key in this picture is that although market research firms deliver many or most of these analyses in the course of business, they are often – as are the data-collection mechanisms – separate, individual divisions, processes, or solutions. The difference apparent with the integrated online system is the ability to integrate, coordinate, and cross-inform analyses. This functionality is built into the enabling architecture's systems and structure. Thus, the major forms of studying and understanding customers or consumers can be linked, affording the potential to build a deeper, more complete picture. Up-selling research solutions, commonly associated with higher value, more complex analyses or procedures, now becomes part of a continuum of services that are naturally connected. Clients can buy in at any touch point of the system that makes sense and is appropriate for best informing their needs.

The combination of behavioral, attitudinal, and demographic data, including the appending of robust readily available third-party data, provides the raw data stream that can be accessed by the market research analyst, consultant, or knowledge worker to drive primary segmentation, prediction, and testing approaches. Easily incorporated are such things as:

- registration/membership forms' data: from panels, or through customizing, personalizing, buying, or selling experiences;
- transactional/scanning data;
- original survey research; testing and modeling discoveries;
- secondary research used for benchmarking purposes.

With this enabling system, the Holy Grail of the 360-degree view of the consumer is on the horizon. Thus, such activities as anticipating customer needs through prediction and understanding become more feasible. And the

Figure 6.3 Studying customers

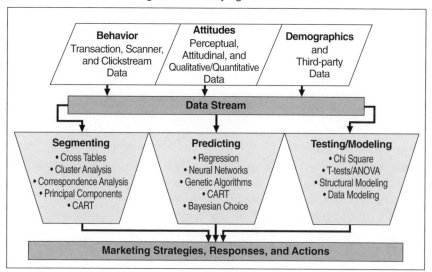

opportunity for the market research professional to delve into deeper, more sophisticated, and potentially more useful executive/management decision and marketing support solutions is enhanced.

ONLINE MARKET RESEARCH AND CRM ANALYTICS

Perhaps the strongest card that the market research industry can play in the race to understand the consumer and guide business decisions and actions is not being used today. Figure 6.4 depicts a generic CRM model that is currently in place in many corporations around the world. Note that data from customer interactions at many touch points are entering into the data warehouse or data store. That data are then accessed in numerous ways to support both the front and back office. What is particularly clear is the fact that market research is but one component of this larger system. However, it is a very important one, since it is the only one that can robustly and directly inform the customer-facing front office about who their customers are, why they are here, what they are looking for, whether they are satisfied, and what would make them loyal consumers. Yet, in the typical "picture" we have of marketing and sales processes, market research is not an integrated component but is seen off in a peripheral corner with an arrow going to the marketing function. This is not a compelling or vital portrait, even though the insight and understanding research can bring delivers great value on all sides of the communication and "relationship improvement" equation.

Currently, CRM analytics comprise a weak solution for learning about and understanding the consumer. OLAP is essentially most useful when accessing, analyzing, and reporting back office data collected in the data warehouse or data mart. Its ease of use via the web browser is an attractive feature, but it does little to add value to the deeper issues that marketing, sales, and customer service personnel face.

Likewise, automated data-mining algorithms (sometimes in a templated format to afford some element of ease-of-use, control, or customization), although they fit very well into the CRM architecture and system, they are fairly limited in their ability to provide actionable insight to marketers. In most cases they work very well for certain precisely defined types of prediction or classification problems, where they can generate a quick response to a situation for a sales or customer service representative. But, generally, they cannot provide the depth of insight or learning that a well-planned, expert market research study can provide.

The CRM architecture and the ability of market research firms to adapt a technology-driven system and solution serves to right the picture so that market research can assume the proper function and value it possesses. Thus, an online market research system supports the role of market research as a key agent in the customer management and relationship process.

In fact, it can be argued that market research essentially informs the pillars of customer loyalty, satisfaction, and care by going beyond CRM's limitations. CRM systems, although elegant, still look at the customer through the lens of the organization, when instead they should be looking through the lens of the customer.[1] Market research can deliver that customer-facing focus. It can assist in the deeper understanding and advancing of the buyer-seller bond by accessing vital consumer knowledge not touched by CRM systems. Indeed, market research may well be the "missing ingredient" in the CRM solution that can be brought to bear to achieve

Figure 6.4 Online market research in the CRM process

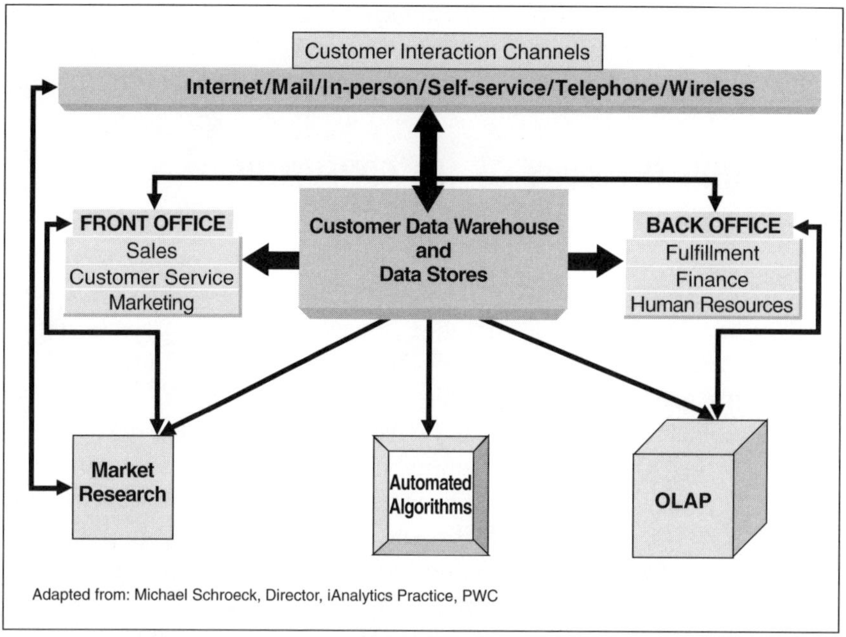

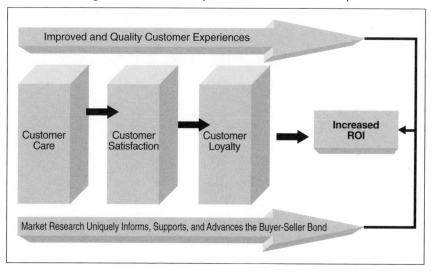

Figure 6.5 Pillars of improved customer relationships

success. Perhaps in response to this need, there is emerging on the horizon a new class of solutions termed "customer experience management" (CEM) that are attempting to marry the power of technology and the power of market research into one integrated and complementary system.

CAPTURING THE VOICE OF THE CONSUMER[2]

Solid CRM is a critical business asset, but most companies do not understand the integrative complexity involved in this concept. Too often they accept anything called "CRM" as a magical cure and expect it to work "out of the box." CRM is not just about automating or speeding up operations; rather, a major facet is optimizing data and information to intelligently manage customer relationships.

The realization of this deficit in the CRM system has organizations frantically reaching for CRM optimization "fixes" via analytics. This change, currently underway but incomplete, will affect current methods of market research, campaign management, and marketing protocols by directly and purposefully infusing technology-driven analytical and market research solutions into CRM operational systems.

Marketing and sales personnel, for example, strive to capture and retain customer loyalty by focusing on customer satisfaction. This goal will not be met, however, if directed only by the operational side of the equation. Rather, data analysis must lead to a deeper and richer understanding of the interactions that may result in customer satisfaction or dissatisfaction, loyalty, and improved service. Leveraging analytic techniques, such as profiling, segmentation, and prediction, will boost the potential to influence customers through an informed understanding of them. However, only market research has the added ability to infuse the qualitative side of the picture. These techniques, tested and proven over time, tap directly into the consumer's mind, feelings, perceptions, and attitudes. They truly can inform the customer experience. The resulting satisfaction, loyalty, and profitability gains – the mission of CRM – are then actively supported and powerfully enhanced by market research and analysis.

Enabling Interaction and Collaboration

A system for improving customer interactions requires an information core for centralized access to data on customer behavior, attitudes, and perceptions. Through this system, the company can measure and probe customer experiences, reveal insights, and capture the voice of the consumer.

The software available for improving customer experience understanding and management is just appearing from many of the CRM suite providers.

Vendors, such as Siebel Systems and e.piphany, having realized the Achilles' heel in their systems, are rapidly moving toward the increased application of analytics to better understand customers and drive improved relationships. To be successful, however, all CRM vendors will need to ensure they provide application integration points for adding customer-facing software packages – including Net-centric market research components – to drive a more complete solution.

Meeting customer expectations will require that businesses continue to invest in new technologies that can deliver on the promise of CRM. It is doubtful that CRM analytics alone can do the trick. The idea of efficiently "shaping" customers throughout their consumer life-cycle is becoming widely accepted, and companies need to adapt to this change by evolving their existing CRM infrastructure and considering the improvements that online market research can bring.

The Marriage of Customer Experience and Market Research

Although the term may be considered "new," customer experience management has always been a fundamental consideration in the way most companies do business. A major part of serving and satisfying consumers is accomplished by influencing what they experience – in relation to products and services – through advertising, merchandising, store design, lighting, music, and, of course, personal service. E-commerce has its own set of experience motivators: ease of use, attractive graphics, convenience, and so on. Thus, attempts to provide a consistent set of cues, messages, and human interactions that, taken together, create "a customer experience," are nothing new. In addition, market research has been, and continues to be, the primary component for learning about customers and guiding customer experience decisions.

A technology-driven customer experience management solution is not, however, simply old wine in new barrels. The fundamental changes occurring in the business environment have been fueled by technological advancements, which have expanded the range of services available to customers – and fragmented customer experiences and expectations. The paradox is that although more services and products are available via more channels than ever before, customer satisfaction and loyalty appear to be at an all-time low. E-retail loyalty on the web, for example, has been particularly elusive. Within this framework, market research can help reverse this situation by providing efficient business tools, procedures, and methods that rapidly inform interactions between companies and customers. The combined effect of improved consumer insight with rapid insight delivery can advance the buyer-seller bond to new levels of satisfaction, loyalty, and ROI.

Notes

1   Johnson, M.D. & Gustafsson, A. 2000. *Improving Customer Satisfaction, Loyalty, and Profit: An Integrated Measurement and Management System.* Jossey-Bass: San Francisco, CA.

2   Kinesis Corporation 2001. "White Paper: Customer Experience Management." www.kinesis-cem.com.

CHAPTER 7

Global Access Panels

M arket researchers have at their fingertips the techniques and methods to be leaders in global marketing and business insight delivery. Due to accelerating global market dynamics, information about new trends and feedback on new products or services are increasingly required on short notice. Thus, global access panels are emerging as an effective way to reach consumers around the world to assess their satisfaction, attitudes, and perceptions. An online panel, carefully structured and maintained, can establish a worldwide pool of people who agree to take part in research studies on a regular basis. Using an integrated collection, management, and access platform, online global panels can be constructed that support a wide range of research techniques, methods, processes, and analyses. The result is the ability to serve the pressing global research demands that clients present in a reliable, efficient and timely manner.

Figure 7.1 depicts a standard online platform for managing panels. Primary components consisting of a set-up, management, and delivery system all feed into and are tied to a central database. The primary components include:

- **Panel set-up**: a web-based interface that enables the initiation, identification, and details of a panel to be planned and arranged. This includes, but is not limited to, such things as naming the panel, setting quotas, and establishing the specifications for each panel.
- **Import and export**: the database functionality contains features and assists for importing and exporting data of all kinds that are relevant to the panel or client need.
- **Panelist management**: once panels are established, a Net-centric management system allows all aspects of the panel to be controlled and tracked through a common web interface. Individual panels can be sized, profiled, validated, and maintained using the panel management system.

- **Panalist recruitment**: recruitment can be optimized through the effective application of campaign management techniques. Different demographic, technographic, and psychographic groups can be approached with different companies, optimally tailored to provide maximum ROI.
- **Portal management**: portals are "entryways" for panelists, as well as "connectors" to clients. Portal management is a key process and communication feature of online panels. It enables the gateways for panel development and maintenance, as well as the pathways for clients to access raw data or completed reports.
- **Incentive management**: a well-designed online panel system will afford the capability to manage incentives on an individual panel and global scale. Integrated into the system, this important function enables control of incentives in a flexible and customized manner, conducive to cultural expectations and norms.
- **Customer service**: a final, but oft-neglected, feature of an integrated panel management system is the ability to provide both automated and in-person customer service. web technology affords the establishment of automated responses, help, and assistance for efficiency, while the capability to tie in vital phone, e-mail, and/or in-person assistance is incorporated as well. All of this is built into the integrated panel management system.

Figure 7.1 Panel management model

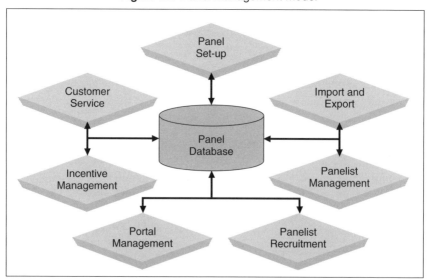

BUILDING GLOBAL ACCESS PANELS

Traditionally, panels have been used for longitudinal studies that collect data from the same individuals, on the same variables, over time. The unique power they hold is in allowing analysts to accurately assess change. Related to this classic design are trend panels, where the same information is collected from comparable groups of people across time. Both methods have various advantages, strengths and weaknesses that are well documented in research literature.[1]

Somewhere in between the poles of longitudinal and trend designs exists a variety of hybrid panels termed "access panels." Although not a new phenomenon, they are given new power and flexibility when supported online. For example, by having a ready group of people representative of a broad population of interest, the flexibility to run the gamut from cross-sectional to time-series studies is enabled. As well, other useful deployments include targeted research snapshots from very broad to very specific cohorts found in the established panel; the ability to recruit for qualitative, as well as quantitative, ad hoc studies; and the option of enriching panel results by appending opt-in membership information, behavioral/transactional, and/or third-party data matched at numerous levels.[2]

Two key characteristics of the online panel extend its usefulness in the Internet Age: (1) the online panel can be globally populated, managed, and driven; and (2) the integrated structure of the online panel system enables complete research coverage for global clients, as well as the ability to deliver comparative analyses based on multi-mode and multiple-method research capabilities. The advantages of an integrated multi-country panel that can be managed directly within one system bring awesome capabilities to meet the extended needs of an ever-expanding global client base.

Thoughts on Building Representative Global Panels

Global access panels are collections of a broad representative sample of people or households within countries, regions, or well-defined segments. Strictly, an online system, by its very nature, excludes those people without access to the Internet. However, the flexibility and integrative structure of the online system can accommodate a global access panel that is made up of those with Internet access, those who can only be reached by phone, and also those who can only be reached by mail. Thus, within a planned effort, a representative panel can be built using the online platform to store all panel access information. Then, in the data-collection process, multiple ways of reaching people are possible.

It is well accepted that the online system is used most effectively where the online population in a given country or consumer segment of interest is a significant proportion of the general population, the interest is only on the online consumer, or both. Here, also, a variety of standard and proprietary weighting schemes can be employed, as needed, to bring results into line with general reliability and validity expectations supported by statistical theory. A general consensus is evolving that online usage will only be increasing (including wireless access) and that at some point in time the representativeness question will become a non-issue from the statistical and methodological side.

The potential also exists in very large panels (100,000 or more) to approach analysis from the data-mining perspective (inductive rather than deductive), particularly if a large number of relevant additional fields or variables are appended. These techniques are best used when seeking to make sense of CRM behavioral data flowing into the pipeline. With them, market researchers have in their arsenal a way to work with both crystallized business intelligence and the more fluid business intelligence potentially locked within the transactional/behavioral data generated by the CRM system. Market researcher's propensity to avoid the "segment of one" and the industry's well-documented pledges not to impinge on privacy can be alleviated by an approach that takes the best features of an aggregate and atomistic approach.

How are these panels built? Remarkably similar to traditional panels, except that the whole process and design are hosted online. The most common approach is a continuous process flow that follows these actions:

- **Recruit**: drawing and attracting people to join the panel.
- **Build**: specify and plan the make-up of the desired panel.
- **Profile**: study and track the actual panel membership to desired quotas, demographic, or lifestyle – or even behavioral specifications.
- **Validate**: establish regular protocols to address panel membership validity concerns. This involves random recontact to verify information, tracking and studying profiles, and devising appropriate weighting schemes.
- **Manage**: management occurs directly through the online system and involves panel member service, satisfaction, and assistance, as well as corporate customer service and training for maximizing the use of the online system.
- **Maintain**: maintenance of the panel refers to keeping member participation, motivation, and interest at acceptable levels. It also signifies the feedback loop to recruiting, or replenishing and refreshing, panel members based on profiling, validating, and managing activities and outcomes.

The quality of online panel survey data can be improved by consistent care and attention to panelists. Such simple facets as completion bars/completion counts on survey forms, regular profile and membership form updates, procedures for following up on non-response to survey invitations, reduction of panel attrition through protocols of panel maintenance, and regular random identity checks via offline contact can go a long way in maintaining a viable and reliable global access panel.

Figure 7.2 Building Global Access Panels

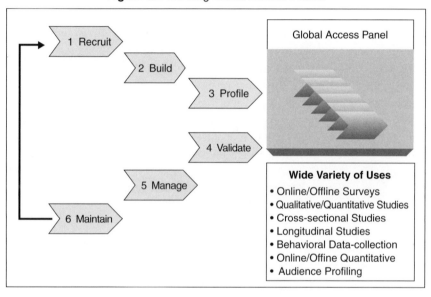

Ultimately, the greatest strength of online panels is the opportunity to plan and deliver market research techniques and methods on a global scale that best fits clients' needs. A flexible and wide array of uses is enabled that includes:

- **Online/offline surveys**: perhaps the most common use is for surveys that inform ad hoc, trending or longitudinal studies. These can be deployed both online and offline, via the multi-mode panel, and managed with the online system to take advantage of its inherent speed, global capacity, and efficiency attributes.
- **Qualitative/quantitative studies**: the results of combined methods can be integrated by the online research system. Opportunities to include ad hoc online surveys during online focus group explorations, or to drive selection for qualitative research studies via a quantitative filtering study are quickly and easily accommodated. In essence, the wall is broken down

between methods that can stimulate new and creative solutions to a variety of consumer research questions, while also allowing global coverage.

- **Cross-sectional and time series (cohort) studies**: panels, if of a sufficient size, can be leveraged for trend studies via the online system. An additional advantage is the ability to manage more efficiently and effectively, and to deploy these studies on a global scale where it is easier to standardize, arrange, and support comparisons.

- **Non-reactive observations, behavioral, and transactional data**: clickstream data on online panel members can be gathered automatically for a study, if desired. As well, individual members from the panel can be identified and tracked through client-side (cookies) or server-side (user agent identification) techniques. Behavioral data from this online, as well as offline scanner and other behavioral measurement techniques, can be incorporated in the panel results as needed for a particular study. Finally, transactional, lifestyle and preference (from panel membership forms), and third-party appended data can be assessed and integrated into a global access panel's data core, thus providing the foundation for the use of advanced analytic or data-mining techniques.

Figure 7.3 Online panel process survey model

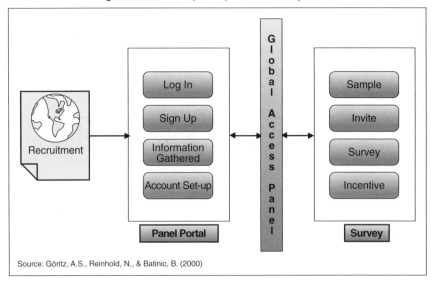

Source: Göritz, A.S., Reinhold, N., & Batinic, B. (2000)

REPRESENTATIVE SAMPLING

Perhaps the strongest criticism from research corners is that online panels are not representative of the general population. While this is strictly true, many uses for online panels of certain populations, segments, groups, or subgroups (pseudo-panels) remain that are perfectly suitable and that meet acceptable statistical criteria. In addition, it is possible to build representative panels using strict traditional techniques, or multiple methods (online/offline), that are merely hosted on the online system. Thus, the advantages of online efficiency and integration are leveraged while still allowing the management and deployment of multiple methods of data-collection to assure the representativeness issue is addressed at the study or project level.

It should be remembered that representativeness of the sample is only necessary when projections from the sample to the defined total population of interest are attempted. Many common research situations in marketing and advertising are not based on this assumption.[3] For example, often a client's interest is centered on what panelists say; that is, their verbatim or individual comments. If a universe is well defined and accessible, it can be represented by an online panel and deliver the strength and richness of insight that a client may seek.

While it is possible to construct quite sizable online access panels (in the millions), size alone does not wash away statistical theory. While numerous weighting schemes abound and are utilized appropriately in market research, social science, and government census calculations, it is still impossible to weight zero. In a similar vein, very large online panels also present challenging bias and estimation problems. Thus, an online access panel that can incorporate online and offline members can be constructed that is less costly to maintain than a mega-panel and will be just as accurate for statistical projections when needed.

The best technique for reducing strong sampling bias is to use a number of online and offline recruitment techniques. If a supplier or client has the time and resources, a validation of online panel profiles or data through parallel representative offline surveys can quickly reveal influences of the research medium and/or the sampling. This can become an expensive and time-consuming activity, however, and the benefits of an online panel could be severely hampered by this procedure, so a judicious approach is always recommended.

Using multiple modes to recruit panelists can be a way to solve the representativeness problem. This way, the recruitment of online participants is blended with offline recruitment (for example, through Net-CATI or Net-CAPI). Offline recruited members are easily incorporated in the access panel database and tagged for the appropriate data-collection method. Thus, if properly constructed, the online access panel infrastructure can become the standard platform for the management and maintenance of a fully representative panel.

One other bias issue, however, needs to be addressed. When participants can self-select to complete online surveys, a bias is introduced that distorts representativeness for the general population and the population of Internet users. A better process is to have people decide for themselves whether to join a panel, but not to select what surveys they wish to complete. Thus, the access panel becomes the sampling source for probabilistic samples.

Probabilistic and non-probabilistic samples can be drawn for separate surveys from an existing access panel, regardless of whether it was recruited online or offline. For the results from a quota sample to be generalizable at all, the criteria for the quota need to be relevant to the research question and to be as exhaustive as possible. Unless a quota sample matches the distribution of characteristics within a desired universe they are not, in general, an adequate means to attain representativeness. Nonetheless, panel project managers, by using global panel management system software, have an advantage in that they can choose panelists using less biased or subjective methods. In using reliable estimates of the size and composition of the population universe, a careful and rigorous panel methodologist can meticulously glean and carefully study panel membership and registration information to gain a complete and expert understanding of the characteristics of the sample under study. In extreme cases, panel members can be submitted to a strict screening or pre-study to ascertain these characteristics. In this case, the panel management system is not a replacement for, but an enabler of the market researcher's expertise.

Once a panel is constructed, an ongoing challenge is to assure that it continues to accurately represent the reference population. This is achieved by active and intelligent panel management that has two components: (1) ensuring ongoing cooperation and participation from existing panelists; and (2) bringing new people into the panel. This is a particularly acute concern due to the dynamic state of the online environment and the fact that it can be costly to keep an online panel refreshed and representative. However, as the growth of Internet accessibility and usage continues, web access will become as ubiquitous as phone access, thus ensuring its place as a primary research tool.

Advantages of Online Panels

Global access panels have numerous economic and methodological advantages over offline studies and over ad hoc online studies. These include:

- fast and cost-effective turnaround of results;
- the opportunity to obtain large and heterogeneous samples;

- freedom from the constraints of testing people at a particular time or a specific place;
- support of complicated survey logic and question routing patterns;
- diminished intrusiveness because respondents can self-schedule;
- real-time validation of survey inputs;
- broader stimuli potential through the integration of multimedia elements;
- standardization of experimenter effects;
- possibilities of conducting cross-border research without the expense of traveling;
- error reduction due to automated data-handling;
- respondent monitoring through log-file analyses;
- elimination of question bias through randomized ordering of items and alternative answers.

When considering a mixed-mode panel approach, managed via a Net-centric system, additional advantages accrue:

- greater study design flexibility;
- the realization of the entire range of both time-based observation plans (cross-sections and longitudinal studies) and designs for variance control (experimental and non-experimental);
- true representativeness can be accomplished and accommodated in the online panel system through standard offline recruitment;
- with a large access panel, quite specific target samples (for example, Hispanics over 55 years of age) can be drawn without the costly prescreening of large portions of the population;
- when needed or driven by business demand, specific or low-incidence segments of the population can be incorporated into the online panel by means of highly tailored recruitment campaigns;
- since panelists' profile data, membership/registration information, and history are accessible via the data store, survey/questionnaires can be pared down to the most essential questions, and appropriate appends can be retrieved later to enrich analysis;
- survey non-response rates can be calculated more accurately. Profiles of non-respondents can be examined and thus provide the information that allows the estimation of sample bias;
- since researchers can continually count on a stock of potential respondents, the time and expenses of recruitment are drastically reduced. Considering the potential survey participation fatigue of the population at large, it is likely that these economies will be maintained even as the costs of panel maintenance rise.[4]

MANAGING PANEL GROWTH

The term *panel maintenance* refers to all protocols, processes, and activities that aim to reduce panel attrition. Panel maintenance can be divided into two components: (1) respondent motivation; and (2) participant tracking. Motivating respondents includes measures taken to spark interest, facilitate participation, and create an atmosphere of mutual trust. This can be achieved through personalization and/or the creation of an online/offline community of interest or reliance. Such things as sharing information on the research subject, payments, gift certificates, or lotteries are useful. Thoughtful concern for panel respondents demonstrated through the use of concise questionnaires, a reasonable survey demand, and a careful selection of questions can go a long way to increase panel satisfaction. Trust can be ensured by forthrightly informing panelists about issues of data confidentiality. Customer service that is multichannel, persistent, and displays care and concern is vital to panel maintenance. Personal contact should always be available for panelists. An online advantage is inherent in the ability to access web page logs that allows the researcher or panel manager to precisely monitor the participation process.

The Internet and an online global panel system enable the utilization of innovative and easy-to-administer panel maintenance features, such as newsletters, online games, and redeemable bonus points. While the effect of incentives on data quality and drop-out is not established, there are first indications that online survey drop-out can be reduced by material incentives.[5] The bottom line for rewarding panelists appears to hinge on establishing an equilibrium between enhancing their participation and discouraging incentive-hunters.

An enhanced set of features for online access panels exists today. In addition to panel and panelist management and administration features, an integrated system incorporates project and incentive management under one umbrella. Increasingly, private/personal portals for clients and individuals are emerging as the interface of choice. These portals, as well, can be managed via the system's supporting features. Finally, systems need to provide integration capabilities to other online research panel systems, to afford cross-connections. Until one distinct and primary online research platform emerges, this will be a necessary component for successful and robust deployment.

Notes

1   Göritz, A.S., Reinhold, N. & Batinic, B. 2000. *Marketforschung mit Online Panels: State of the Art*. Planung & Analyse, 3, 62–7.
2   Göritz, A.S., Reinhold, N. & Batinic, B. 2000.

3   Myers, J.L. & Well, A.D. 1995. *Research Design and Statistical Analysis*. Lawrence Erlbaum Associates, Publishers: Hillsdale, NJ.
4   Göritz, A.S., Reinhold, N. & Batinic, B. 2000.
5   Frick, A., Bächtiger, M.T. & Reips, U. 1999. "Financial Incentives, Personal Information and Drop-out Rate in Online Studies." Paper presented on GOR 99. Available: http://dgof.de/tband99/pdfs/a_h/frick.pdf [1999, Nov. 5].

CHAPTER 8

Online Market Research Project Management

INTEGRATING THE INTERNET INTO THE MARKET RESEARCH VALUE CHAIN

A key weakness that exists in the market research value chain is a preponderance of outdated workflow and process models. Frankly, clients are demanding – and new technologies are providing – faster turnaround times at every corner. The ultimate product that a research firm delivers – insight, decision support, and carefully studied recommendations – is not at issue here. What can be improved is the management, deployment, collection, and delivery of professional service.

Real Advantages of Integration via an Internet System

Most traditional market research is delivered on a project basis. The value of an online system designed for market research becomes apparent when it enables the integration of the processes and activities required for successful project delivery. The result of this integration is new value creation in the form of:

- Elimination of redundant data entry: information entered into the system during the proposal phase flows into the project phase upon client approval. In turn, project assumptions control the quota sample. Finally, integration with the billing process assures that the invoicing basis is consistent with the original proposal.
- All project information is accessible centrally: with project personnel working around the world, increasingly with external vendors and partners, the ability to provide secure access to project information is a source of efficiency gain. External project personnel can access the

information needed to contribute to project delivery. External client representatives can also monitor progress.

This chapter will focus in detail on the process and workflow of a typical and probably the most common activity of the market research industry: the survey. A series of steps, feedback loops, and decision points within the context of an online enterprise market research system will be described. Note, this system can accommodate qualitative data-collection, merge data from multiple sources for analysis, and be customized for delivery via a corporate portal. These aspects will be covered in more depth in later chapters.

Putting the Pieces Together

A generalized model of a Net-centric or Internet-enabled online research management and delivery system is depicted in Figure 8.1.

Figure 8.1 Online project management and delivery

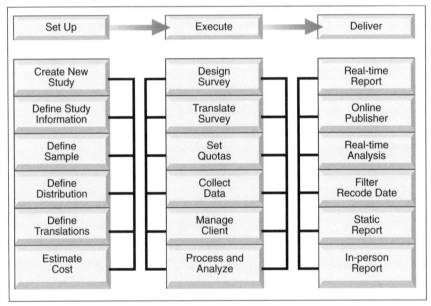

The key features of the model include:

1 **A robust set-up or planning module**: this component enables interaction between client and research supplier to create surveys, define key aspects of the method and project, and estimate/bill costs. The web-based interface allows rapid communication, while all information is stored in an accessible database format.

2 **An execution and action module**: all aspects of survey design, deployment, and data-collection are handled within the Net-based system, affording an efficient and interactive medium with secure access to either static or real-time information during the fieldwork phase of the project.

3 **A robust and variegated delivery module**: to fully exploit the communication and interactive features of the Internet, multiple delivery methods are expected. Thus, real-time, static, and in-person deliverables afford the market research supplier the ability to deliver the end-product in the format(s) that is appropriate for the project.

All modules in a robust online system are seamlessly integrated, and presented to the user in a familiar tab/folder interface. The client can expect secure access within the market research firm, when interacting via the system, or in receiving real-time desktop delivery of results or data for analysis.

FROM A REQUEST FOR PROPOSAL TO INVOICE: AN INTEGRATED PROCESS

The historical process for initiating a request for proposal (RFP) for vendor proposals is in many regards woefully outdated. It represents inefficiency at several levels due to the manual process of extracting unstructured specifications and entering relevant information into incompatible systems for evaluating feasibility and generating a cost estimate. This is a key area where Net-centric research information systems can provide a substantial productivity advantage.

A workflow diagram of the standard market research project process, with description to stress technological touch points or improvements, best depicts the integrated process involved. A model of the research project workflow is presented in Figure 8.2. This model contains five primary workflow blocks:

- from an RFP to submitting a proposal;
- from registering a project to piloting a study;
- from data-collection to data-processing;
- from cross-tabulation to report delivery;
- from tracking project expenditures to collecting payment.

Figure 8.2 Online research project workflow

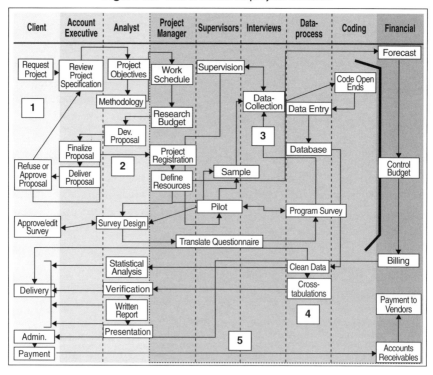

Step 1: From RFP to Submitting a Proposal

A market research project can be initiated in two ways: first, it may be generated by a visit, an event, or a call from the market research supplier. This is referred to as a **proactive project**. Second, it may be generated by direct contact from the client (or its representative) this is called a **passive project**. In both cases, the client must provide general or quite specific information regarding the project. Most market research firms review requests to assure that they have all the essential information with which to act. Such information facilitates the accurate study design, resource planning, and cost estimation of the project.

It is also a wise practice to take a consultative approach whenever possible to confirm the request and to identify, or suggest, the main and specific objectives of the project. Objectives are the key questions that must be answered by the researcher. With objectives clearly stated, the researcher can also define and/or determine the most appropriate methodology. The time spent in these early stages is not wasted, but often forms the basis for closer customer relationships, better understandings, and clearer answers to:

1 **What is the appropriate sample?**: When reviewing or determining the objectives, the researcher must also figure out who the most appropriate people are to participate in the study. By identifying the "who," the researcher can determine "how" the data are best collected. Areas to consider when setting up the "who" include:
- target market: global, region, country, city, postal code;
- respondent profile: demographics, lifestyle, psychographics, technographics and so on;
- sample size: number of interviews to complete;
- incidence rate: estimate of how many will qualify to complete the full questionnaire;
- margin of error for the total and segment levels: gender, age, and so on;
- weighting parameters;
- contact method, recruitment, and selection procedures.

2 **How will information be collected?**: The researcher has options regarding how the data will be collected. A project may employ individual or multiple data-collection methods, such as:
- in-person (central location or home visit), using a computer-assisted personal interview (CAPI) system via a laptop or handheld device;
- paper and pencil, in-person;
- telephone;
- computer-assisted telephone interviewing (CATI);
- interactive or automated voice response (IVR);
- Internet: computer-assisted web interviewing (CAWI);
- Website intercept: "pop-up" or interstitial delivery;
- targeted database (B2B or B2C) response online;
- e-mail invitation;
- central location (cyber café);
- standard mail;
- video or audio recording for qualitative research;
- CD-ROM or disk by mail.

Also, in this step an operational person within the market research firm will review the detailed project specifications and the estimated work schedule to determine the cost for executing the project. Information that is necessary to adequately calculate a research budget includes:

- **Project scope**: questionnaire length, stimulus, product usage, routing logic.
- **Sample definition**: respondent profile, sample size, incidence rates, contact, recruitment method and selection procedures, sample source, list or panel costs, incentive costs.

- **Questionnaire programming**: the structuring of the questionnaire can have several forms and may impact the budget, depending on the data-collection method. This calculation is for the professional programming time (for computer-assisted methods) or formatting (for paper and pencil methods).
- **Supervision and validation**: the cost depends on methodology variables, such as sample and data-collection method(s), percent of validation (indirect supervision), percent of direct supervision, and professional hours involved.
- **Pilot phase**: if a pilot is conducted, it must be reflected on the budget since there will be costs incurred with the sample, data-collection, supervision, data-processing, and analysis.
- **Data-collection methods**: all have variable and fixed costs.
- **Coding**: when a questionnaire contains open-end questions, or text questions, a coder will review the written information. The cost calculation is based on the number of open-end questions, or total of open-end questions per project, and by the number of completed surveys. A rate per question may be used instead.
- **Data-processing**: all costs here are typically reduced with an online system, perhaps to the point that a separate line item is not needed.
- **Data-cleaning**: depending on the data-collection method, this step may require a lot of time from the data-processing department, or it may not be necessary when using computer-assisted data-collection methods. The cost is based on the amount of professional time required.
- **Data delivery**: if these are requested as part of the deliverables of a project, the cost must be calculated based on the amount of professional time required to produce the tabular report and exported data set. Note here also that a web-based system results in the immediate production of standard tables directly to the client desktop at a great cost saving.
- **Online deliverables**: depending on what type of deliverable the client has requested, various calculations may need to be made. Calculations in this area are based on the cost of professional time involved, usually at a rate per hour. Online deliverables (raw data for analysis using an embedded online analyzer tool, basic to advanced top line reports, fully published reports, and tracking/trending data streams) are the least costly.

By using information from project objectives and methodology the operational person assesses the departments that will be involved in the execution of the project. Milestones are created and a timetable is generated. Two timetables may be used: one for internal tracking and one for the client.

In this step, the research department compiles information given by the operations department and formalizes the project proposal. The draft version of this document is then sent to the sales department for final pricing and revision. The sales department reviews the draft proposal sent by the research and operations departments. Prior to finalization, they may negotiate time and cost details. As a final step, the sales department formats the proposal and includes margins for the final pricing.

The final version of the commercial research proposal is sent to the client. Upon receipt of the proposal, the client may either:

1 approve;
2 refuse;
3 request method changes;
4 request time changes;
5 request price changes.

Steps 1, 3, 4, and 5 require action to be taken by the market research firm.

Upon approval of a proposal, the project is registered in an internal online study tracking system. Study tracking systems may vary. Some essential details to include are: client name, objective, cost, time, and people involved. Upon the change of status of a proposal to "Approved," the online system will use the proposal data to register a new project. The new project will be automatically displayed in the project section, and will have a project ID associated to it.

Step 2: From Registering a Project to Piloting a Study

In this step an operations person assigns the various activities needed to complete the research process to departments and individuals. A predicted time to complete each activity is also assigned. This assignment information is communicated to all parties involved via the online system for accurate planning.

The research manager reviews the objectives of the project, and in some cases reviews qualitative data or results, to inform and author the questionnaire to be used for data-collection.

When completed, the questionnaire is sent to the client contact for review. This is historically a Word document sent as an e-mail attachment, but increasingly it is delivered as an online interview that replicates what the user would experience regardless of modality: CATI, CAPI, web survey, and so on. Iteratively, the client may request changes or approve the questionnaire as is.

Once the end-client has approved the questionnaire, the market research firm may choose to have the questionnaire translated in-house or outsource the translation service. Within an online system, translation features are built in that expedite this optional process by allowing multiple translators around the world to work on the system remotely, and conveniently.

Concurrently, the sample specifications for the approved project are passed on to the sampling department. Depending on the specification, several different actions may be taken. Sampling activity can range from very simple operations to extremely complex protocols that must be developed by highly expert sampling professionals. The online system provides the ability to deploy basic to advanced customized sampling procedures based on the knowledge and expertise of the sampling professional.

A final approved questionnaire is formatted for paper or pencil application or programmed for CAPI, CATI, CAWI, IVR or scanning methods. Formatting and programming include the setting up of question types and the logic of the questionnaire (skips, rotations, screening, quotas and so on), all enabled within the online system. Often a test or pilot run of the survey is done to check design, length, and incidence (completion) rate.

Step 3: From Data-collection to Data-processing

Data-collection is the process of reaching the target respondents and having them return a completed questionnaire. Data-coding is necessary when a survey includes open-ended questions. These are questions where the respondents may express or elaborate on their point of view in written form. Coding uses a process of association. The coder must tabulate the number of times a certain response appears, and if it appears a significant amount of times, then a code is created for that response. Thus, the information is categorized per respondent and it can be quantified.

Supervisors of the data-collection process usually conduct direct and indirect supervision. Direct supervision involves observing or listening to an interview or survey as it is being completed. Indirect supervision is accomplished by recontacting an interview or survey respondent to check certain responses. An internal quality report is often generated as a result of this process. With online surveys, incoming results can be validated during the interview.

When using paper and pencil data-collection methods, the data must be entered into a database, which is a time-consuming and error-prone process. A program interface is used to capture the data. Typically, a validation process is in place to minimize entry errors and assure accuracy.

In many cases, an automated data-cleaning process is used in combination with an online web-based system that employs a built-in validation system.

Step 4: From Cross-tabulation to Report Delivery

Cross-tables are a traditional deliverable in market research and often the initial one in the reporting phase of a project. Usually, the analyst has predefined the "banner points," or column headings for the cross-tab report. Standard banner points are most often based on easily assessed or important respondent demographics.

A wide variety of statistical techniques are employed in the process of analyzing data. This serves several purposes and is done by a research analyst. In this step, the tabular report is checked to make sure that the information is correct and structured according to the request of the client. The analyst may also start to identify areas of interest or insight for the written report at this point.

The written report, if required, is a document that includes the study objectives, methodology, and any other relevant specifications or information. Mainly, it consists of written conclusions, recommendations, or insights, as well as the interpretation of the data collected. This report, authored by the research analyst, delivers the value-added answers to the questions and objectives stated in the proposal. With an online system, the report can be published electronically and delivered directly to the client desktop, or presented in static or active form, in-person or via printed form.

The presentation of the results may or may not precede the delivery of a written or web-published report. It consists mainly of visuals – such as charts, graphs, and tables – delivered in person to a client group, usually by an experienced senior researcher or consultant. Distribution can be in any of the following forms: clean data file, a tabular report, written report, or presentation.

In a Net-centric model, the project number can extend the form of distribution while simultaneously speeding up the process of actual delivery. For example, clients can see online survey results in real-time, the market research firm can merge or append files to allow greater in-depth analyses, and any number of reports can be delivered in varying formats directly to the desktop.

Step 5: Tracking Project Expenditures and Payments

Upon finalization of the internal resources involved in the execution of the project, the general and administrative department of a market research firm develops the client's project cost by activity, final price, and billing schedule. An online system enhances and streamlines this function. In an integrated research management system, expenditures are continuously compiled and updated for a specific project. Project managers and department managers are able to review this information while the accounting department can execute the billing schedule and manage collection.

Extending Beyond Surveys

With an integrated online market research system, all processes of project management coalesce around a common Net-centric interface. Although this chapter used a custom survey as an example, in principle all forms and methods of research can be accommodated by the interactive and communication features of an online system. Thus, the entire research product range can utilize the various capabilities to support activity extending along the entire market research value chain.

CHAPTER 9

Mixed-mode Data-collection

Mixed-mode data-collection ordinarily refers to research situations where two or more different types of data-gathering are completed to address, study or project objectives. Due to the flexibility and integration of an online-enabling research system, however, we can broaden this definition to include, for example:

- telephone recruitment followed by online self-administered interviewing by some or all of the recruited respondents;
- panel survey results gathered both online and offline for the same study or project;
- panel survey results appended with profile, scanner, or aggregate clickstream data from the same respondent;
- online focus group participation, followed up by an online survey, or vice versa;
- an online survey completed as part of an online focus group;
- CRM analytical data that triggers an online or telephone satisfaction survey (based on business rules and knowledge of the customer's preference for survey interaction).

It is clear that multiple opportunities exist to capture responses and, with the online system, to integrate and collate the findings for analysis. The potential to do this extends the research function to all customer-facing channels, allowing for interaction and collaboration in analysis that currently is not available or is very difficult to arrange.

Figure 9.1 presents a research-based data-collection model that utilizes a core database, or storage unit, and access to global results, panels, and quota segments. Note the distinction in naming these solutions "Net-centric." The term "web" is limited to a browser interface. "Net-centric" means anything that is TCP/IP compliant, and thus can send information back and forth through the Internet via any of the various protocols: HTTP, FTP, SMTP, and so on. The primary elements that feed into the analytic data-access center, and that can deliver back analysis or real-time reports, potentially include the results from both structured and unstructured data-collection:

- web surveys, with results going directly into the database;
- Internet-based CATI, or results gathered over the phone (including wireless devices) and input directly into the database;
- Internet-based CAPI, or results gathered through personal interviews and input directly in the database via laptop, desktop, or hand-held device;
- imported data sources: these include membership/registration information on panelists, third-party demographic and lifestyle information, and scanner or clickstream (behavioral) data on individual or panel segments;
- Internet-based focus groups, or the results from online focus groups, including transcripts, summaries, coded responses, and so on;
- Internet-based discussion boards, similar to focus groups: the transcripts, summaries, text-mined, and/or coded responses of online discussion board research participation.

Figure 9.1   Mixed-mode data-collection model

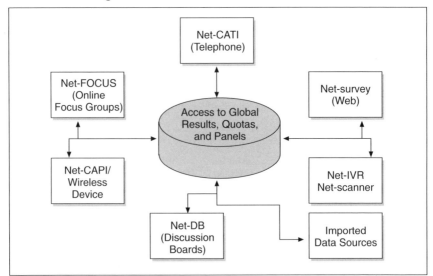

This chapter focuses on the variety of data-collection modes available within the online system: web surveys, Internet-based CATI, CAPI, and wireless. Later chapters will focus on multi-method topics, such as Internet-based focus groups, discussion boards, and mixed-method/qualitative–quantitative approaches for gauging advertising and brand effectiveness.

WEB SURVEYS: WHAT WE HAVE LEARNED

Just as e-commerce brings unique features to the buying/selling experience, but does not change fundamental laws of business,[1] the same is true of the online survey. Effective online surveys are generally:

- **Graphical, attractive, and clear survey presentation**: online surveys have a visual component that conveys an effect in the survey-taking experience.

- **Complexity is hidden**: sophisticated and complex survey designs can be programmed in the online environment that are self-directed; that is, the respondent is unaware of the underlying logic as the survey adapts to the answers provided.

- **Quick, easy completion**: the most oft-cited advantage of online surveys is their quick completion. From the respondent's perspective a latency of more than a few seconds between screens is known to significantly reduce completion rates.

- **Media incorporation**: the ability to incorporate audio, video, and pictures into the survey process has been demonstrated. In fact, it is currently feasible with a broadband, T-1, or DSL connection. In reality, the world has not caught up to the promise yet, as connection speed is a limiting factor in robust delivery of this enhancement. This has not, however, stopped marketing and advertising research firms from exploring and developing approaches that are being tested and refined.

- **Incentives**: the online system provides for an efficient method of rewarding survey participation and in the case of online panels, a variety of flexible solutions to track and deliver incentives.

- **Adaptive content**: for both client and respondent, the real-time aspects of data and result delivery are evident. In addition, the online environment can be equipped with algorithms, running in the background and invisible to the respondent, that can adapt surveys based on the responses given. Some high-end automobile companies have experimented with this approach through adaptive online customer satisfaction and preference surveys.

In conjunction with a discussion of web-based surveys, web usability is an area of research that has received much attention. Web usability studies are focused on the broader issue of how to make the entire web experience most effective and efficient for users. Web usability is a key component of a successful e-business or e-commerce effort.

INTERNET-ENABLED CATI SYSTEMS

A Net-centric CATI system is an Internet-driven application for conducting telephone research. Net-CATI systems have the potential to make traditional phone research fieldwork more efficient and cost-effective, while providing integration and access to online modules for project management, panel management, mixed-mode data-collection, and online data analysis. The key features of a Net-CATI system include:

- fully Internet-enabled application;
- integration of both supervisory and operator functions;
- optional use of Voice-over Internet Protocol (VoIP);
- integration with a Net-centric enterprise research system.

Internet-enabled Application

Net-CATI applications contrast with conventional CATI in that they are deployed over the Internet. This can be accomplished in a variety of ways:

- **Browser-based**: in the preferred embodiment, Net-CATI is deployed via conventional web browsers. This enables the immediate application of a standardized solution whereby minimum integration effort is required at the site location. The CATI application itself may make heavy use of browser-based applications such as Java applets that can reduce the amount of iterative data communication back to the central web server or database server while interviewing is in progress.
- **PC or terminal-based**: the application may alternatively use the traditional dumb terminal infrastructure. This requires some amount of LAN server technology to mediate transactions at the site level back to the central server application. This approach requires additional adaptation of the local call center environment to accommodate the legacy hardware.
- **Hybrid**: terminal emulation applications can in some instances provide the means to emulate a browser-based application in a call center utilizing dumb terminals.

Integration of Supervisory and Operator Functions

Net-CATI applications go far beyond the interviewing application. As a full replacement of the traditional call center management application, Net-CATI treats the world as if it is one giant call center with minimum hardware required at the operator level, and an infinitely scaleable number of operator sites that can be administered centrally and remotely from the various data-collection locations that are operator-driven. Some key components of the CATI application include:

- **Operator terminal**: the CATI operator is able to manage all of the activities related to telephone interviewing of respondents.
- **Supervisory control panel**: concurrent to interviewing, supervisors are able to manage all aspects of the planning and interviewing process, including loading sample, managing interviewers, controlling quota progress, reporting productivity, monitoring operator calls, and scheduling personnel.
- **Client-driven observation tool**: throughout the data-collection period, the external client has the ability to listen to the activity of the operator in dialoging with the respondents. Any operator can be tapped that is currently interviewing a respondent for a given client project.

About Voice-over Internet Protocol (VoIP)

VoIP is a technique that makes it possible to transport the human voice over the Internet. Internet Protocol Telephony (IPT) is defined as the transport of telephone calls over the Internet, using traditional telephony devices, multimedia PCs, or dedicated terminals. The definition holds for calls made entirely or only partially transmitted over the Internet.

As VoIP networks continue to evolve, it will be possible to make phone calls from an interviewer's computer to any phone line in the world, based on local telephone rates. Thus, the cost of a connection with an Internet Service Provider (ISP) will increase slightly to accommodate an additional fee for a networked Internet Telephone Service Provider (ITSP) connection. Since the quality of the call center's voice network services is a critical aspect of assuring reliable IP-telephony, users should only accept superior network performance for voice services.

The most significant benefits of IPT, and the primary drivers of its evolution, are the cost-saving potential and easy implementation of innovative services:

- In the near future, ITSPs will use a single infrastructure for providing both Internet access and Internet telephony. Multiplexing data and voice will result in improved bandwidth utilization as both providers and clients profit from the lower costs of a single network.
- Currently, customers can take advantage of flat Internet rates versus hierarchical Public Service Telephone Network (PSTN) rates, and save money by letting their long-distance calls be routed over the Internet. This is particularly evident in Europe, where the prices of long-distance calls are still higher than in United States.

- IPT users will profit from the software-centric nature of the systems: software solutions can be easily embedded and integrated with other services and applications, such as online whiteboards, electronic calendars, online focus or discussion groups, and online interviewing. Deployment of new IP telephony services requires significantly lower investment versus traditional PSTN environment, particularly when hosted services and applications are used.

It is precisely because of the lower telephone costs using VoIP that geographic distance between call center and respondent is becoming increasingly irrelevant. For example, an operator in the United States can now also conduct interviews in the United Kingdom – 9 a.m. on the US West Coast is 5 p.m. in the United Kingdom, making it possible for a single shift to be working during prime time during the entire day. A multilingual call center could even run extended hours (nearly 24/7), thereby expanding the possible client base of the call center and the use of the facility itself.

Architecture of the VoIP System

The Internet telephony system is composed of the following elements:

- **End devices**: these may be either traditional telephones, audio-equipped personal computers, or single-use appliances.
- **Gateways**: if a traditional telephone is used at either calling side, the call (that is, its transmission format, signaling procedures, and audio encoding), has to be translated to/from the format for transport over the Internet.
- **Gatekeepers/proxies**: the gatekeepers/proxies provide centralized call management functions; that is, they provide call admission control, bandwidth management, address translation, authentication, and user location.
- **Multipoint conference units**: these manage multiparty conference calls, e.g. for remote monitoring of phone calls.

The components may be implemented as hardware or software, and may be integrated into single units. They communicate with each other using signaling and voice-transporting protocols. To ensure interoperability between products of different vendors, standardization bodies have elaborated standards for both hardware and software classes of protocols.

Conceptually, Internet telephone gateways that enable Internet-based CATI work like this:

- **From the interviewer's end**: the gateway connects to the telephone world. It can communicate with any phone in the world. A phone line plugs into the gateway on this end.

- **On the receiving end**: the gateway connects to the Internet world. It can communicate with any computer in the world. A computer network plugs into the gateway on this end.
- **The gateway takes the standard telephone signal**, digitizes it (if it is not already digital), significantly compresses it, packetizes it for the Internet using Internet Protocol (IP), and routes it to a destination over the Internet.
- **The gateway reverses the operation** for packets coming in from the network and going out the phone.
- **Both operations** (coming from and going to the phone network) take place at the same time, allowing a full-duplex (two-way) conversation.

A number of variations can be configured from this basic operation. Phone-to-PC or PC-to-phone operation can take place with one gateway. Phone-to-phone PC operation can occur with two gateways. To offer international long-distance service using gateways, for example, an organization or service provider can host one gateway in each country. By bypassing the international connect charges, even paying in-country long-distance rates, this configuration costs significantly less than traditional circuit-switched services.

VoIP: Dialing Methods

In addition to Random Digit Dialing (RDD)-based or quota sampled techniques, phone interviewers can also use existing online and offline respondent panels for telephone research. There are three basic methods for outbound calling with Internet-based CATI systems:

1. **Normal landlines**: existing PBX or direct outside lines connecting the workstations to the Internet can be used. Adding a voice-modem (either analog or ISDN) to interviewer workstations affords the opportunity to dial automatically using an autodialer.
2. **VoIP hardware**: when using the VoIP protocol, the best way to assure proper compatibility with a provider is to install a VoIP gateway from a standard-bearing manufacturer such as Cisco. Interviewer workstations need to have a voice modem (analog) from which the connection is made (directly) to the gateway. When using VoIP software, the only hardware needed in a call center is a router connected via a 1 Mbps connection (for a 60-user call center) to a provider. Then full use can be made of advanced dialing routines such as power dialing, progressive dialing, and predictive dialing without the need for extra hardware.
3. **VoIP software**: the software to operate CATI functions is generally part of a hosted online-enabled system.

Figure 9.2 How Internet-based CATI works

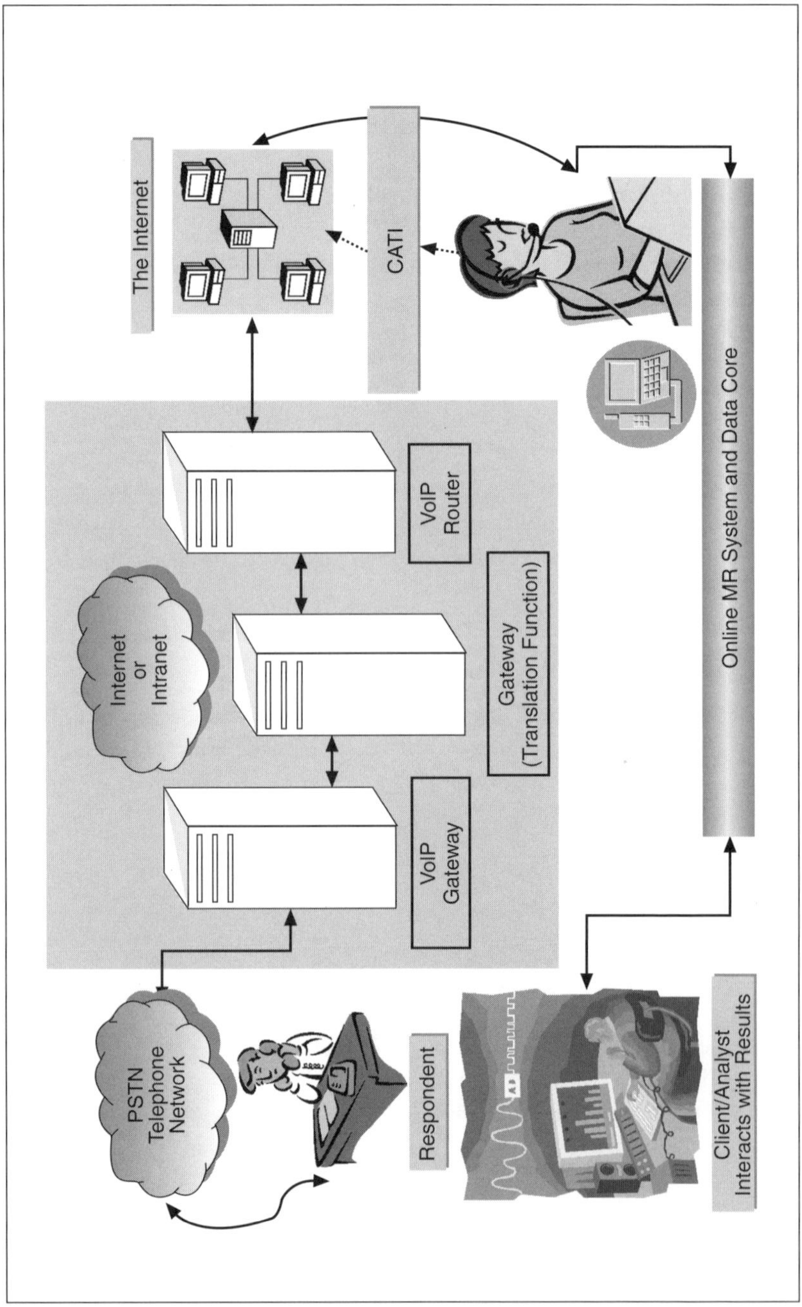

An Internet-based CATI System's Caller Logic: The Self-learning Sample

To further enhance the low-cost connection, online systems employ RDD software – required for statistical sampling validity – and some means of "learning" or adapting to improve the system's contact rate. When calling an RDD sample, it is often difficult to determine who is behind the telephone numbers and to keep an accurate record of that information. A *self-learning sample* is a software solution that automatically edits the contact information from every telephone number dialed to reflect the following critical elements:

- disconnected numbers;
- refusals;
- constantly busy numbers.

A system that permits an interviewer to choose whether or not to include telephone numbers that are disconnected or were busy for more than a set number of times, as well as telephone numbers where the respondent refuses to cooperate, enables the construction of a solid database of usable telephone numbers that can yield improvements in productivity, particularly when a vast number of operators are working with a common Net-centric database-storing call activity.

Another key advantage is the ability to store all information from every question out of every questionnaire in one aggregated database; for example, a survey that has a target audience of only females aged 18–24. Using traditional CATI-systems, you can expect a 3 percent incidence rate at the household level just to locate this sample. With an adaptive and self-learning system, however, the sample is built into the database and can be called directly within the target group. Since the database holds all results in a centralized repository, it is cumulative, enabling it to be used for all surveys.

With Internet-based CATI systems, RDD samples generally are integrated for every country in the European Union (15) and the United States. Because most clients use these samples as their standard, the self-learning technique quickly builds efficiencies.

Advantages and Features of Internet-based CATI Systems

- **Voice-over Internet Protocol**: by using VoIP, reduced telephone costs, particularly when conducting telephone research across borders, can be realized. All calls, even international calls, can increasingly be completed at costs that are at, or near, the cost of a local telephone call.
- **Self-learning sample**: adaptive caller logic enables the storage of all outcomes of all contacts in one integrated database. A sampling manager

can therefore make intelligent use of cumulative information on dialing history and avoid dialing numbers with a high probability of refusal.

- **Call centers can easily be linked together**: since the whole application runs via the Internet (or intranet), and is hosted on a central web server, call centers can be linked to each other by simply logging on to the same web server(s). This substantially simplifies the process of distributing data-collection work across multiple locations.
- **Virtual call centers are easily deployed**: when interviewers prefer working at home rather than at a call center, they only need a computer with an Internet connection. For using VoIP, interviewers need a dedicated 8–12K connection, a Cisco VoIP gateway with connection to an ITSP, or a normal landline. Since they are linked via the Internet, they can use the same functionality as the interviewers who are physically located in the call center.
- **Hardware investments are significantly reduced**: to run Net-CATI systems, workstations need only an Internet connection (via a router), a soundcard, and the ability to run a standard web browser. With hosted applications, a server is not needed, thereby reducing hardware investment costs.
- **Mixed-mode data-collection is enhanced**: one study can be accommodated using different types of data-collection. For example, in an online survey of consumers, it is possible to fill in any gaps in the quota cells or to meet representativeness standards via computer-assisted telephone interviews. No realignment is necessary as quota cells and surveys are all running and integrated within the same online system.
- **Different CATI systems can be run but still retain the advantages of an Internet-based CATI system**: interfaces to traditional CATI systems, can afford rapid migration from phone-based systems to web-based systems. In fact, it is possible to run both systems simultaneously while having the advantages of real-time reporting over the Internet available.

Call Center Comparison Costs

Figure 9.3 illustrates a detailed comparison of traditional and web-enabled call centers. Note that this comparison is done without factoring in interviewer costs. Significant additional savings with VoIP may be accomplished via:

- using call centers to cover remote locations to extend and increase call center utilization;
- using intelligent, adaptive sampling to reduce the incidence of refused interviews and generate productivity gains;

- accessing lower cost operators in remote call centers or home-based locations to generate cost and productivity gains.

MOBILE AND WIRELESS DATA-COLLECTION

Computer-assisted personal interviewing (CAPI), mobile phones, and wireless devices serve to extend data-collection channels. Generally, the emergence of channel independence has already appeared. Businesses are realizing that they have to deliver content to any channel, if they wish to remain viable. While not as evident in other parts of the world as in Europe and Japan, mobile phones are rapidly infiltrating consumer households. For example, Ulf Andersen, CEO of ResearchLab in Norway, said: "Many people in Norway now only have mobile phones, and no fixed line phone. Our current estimates are running as high as 10 percent of the population. In addition, these people are significantly different from others: they are typically younger people, either students or similar to the old 'yuppies.' These people are now inaccessible via normal omnibus and traditional sampling routines. Thus, in order to really get a population representative sample, we have to revise our sampling methodologies in order to also include these 10 percent."[2]

Case Study 11

The Emergence of Wireless Technology Changes the Quality of Our Established Methods: ResearchLab Report December 10, 2001

Despite the fact that today's telephone surveys are limited to households with fixed-line telephones, results from these surveys are presented as representative of national populations. This practice comes from an assumption that households available on fixed-line telephones are no different from households who are not available on fixed-line telephones. This assumption does not hold true in countries where mobile phone penetration is exploding. In Norway, 10 percent of the population can now only be reached via mobile phones. They no longer have a fixed-line subscription and, consequently, are no longer included in our nationally representative samples and surveys.

A Fundamental Change

An important development in many countries is the growing proportion of the population who can only be reached by mobile phone. One of the most

Figure 9.3 Call center comparison

Net-CATI VoIP Hosted	Web-centric using VoIP-hosted system	Traditional CATI system using landlines
	All prices are in US dollars	
Set-up Costs		
Servers	0	15,000
Workstations	62,500	62,500
PBX	0	60,000
Router (with Voice-over IP)	25,000	0
Backup facility	0	2,500
Installed software on own server	0	10,000
Dedicated predictive dialer	0	170,000
Total set-up investment	**87,500**	**320,000**
Annual Operating Costs		
Software license fees	40,000	25,000
Application usage costs	72,000	0
Telephone costs	83,300	250,000
T1 connection with an ISP	20,000	0
Dedicated IT personnel	20,000	50,000
DP personnel costs	39,000	65,000
Total Annual Operating Costs		
Year 1	**274,300**	**390,000**
Year 2 and beyond	**<274,300**	**<390,000**

Comparison is done without interviewer costs.

Benefits of a Net-centric System

Significant additional savings with VoIP may be accumulated via:

- the use of call centers to cover remote locations and increase call center utilization;
- productivity gains from use of intelligent sampling to reduce incidence of refused interviews;
- cost savings from access to lower cost operators in remote call centers and/or ability for home-based work;
- faster turnaround time;
- reduction in project management and charting/reporting costs;
- labor saving on mixed-method projects.

interesting elements with wireless technology is how usage and attitudes toward mobile usage have changed radically. Even the youngest in our populations – those under eight years – are often included in statistics over mobile usage and penetration. And age is often that which corresponds closely with usage, penetration, and availability. In 2001 in Norway, 95 percent of all persons age 16–20 had a mobile phone.

The key here is variation in accessibility in different segments of the population. A growing number of people are exclusively accessible via mobile phones. These people no longer see the need for a fixed-line phone. When MR companies today run nationally representative surveys, these surveys are almost always done by using a random sample of fixed-line subscribers.

As a consequence of this ResearchLab has worked on an approximation for including the growing proportion of people exclusively accessible via mobile phones. Our research shows that in November 2001, over 13 percent of the population in Norway claim that they do not have a fixed-line telephone at their disposal. Adjusted for the small proportion who physically actually have a fixed-line telephone in their household (but claim they never use it), the proportion of the population with exclusively a mobile phone is 10 percent. *In other words, one in 10 Norwegians is now excluded from our nationally representative surveys.* Moreover, this segment of the population shows definite deviation in attributes like gender, age, and geography. The segment is dominated by males, often in one-person households living in urban areas.

Important Attributes

The important issue is not first and foremost that the sample mirrors the population on demographic variables. That the sample is representative on these attributes is only of interest if they covariate with the attributes and variables being measured. The problem arises when we systematically under-represent segments of the population with different attitudes, preferences, and behavior.

It is mainly in the age group 20 to 29 where the under-representation is highest. In this age group, 30 percent do not have access to a fixed-line telephone at home, and are consequently only accessible via mobile phones. This is a phase of life where they are moving out of their childhood home and establishing themselves for the first time. This segment, also called the education generation, is the key segment for defining the modern way of living. Many of our values and beliefs are formed during these years, and important choices for life are taken now. Young people shape and define their identity through consumption, fashion, symbols, codes and interests, and, to a lesser degree than before, through family background or social class.

Known Problem – New Approximation

Are we able to capture these differences by only interviewing households with a fixed-line telephone? What are the consequences of excluding this age proportion of the population, especially into the future as mobile telephones continue to gain ground? Even with a "correct" distribution on the traditional background variables, we will with almost certainty have replaced hard-to-reach respondents with respondents who are more easily reached in a fixed-line telephone sample. Under an assumption that these are different, a post-stratification will only increase the bias incorporated into our samples. In all essence, a fixed-line telephone sample will only be able to generalize over the fixed-line population, and not the entire population in a country.

New Channels – Greater Flexibility

A key challenge facing our industry is the client's demand for flexibility as the number of data-collection channels increase.

Perhaps group-belonging and differences in characteristics related to channel will make it necessary to utilize complementary channels in order to be able to generalize on behalf of the population in a country. Respondents are increasingly becoming channel independent, which in turn requires the possibility for interviewing in multiple channels. This channel independence will affect the market research industry in the sense that data-collection in the future increasingly must become channel independent as well.

The fact that a major proportion of the population in several countries no longer can be reached by our traditional telephone surveys because they now are only accessible via mobile phones, is only the first sign of a development our industry must take very seriously. And the development will only reinforce the problems and imperfections of today's sampling and interview methods.

Source: Ulf Andersen, Managing Director, and Marius Kongsgarden, Director Research & Statistics, ResearchLab, Norway.

This trend, evident today in Norway, is a signal of what the future may bring regarding how data will be collected, stored, and analyzed, and how the relationship between market researchers and research respondents may change. In all probability, wireless devices for market research will include phones, personal digital assistants (PDAs), possibly laptops, and future inventions, such as wireless screens, embedded microchip cards, and "tubes" that amount to simple devices dedicated to Internet access. Currently, four options exist for doing research on wireless phones – Wireless Application Protocol (WAP), Short Message Service (SMS), the Internet, and standard voice.

- **WAP**: the phone accesses one question at a time in a survey on a server, and the respondent keys in an answer. The server then delivers the next question. This technique is acceptable for filters or minimal surveys, but the usability is very poor, mostly to do with the inadequacies of keying in a response.
- **SMS**: this technique works by sending an SMS to the respondent, and the respondent replies with an SMS giving only the letter (a, b, c, and so on) that corresponds to the answer he or she wants to give. The server then sends a new SMS with the next question, and so on. While fairly expensive (currently you pay per SMS transmission both ways), it can be used with targeted precise samples for better efficiency. Thus, for example, if you know you are reaching the college student you want to survey, this can be a precise method for collecting point-in-time survey results.
- **Internet**: phones are beginning to come with Internet/browser capabilities, making it possible to access standard web surveys. Currently, limited screen real estate results in less than adequate usability. Access speeds could also be a problem, but as high-speed transmission and 3G/UMTS become more common, that will be alleviated. When phones migrate to PDA-type screens, usability will definitely improve. Already, devices such as Motorola's Accompli 008, which is equipped with a larger screen, are available.
- **Voice transmission**: using the mobile phone in the same manner as a traditional fixed-line CATI survey, people can be contacted directly to participate in surveys or interviews.

For accessing respondents, three options are available: (1) a pre-recruited panel; (2) client lists (normally from telecommunication companies); or (3) an RDD system based on a number series allotted to mobile networks (just as with e-mail addresses, in most countries there are no White Pages for mobile phone numbers). Finally, although research itself can be performed over the wireless phone, there are also other possibilities; for example, sending an SMS to respondents and asking them to log into a survey via a normal PC-based Internet connection.[3]

INTERNET-BASED CAPI

Internet-based CAPI solutions utilize state-of-the-art technology for offline data-collection via personal computers. This allows the user to conveniently collect data using a software tool that can run on a conventional PC without any connection to the Internet. Data can be collected on stand-alone PCs and periodically uploaded via a hosted web page, or via a special e-mail address, for the central processing of results.

The components and characteristics of a Net-CAPI system include:

- **Software**: the Internet-based CAPI survey engine uses Java and XML technologies to drive offline interviews. A complete application is capable of handling complex routing, logic, and multimedia stimulus. The administrative software runs on the web. The CAPI application itself runs offline as an applet.
- **Questionnaire development**: CAPI questionnaires are designed to relieve the interviewer of much of the decision-making burden during the interview and to improve the quality of data by taking full advantage of computer technology. Questionnaires with thousands of unique questions, nested loops, and complex logic can be processed.
- **Authoring system**: to facilitate questionnaire development, Internet-based CAPI uses the same standardized authoring system found in the online market research system. This process allows those responsible for instrument development to create and centrally manage the specifications that can be read into the CAPI system.
- **Testing protocol**: a standard protocol for programmers and instrument development experts to follow in testing CAPI programs is essential. Programmers thoroughly test and debug the program. Thereafter, demonstration cases are collected and uploaded to the central server where results are aggregated in real-time.
- **Foreign language translations**: all CAPI software packages should allow for the administration of interviews in foreign languages. Multilanguage interviews are typically developed as one instrument, sharing the same program logic. This eliminates the need for reprogramming and streamlines the testing process to focus only on the translated text.
- **Case management**: as part of every Internet-based CAPI application, interviewers are linked to an integrated field management system. This system allows them to update the status of their cases daily and to transmit the updates to a hosted or internal service, where daily status reports can be generated online for interviewers, supervisors, project staff, and clients. The system is also designed to deliver software updates to field staff computers in the event that problems arise during data-collection.

A New Wave of Data-collection?

When viewed through a global lens, the emergence of a mobile Internet and a robust and flexible CAPI instrument has the potential to drastically alter the way we reach consumers. For the market research industry, new ways to survey respondents can be created, engineered, and deployed. As a result of the mobile system, consumers will be able to access the Internet from more than one device, forcing market researchers to accommodate this channel independence. The diversity and flexibility of Internet-based CAPI for capturing, managing, and collecting structured and unstructured data will be unparalleled for use in mall, one-on-one, business, or in-home surveys. What will be required are new protocols and relationships for interacting with consumers and businesses for research purposes.

From the CRM perspective, Internet-based CAPI and wireless solutions take the power of market research out into the field, yet capably link it back to the central database for storage, analysis, and reporting. Within the corporation, human resources (HR) interviews and on-the-spot surveys of employees can be deployed quickly and easily. The possibilities are endless: customer service supervisors can rapidly gauge customer satisfaction on the floor by randomly sampling service quality. Sales, marketing, and public relations professionals in the field can be equipped with devices that permit simple to extremely complex interviews to be completed. Engineering, scientific, and technical workers, as well, can utilize wireless or Internet-based CAPI technology to gather information on sites or in distant or remote

Figure 9.4 How Internet-based CAPI works

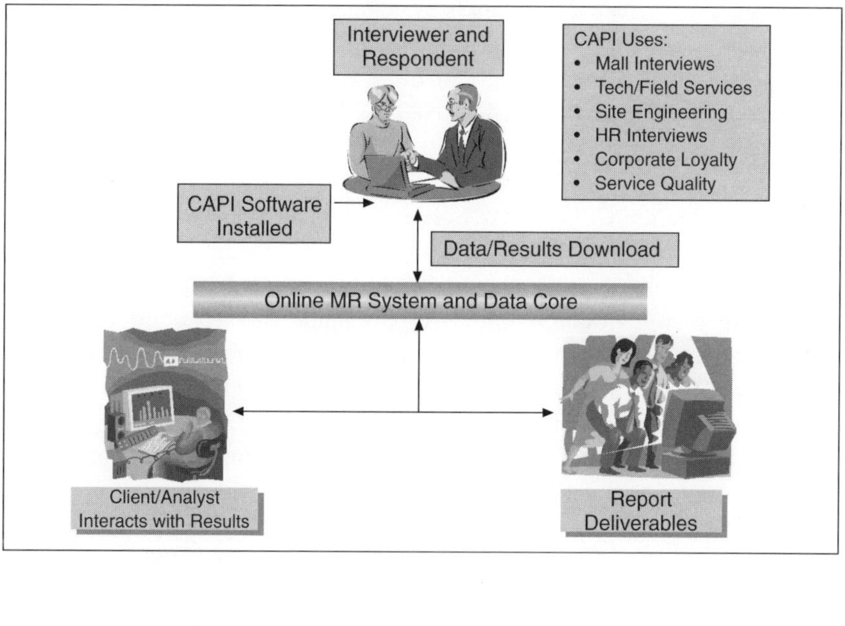

locations. The key is that all data collected go into a centrally managed database that can be accessed, manipulated, and reported on in a number of ways.

Folding this channel independence into an online, web-enabled system, or as a component of an existing analytical CRM solution, will encourage the exploration, development, and adoption of such things as online access panels, efficiently integrated and managed systems, and a new technological focus for the market research industry. Moreover, systems, such as described in this book and found in abundance in CRM offerings, will become a necessity for firms hoping to achieve the necessary research coverage most businesses and organizations will require.

INTEGRATING DATA SEAMLESSLY FROM MULTIPLE COLLECTION SOURCES

Emphasis has been placed on an accessible data core as a necessary component of an enterprise online market research system. The objective of this book is to focus on ways to extend market research capabilities, processes, and techniques to meet increasing global client demand. It is not a discourse on technical database or warehouse issues. Thus, the descriptions and terminology used have not been particularly rigorous, or have been deliberately generic in nature. The fundamental point is that data from multiple sources are stored and accessible in a format that market researchers, analysts, and executives can use. From this data stream can be extracted the breadth and depth of knowledge that is truly useful to business. A robust enterprise-wide research system, as well, must have numerous components and tools that afford the whole range of research techniques to be applied, while also ensuring that these components, tools, and data can be accessed, managed, and deployed within a logical, consistent, and integrated framework.

The integration of data and databases remains a difficult and challenging task. David Marco, CEO of EW Solutions, and an acknowledged expert on meta data repositories and data integration, likened the integration process to the IT equivalent of using chewing gum, string, and paper clips to hold things together.[5] Although initiatives are underway to help resolve the integration issue – such as those through the efforts of the meta data coalition (MDC), and object management group (OMG) – an industry standard for integration architecture still does not exist. Fortunately, work by Marco, and others in the industry, will remedy the situation through the use of meta data, a semantic layer that unites the technical system and the business user.[6]

Concerning databases, briefly, *enterprise data warehouses* are the major repositories of corporate data. They are designed to efficiently and effectively store data, not to explore, access, or analyze it. Thus, *data marts* or *data stores* were created to enable analysis, mostly via OLAP tools and/ or Structured Query Language (SQL) queries. Data stores can also be broken down into *operational* and *analytic*. The next stage in the development has led to *exploration warehouses* that are even better equipped to access data and, finally, the web versions of data warehouses, stores, and marts. Currently, the procedure allowing all of this data to be integrated and accessed rests on XML, or Extended Markup Language. XML enables many of the process, techniques, and potentials of the market research, analytic CRM, OLAP, and data-/web-mining systems to function together.

Exploration Warehouses[7]

The exploration warehouse is a separate warehouse, data mart, or store intended specifically for end-users who want to conduct ad hoc queries and unrestricted exploratory analysis. The exploration warehouse is primarily designed to support analysts whose needs go beyond the preformatted templates developed for the average user. Advanced analysts need quick and ready access to multiple streams of data and to be able to use OLAP, data-mining, market research, and other business intelligence applications directly, rather than having to channel through an IT department or person.

Although the exploration warehouse receives data primarily from an enterprise data warehouse, the exploration warehouse is kept separate from these operational warehouses in order to avoid overtaxing system resources and grinding these systems to a halt. In addition, since exploration warehouse users frequently need to integrate external data (for example, marketing, census/demographic, Internet, or other data acquired from third-party data providers) to conduct their analyses, it is imperative that this data not be mixed in with the operational data warehouse.

For an exploration warehouse to be effective and provide truly ad hoc, flexible, and robust analytical capabilities, the elimination of explicit data structure creation and maintenance are required. In addition, it must possess the ability:

- to quickly and easily load data from a variety of sources, including databases, flat files, legacy systems, and other third-party data sources (for example, geographic, marketing, and Internet data);
- to build ad hoc tables in real-time that are fully indexed in order to support robust and complete analytical processing;
- for users to immediately start analyzing data once they are loaded into the database;

- to add additional data on the fly at any time without the need for the database to be restructured or redesigned.

In addition, the exploration warehouse database must be able to handle complex non-optimal queries, frequently written by end-users possessing a limited knowledge of SQL. For efficiency, the exploration warehouse database should provide automated management capabilities to reduce, as much as possible, the need to call on IT personnel for assistance and support.

The biggest drawback to conventional database systems – and a limiting factor for the exploration warehouse – is the amount of effort required to set databases up before users can actually start analyses. With relational databases, this effort requires that IT professionals first model, build, and then create the database schema before any data can be loaded. This is followed by considerable fine-tuning to support the types of queries that end-users are expected to generate once the warehouse goes into production. With multidimensional databases, this upfront effort involves precalculating the database and generating the OLAP cube that can then be "sliced and diced" by analysts in a fairly free-form manner.

With an exploration warehouse, however, the requirement shifts to supporting a database that demands no upfront data-modeling or cube-building to function. The exploration warehouse also does not require reorganization, reindexing, rebuilding, retesting, and reoptimizing every time users want to perform new unforeseen analyses or incorporate new data (formats) into the database. Obviously, any database used to implement the exploration warehouse must also work with traditional databases in order to efficiently integrate into the organization's overall data warehouse architecture. Therefore, it should also support industry-standard APIs for data access and for integration with familiar front-end analysis tools.

The exploration warehouse is an important development for the analytic community because it offers two important benefits. Used in a prototyping role, it provides a development database platform for speeding up the construction of data warehouses. In an analytical role – more important for market researchers – it offers end-users the ability to quickly create data marts and warehouses for conducting exploratory analysis not supported by an organization's existing production warehouse. Hence, the exploration warehouse is an important supplement to, rather than a replacement of, traditional data-warehouse architectures.

Figure 9.5 depicts a generic model of data integration and access for a variety of analytic needs. While the concept is fairly straightforward, the execution can be complex. However, the benefits of analytic component integration, business-user access to data, and the potential to approach a 360-degree view of the consumer are profound. Add to that the skill, experience,

Figure 9.5   Data integration model

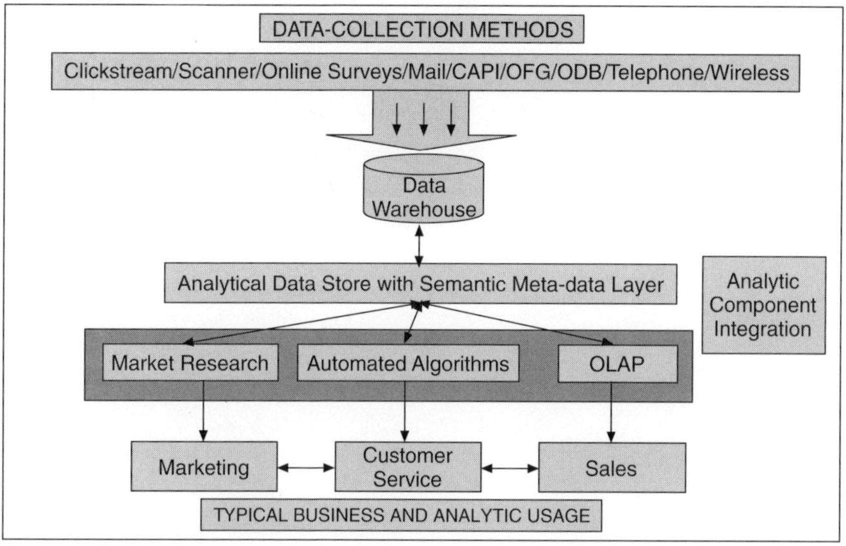

and insight of market researchers and analysts, and the benefits continue to compound.

Notes

1   Shapiro, C. & Varian, H. 1999. *Information Rules: A Strategic Guide to the Network Economy.* Boston, MA: HSB Press.
2   Ulf Andersen, ResearchLab, personal interview, September 2001.
3   Ulf Andersen, 2001.
4   Source: Global Market Insite, Issaquah, WA. www.gmi-me.com.
5   Marco, D. 2000. *Building and Managing the Meta Data Repository: A Full Lifecycle Guide.* John Wiley & Sons, Inc.: New York, NY.
6   Marco, D. 2000.
7   Hall, C. 1999. "Exploration Warehouses: Techniques and Products." *Data Management Strategies,* Vol. 3, No. 3. Cutter Information Corporation: Boston, MA.

CHAPTER 10

Analyzing Data and Reporting Results

This chapter focuses on the "pay-off" side of the research equation: analyzing data, deriving insights, and delivering results efficiently and directly to the client. As we saw in Part 1 of this book, the convergence of trends toward rapid, broad, and thorough delivery of results presupposes that the collection and analysis of data can be accomplished quickly and effectively. An enterprise-wide online market research solution supports the accomplishment of those objectives.

Figure 10.1 depicts a generic model for online analysis and delivery. Note that some sort of online client delivery channel must first be realized. Whether the delivery is dedicated just to the researcher-client channel or

Figure 10.1   Basic online analysis model

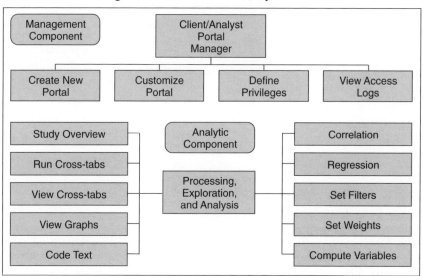

embedded within an existing corporate portal, both require an online management component and interface. The processing, exploration, and analysis features presented are just one possibility. Many variations and/or customized versions – from extremely simple to very complex – are feasible.

THREE PRIMARY CATEGORIES OF QUANTITATIVE ANALYSIS

In the online environment – and in the context of generating consumer insight and market measurement – three well-defined categories of analysis exist: (1) statistical processes and techniques used traditionally by market researchers; (2) OLAP; and (3) data-/web-mining procedures. The advantage of the online system in bringing these techniques together is reinforced by the fact that the analytics share a common data core and data-/report-delivery mechanism. Thus, the integrative features of the analytic and value-added insight delivery side of market research can be exploited in ways not feasible or commonly attempted in the recent past. As well, the ability to interact and collaborate on research and analytic activities within a closed system fits well with the technology-based CRM/eCRM framework increasingly adopted by global corporations.

Figure 10.2   Three categories of quantitative analysis

Traditional Market Research Analytics	OLAP	Data-/Web-mining

• Cross-tabs
• Means
• Correlation
• Regression
• Segment/Profiling
• Testing
• Modeling
• Conjoint
• Clustering
• Can be Run:
  – Real-time
  – Online
  – Offline
	• Real-time
	• Multidimensional Tables
	• Limited to Historical Data
		• Prediction
		• Segmenting/Profiling Large Datasets
		• Classification of Large Data Arrays
		• Automated Algorithms
		• Still Difficult to Run in Real-time

Online Data Analysis for Market Research

The wide variety of traditional market research analytics listed in Figure 10.2 are familiar to industry professionals. A new power emerges, however, when these well-known and time-tested procedures can be leveraged via an integrated online system. At the very least, a time- and cost-saving advantage is introduced when the breadth of techniques is available for use in real-time analysis of data collected and stored in a centralized and easily accessible data core.

TRADITIONAL MARKET RESEARCH ANALYTICS

To go beyond the traditional data-collection, export–import, and analysis cycle, an integrated online analytical module requires the ability to access data directly from the data core and apply common and familiar quantitative techniques. These include, but are not limited to:

- running frequencies, descriptives, and exploratory data analysis (EDA) protocols;
- constructing cross-tabulations or tables;
- comparing means;
- testing, using t-tests, Chi Square, analysis of variance and non-parametric alternatives;
- running correlations (parametric and non-parametric);
- running linear regression (simple, multiple, step-wise);
- segment/profiling using factor analysis (principal components), cluster analysis (hierarchical and non-hierarchical), regression models;
- modeling, via multivariate techniques, partial least squares (PLS), principal components regression (PCR), and structural equation modeling (SEM);
- consumer conjoint and correspondence analysis (perceptual maps);
- times series, tracking, and trending techniques.

These techniques encompass the procedures found in popular statistical packages, such as SPSS and SAS. They are the foundational methods widely used by market researchers to analyze quantitative data results. Utilizing a Net-centric environment, however, analytics can be deployed immediately on the data set found and accessed in the data core. The basic integrated market research component enables the uninterrupted and seamless workflow of analytics to proceed. Results can be deployed immediately, or can be fashioned into a finished report by the researcher via an online publishing system for delivery to the client desktop.

Additional techniques that are a requirement for a complete online analytical system for market research include:

- **The ability to weight data**: a flexible system for simple weighting (population/sample) to more complex procedures using stratification, finite population correction factors, or multivariable techniques.

- **The ability to filter data**: filtering affords the inspection of more targeted groups within a respondent pool.
- **The ability to recode and/or recategorize data**: market research often requires the categorization of continuous data results, as well as the recoding of existing variables to be able to be flexibly deployed.

Cross-tabs are a staple of market research, and a well executed and customizable online deliverable is a minimum requirement from the market researcher's perspective. But, the online system should be able to deliver an extensive and thorough set of analytic features to be truly world class. Market research analytics, delivered via the enabling and integrated online system, become the foundation for generating consumer insight and market measurement, whether it is through traditional project delivery or as part of a larger CRM/eCRM system. The ability to accomplish this is the first step toward solving the "missing link" problem in consumer analytics so prevalent in today's CRM software solutions.

ONLINE ANALYTIC PROCESSING (OLAP) AND REPORTING

Many misperceptions abound around OLAP tools and delivery. The use of OLAP emerged from recent data-warehouse solutions as a way to access, in real-time, the historical results kept on store in the corporation, to allow the construction of multidimensional cross-tables (a market research staple), and to deliver results in a limited and templated format. OLAP is not a replacement for market research, even though it uses interactive cross-tabs extensively. Instead of delivering information about consumer attitudes, perceptions, and feelings, it allows inspection of past events, such as a concise look at last quarter sales per region, what categories of product may have sold the most and where last year, and how quarterly financials of the corporation may have tracked over the past two years.

The technique of real-time access of data and analysis is a feature of the online market research system, but OLAP itself is quite limited in what it can do with the data; whereas, a complete online analytic system geared for market research can deliver the full range of techniques generally available in third-party statistical software. In addition, a market research system can take advantage of the data deployment features in common with an OLAP system to fashion and deliver results directly to the corporate desktop. This comprises:

- raw data delivered directly to the client, via a client portal, for the client's analysts to work over using the traditional statistical tools accessible from the online system;

- simple top lines, summaries, explorations, and cross-tabs created and produced by the research firm and delivered directly to the client's desktop;
- finished reports, containing analyst insight, recommendations, and decision guidance, produced directly online via a report publisher and delivered to the proper executive or managerial level.

OLAP, as such, does not have this broad and complete ability to afford the delivery of top-level insights that are the market research professional's strength. Combined, however, with market research techniques, OLAP becomes another facet of the delivery of business intelligence directly to the corporate user, knowledge worker, analyst, or executive. Thus, tapping into the data mart becomes an extended effort to offer the continuum of research capabilities inherent in market research through an interactive, scalable, and convenient delivery system.

DATABASE INTEGRATION AND DATA-/WEB-MINING

A relatively new and vastly under-explored area from the market research perspective is data-mining. Traditionally, data-mining is more closely ascribed to direct marketing activities than to market research. However, the emergence of an assortment of behavioral data-collection methodologies and the availability of impressive third-party databases prompt a reassessment and re-evaluation of the value of these approaches. Particularly in conjunction with an online market research system, or even as a component of an enterprise-wide CRM framework, data-mining procedures and techniques can be integrated into a helpful complement to and/or an intriguing framework for:

- **running data-/web-mining procedures directly within the online research system framework**: techniques for prediction, segmenting/ profiling of large data sets, and the classification of large data arrays can be accomplished directly on non-research data, such as:
  - behavioral/transactional data stores;
  - web warehouses of clickstream data;
  - databases of scanner or other behavioral data-collection;
- **appending either/both research data or third-party data**: data-mining procedures can be applied to data sets extended by original research results, appended membership/registration/profile data of consumers, and third-party data;
- **appending behavioral data to existing original research results**: original market research results can be extended by using clickstream,

behavioral, or scanner data, and then submitting to data-mining techniques for a variety of exploratory, classification, or predictive results.

Data-mining techniques essentially fall into three classes:

- prediction, represented best by neural networks, which are really non-linear regression procedures;
- classification, represented best by classification and regression trees (CART);
- correlation/clustering, represented best by association (link) analysis, cluster analysis, and Kohonen networks.

These techniques can be automated or manually deployed, the main advantage being the ability of the statistical algorithms to handle large and complex data sets (cases and variables, rows and columns, and lines and fields). In addition, the techniques complement the traditional market researcher's deductive techniques, as they are employed inductively (from the bottom up) in an exploratory or potentially insight-generating manner.

A little known but very useful project structure for data-mining was developed by a consortium of firms in 1998, called the Cross Industry Standard Process for Data Mining (CRISP-DM). Working from the belief that data-mining provides a way of unlocking the value hidden within the growing store of corporate data, the group's purpose was to codify a generic data-mining process from start to finish as a way of transforming the art of data-mining into well-understood, reliable procedures. The consortium's primary objective was to break down a major barrier to the adoption of data-mining by large corporate users by providing a standard, agreed-upon course of action.

CRISP-DM moved away from a technology focus to address the needs of all levels of users in deploying data-mining technology to solve business problems. This project defined and validated a data-mining process that is generally applicable in diverse industry sectors. Issues addressed include:

- mapping from business issues to data-mining problems;
- capturing and understanding data;
- identifying and solving problems within the data;
- applying data-mining techniques;
- interpretation of data-mining results within the business context;
- deployment and maintenance of data-mining results;
- capture and transfer of expertise to ensure future projects benefit from experience.

CRISP-DM was developed by four companies in various industries:

- **NCR**, a supplier of data warehouse – and through their Teradata Division, data-mining – solutions;
- **DaimlerChrysler**, one of Europe's largest companies covering automotive, aerospace, telecoms, and consultancy industries;
- **Integral Solutions Limited** (ISL), developers of the Clementine Data Mining System. ISL became part of SPSS in December 1998;
- **OHRA**, one of Netherlands' largest independent insurance companies.

The value of CRISP-DM is found in its delivery of a well-conceived and well-prepared template for carrying out standard data-mining projects. It suggests that data-mining works best for certain business circumstances, providing examples and case studies that illustrate practices such as:

- predicting churn in the telecommunications industry;
- segmenting and profiling bank customers;
- associating items purchased in a supermarket to better inform product placements;
- clustering large consumer populations into discrete lifestyle segments.

The informed integration of data-/web-mining capabilities within the online-enabling technology system for market research can extend creative and complex solution- and insight-generation by tying the three components – traditional market research techniques, OLAP, and data-/web-mining – into a powerful analytics platform. As a result, the potential to better understand consumers and deliver marketing and advertising measurement and insight are greatly enhanced.

Case Study 12
An Overview of Data-mining

Introduction

Data-mining lies at the interface of statistics, database technology, pattern recognition, and machine learning. It is concerned with the secondary analysis of large databases in order to locate previously unsuspected relationships that are of interest or value to the database "owners." Today, such data are usually found in a data warehouse, or some form of data mart, data store, or meta-data repository.

Key contemporary problems are twofold:

- sheer size of data sets;
- issues of pattern-matching.

Statistics provide the intellectual glue underlying the data-mining effort and allow users to come to terms with these sizeable issues. There are generally two major views of data-mining:

- The work involves "data-dredging" to vainly "uncover" patterns and relationships without getting to the underlying ("true") structure of the data. The feeling is that a sufficiently exhaustive search will always throw up patterns due to random fluctuations inherent in data.
- Databases are a resource containing potentially valuable information, much of it unexplored. Tools now exist to enable identification and extraction of that information. Data-mining is primarily concerned with "secondary" analysis and becomes very much an *inductive* process.

Defining Characteristics of Data-mining

- size of data sets
- contaminated data
- population drift, selection bias, and dependent observations
- finding interesting patterns
- nonnumeric data
- spurious relationships and automated data analysis

Size of Data Sets

- Data sets are so big (giga/terabytes common) they must be approached with adaptive or sequential techniques.
- Stratified or clustered analytic variants are required to deal with single flat files to multiple interrelated flat files to "distributed" files.
- Sample sizes are so large that miniscule effects lacking any practical value emerge.

Paradoxically, issues of substantive significance actually become more important to guide and structure results culled from the massive collection of data.

Contaminated Data

- In standard statistical analysis, an important part of the process involves cleaning data.
- In extremely large data sets, "going back to the source" becomes virtually impossible.

- However, when data sets are so large and contain data that describe human interaction of some kind (marketing data, surveys, financial transactions, and so on), there are bound to be errors that cannot be located.

Once again we are in the paradoxical position that even though we have so much good information, a miniscule error (say, one-tenth of 1 percent) could involve a *million records*!

Dependent Observations

- Standard statistical techniques are based on the assumption that data items have been sampled independently and from the same distribution.
- Very large data sets are much more likely to have some regions of the variable space sampled more heavily than others at different times; for example, differing time zones mean that things like supermarket transactions or telephone call data will not occur randomly over the whole United States – it will be dependent on the time zone.

This "reality" casts doubt on the validity of standard estimates and poses special problems for sequential estimation and search algorithms.

Nonstationarity

- Nonstationarity (also known as population drift) arises because the underlying population is changing (for example, the population of applicants for bank loans drifts as the economy heats and cools). Unless individual records can be time- and date-stamped, changing population structures may be undetectable.
- Databases like Wal-Mart transactions pose even more problems because they are dynamic; that is, they are constantly evolving. Thus, the results of a shopping day in June may be irrelevant to the organization in September.

Possible fixes, like real-time analytic-processing, pose great challenges to statistical algorithms.

Selection Bias

Selection bias is the distortion of the selected sample away from a simple random sample.

It is highly likely that very large data sets are convenience or opportunity samples. If an objective of the analysis is to make inferences, than any sample distortion invalidates the results. For example, imagine a set of people offered a bank loan. Comprehensive data are available only for those who take up the offer. If these data are used to construct models for future applicant behavior, errors are bound to occur.

Bottom line, what is needed is a model that takes into account all of the above characteristics. Unfortunately, such detailed data are often not easily located.

What Data-mining Does

It Finds Interesting Patterns
The concept of what is "interesting" becomes multifaceted in large database analysis:

- evidence: significance indicated by a statistical criterion;
- redundancy: similarity of a set or flow of findings;
- usefulness: utility to the user or owner;
- novelty: deviation from prior findings;
- simplicity: parsimonious presentation or result;
- generality: the fraction of a population to which a finding refers.

In data-mining it becomes evident that a compromise needs to be made between the specific and the general.

It Affords the Ability to Work with Nonnumeric Data
- Classical statistics deal with numbers.
- Databases contain many kinds of data:
  1 images
  2 audio
  3 text
  4 geographical
  5 web
  6 symbolic.

Data-mining affords the ability to work with both structured and unstructured data.

It Roots Out Spurious Patterns
It is evident that in the analysis of very large data sets, there will be a high probability that chance data configurations will be misconstrued and identified as *patterns*. What can be done?

- use neural networks, flexible models that "learn" patterns in the data;
- restrict the family of models (just examine a subset of models);
- optimize a penalized goodness-of-fit function (based on the number of possible patterns that fit);

- shrink an "overfitted" model (one CART method "grows" and then "prunes" a classification tree).

It Allows Automated Data Analysis
In data-mining we have to accept the fact that programs will drive analysis because it is physically impossible for a human analyst to examine such a large number of records and patterns. Tools like neural networks, classification trees, and others (which essentially are automated), however, must be related to a clear problem and specific objectives.

The methods include:

- **Exploration**: a comprehensive representation of a structure that summarizes the systematic components underlying the data. This is essentially classic exploratory data analysis, as derived from the work of John Tukey at Princeton University.
- **Classification**: imposing a structure that enables exploration of systematic components underlying the data (cluster analysis).
- **Prediction**: a local representation of a structure that summarizes some of the systematic components underlying the data, but which is more useful in predicting a specific outcome.
- **Methods for building models**: cluster analysis, regression analysis, supervised classification techniques, Bayesian networks (conditional dependencies between variables), and neural networks.
- **Methods for finding patterns**: computerized detection systems and graphical displays.
- **Database contributions**:
  - SQL: a basic analytic tool;
  - OLAP: rolling up, rolling down, slicing, and dicing stored and mapped warehouse data in the form of a data cube;
  - Data marts: collected and cleaned transactional data that are integrated and include raw and summarized data, historical data, and meta data. These marts, or exploratory data warehouses, are designed for easy access and analysis.

What's Ahead?
The road ahead is the integration of data-mining into a larger process called "knowledge discovery in databases." This comprises:

- data-warehousing;
- target data selection;
- cleaning;
- preprocessing;

- transformation and reduction;
- data-mining;
- model selection;
- evaluation and interpretation;
- optimization, consolidation, and use.

This full process/project cycle defines the steps needed to deploy a data-mining solution. CRISP-DM is another framework that supports and informs a complete generic data-mining project plan.

TRADITIONAL VERSUS INTERNET-CENTRIC INPUT–OUTPUT MODELS

Figure 10.3 depicts the comparison between the basic traditional input–output approach and an Internet-centric market research model. The starkest difference between approaches is seen in the extensive procedures involving data-handling in the traditional model. The formidable efficiency of the integrated database is clearly represented in the capabilities to access the data, analyze it, and produce reports. In addition, the collaborative and interactive features are enhanced by the web-based network and connection that supports multiple delivery points.

Less obvious are design considerations that allow aggregate and specific data to be combined, thus overlaying levels of research data. This enables new and creative uses of data-mining techniques to explore consumers, customers, and results in more depth. Third-party databases – such as those from Axciom, Experian, and CACI – can be leveraged by incorporating them into the database so that they can be appended to research results, online access panels, and behavioral data sets. All of these features and characteristics serve to extend the market research function, but also to broaden capabilities to improve CRM solutions. CRM analytics, generally, are not providing the robust answers needed to drive customer loyalty, satisfaction, and needs requirements. And, until the onset of online-enabling, solutions for market research, web-based connectivity and communication, and the ability to build integrated, accessible databases, traditional market research techniques have not been able to deliver the speed, agility, and results increasingly required by corporate clients.

Traditional output formats, such as cross-tabs and frequencies will likely remain a staple of market research deliverables. The difference will be in the ability for both client analyst and supplier analyst to interact and work together via the online connection. While import/export issues of data constitute a technical issue that is being pursued and solved on many fronts, the consensus appears to be that new XML and meta-data (data about data) processes and techniques will increasingly allow business information to be turned into business opportunity.[1] In fact, it is the increased emphasis on, and use of, technology to remove interaction barriers, open up collaborative communications, and automate appropriate research functions that reveal a new vista for the market research industry. Freed from many traditional procedural and technical hurdles, market researchers can increasingly focus on, improve, and deliver high-quality insights to decision-makers, tackle complex research problems intractable in the past, and explore and initiate new and creative ways to best understand and predict consumer behavior, perception, attitudes, feelings, and needs.

Figure 10.3   Traditional vs. Internet-centric input–output model

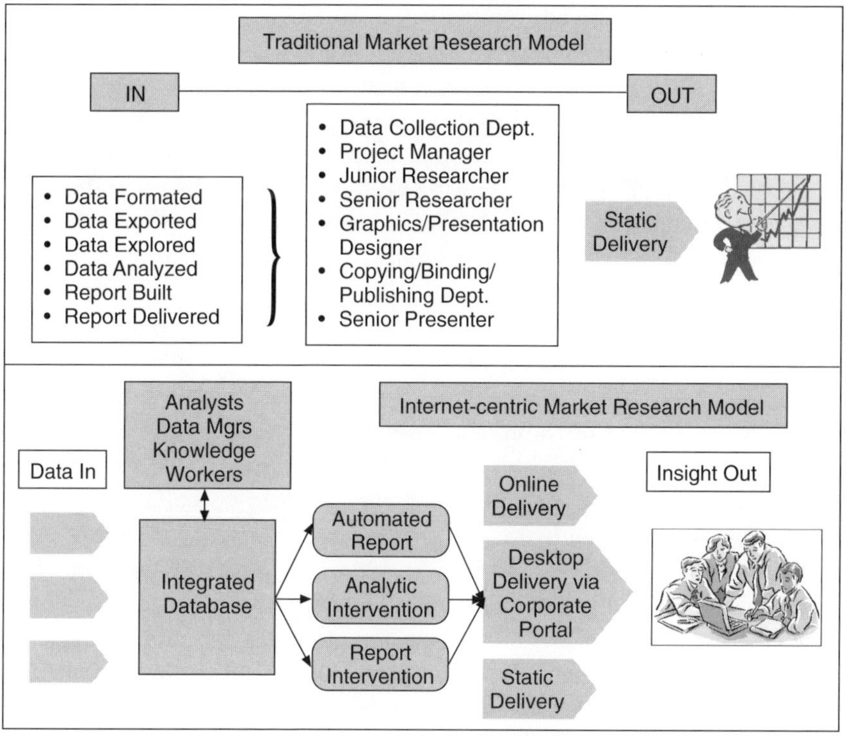

ONLINE REPORT PUBLISHING AND PRESENTATION VIA ENTERPRISE INFORMATION PORTALS

One of the more intriguing potentials inherent in the Net-centric research model is the ability for both client and supplier to interact and collaborate in research activities via a web-browser interface. The ubiquity of internal corporate intranets and, more importantly, the growing presence of corporate/enterprise information portals, enable:

- delivery of proprietary corporate information to all levels of the business;
- access to selected websites, such as those of suppliers, including market research firms;
- the ability to customize the portal, including the provision for a robust search engine for locating internal and external documents;
- the ability to collaborate and interact within and without the organization on research, knowledge documents, analysis, planning, and management.

Enterprise information portals (EIPs)[2] enable the integration of business intelligence and knowledge management techniques. The technologies that support this are the Internet, corporate intranets, and extranets.

The basic value derived from an EIP is borne via information combined from the web, corporate databases, and applications that are delivered using web browsers and search technology directly to the corporate desktop. Data feeding the portal can be either structured (for example, research data) or unstructured (for example, e-mail messages). A key advantage to using an EIP is that the web interface is easily customized. Thus, the portal can be adapted to present information or to provide interactive features based on the needs of an individual user or a group of users. EIPs can also link to information sources beyond the corporation, including Internet news feeds, real-time data streams, news announcements, syndicated research reports, and Internet community discussion groups.

On top of standard EIP capabilities, managers and executives can access additional information sources. This could include real-time event information pertaining to sales and/or the ability to gain an overview of operations by accessing secondary portals – sometimes called subportals. These ancillary sites provide information on a specific business area. Subportals also can be customized, and users can configure their browsers to include or exclude even more specific subchannels. In addition, most corporate users have access to pre-built reports and – at certain managerial levels – the ability to interact with reports (that is, drill down into detail data). Finally, queries can be issued through the portal to construct reports from an analytic data store that can be viewed on web browsers.

Advanced analysts, found in marketing, financial, research, and product development divisions, have additional options to use more powerful reporting and multidimensional analysis (MOLAP) tools. Market research and data-/web-mining are incorporated at this level as well.

Two additional features of EIPs that are important to market researchers and corporate knowledge workers include: (1) the ability to automate workflows; and (2) the ability to enable worker collaboration. Workflow automation provides a means to integrate disparate portal components and to add structure to business processes; for example, presenting users with all the necessary tasks required to conduct an online customer survey, from selecting the proper data to conducting the correct analysis and reporting the findings. Workflow automation also facilitates collaboration by enabling users to communicate with each other. One the greatest strengths of an EIP is found in extending access beyond the organization to customers, partners, and suppliers. For example, market analysts responsible for developing consumer profiles can channel their results to product managers who are in charge of applying the results of these analyses to their product and marketing strategies. Consumer surveys can be deployed to measure satisfaction and marketing effectiveness that can directly feed back to the analysts, managers, sales, and marketing divisions.

THE ROLE OF MARKET RESEARCH AS A COMPONENT OF A BUSINESS INFORMATION OR KNOWLEDGE MANAGEMENT SYSTEM

Market research and business intelligence tools have traditionally been used to apply techniques and processes on structured data – maintained in corporate analytic databases – via applications that cull trends and patterns that can inform business decisions and strategies. Knowledge management (KM), on the other hand, is a practice that blends document management and content-management techniques – typically content search, categorization, and content retrieval – for processing unstructured data (documents, Internet files, news feeds, e-mail, and other text-based information). The goal of KM is to collect, summarize, match, and disseminate an organization's knowledge – including process and business knowledge associated with specific operations, as well as accumulated intellectual capital – to other members of the organization. Typical KM applications employ techniques for aggregating information from many sources and locating and matching appropriate people and resources (for example, documents) through a variety of directory services.

Some aspects of market research involve the collection, analysis, and dissemination of unstructured data. Most often, this is data collected as part of qualitative research efforts (focus groups, discussion boards, open-end surveys, and so on). Thus, market research straddles the continuum of structured to unstructured data and an online market research system must be equipped to handle this. A logical next step for the market research industry would be to pursue the objective as the primary provider of business information; that is, enable the collection, analysis, and dissemination of results and insights across the continuum of information available within and without the corporation, and delivered directly to the client via the EIP or through a KM system as needed.

From the market research perspective, it will be a requirement, as the primary provider of business information and intelligence, for the industry to hold robust capabilities to:

- deliver raw data directly to the client analyst's desktop, including the ability to manipulate data, append third-party information, and complement CRM analytic systems already in place;
- deliver top lines, traditional summaries, and reports directly to the various levels of the corporate hierarchy;
- deliver custom and detailed finished reports, published online, directly to the client;
- push data streams, syndicated studies, tracking/trending reports, and the ability to search robust research repositories via the web portal channel;
- afford interaction and collaboration on all phases of research;
- have the capabilities to handle, manage, and deliver results, insights, and reports from both structured and unstructured data sources.

MAJOR CHARACTERISTICS OF EIPS[3]

- EIPs use both push and pull – two-way – technology to transmit information to users through a standardized web-based interface.
- EIPs provide interactivity: the ability to collaborate and share information via user desktops.
- EIPs can integrate disparate applications including: content management, BI, data warehouse/data mart, data management, market research, and other data external to these applications into a single system that can share, manage, and maintain information from one central user interface.
- EIPs can access both external and internal sources of data and information, and are able to use the data and information acquired for further processing and analysis.

WHAT EIPS ARE CURRENTLY USED FOR

- **General knowledge management**: such applications are typically targeted at document management and content-publishing of large bodies of documents, particularly those that are aggregated from different sources but delivered and updated for use by employees, suppliers, and customers. KM applications often consist of a knowledge repository and accompanying tools that organize similar documents into collections and topics so that users can more easily find and retrieve them. However, certain aspects of market research that deal in the collection and analysis of unstructured data can be deployed here as well.

- **Competitive intelligence**: an EIP typically integrates internal documents, market-share reports, news feeds, press releases, syndicated market research reports and results, data streams and tracks, and other information from the Internet in order to keep track of competitors and gauge how the organization is perceived in the press, in users' minds, and to other analysts.
- **Field and sales support**: corporate portals exist for both sales and field support. Sales support portals typically integrate access to product, market, and customer information, as well as to employees in the field. Field support portals assist customer support calls by enabling field reps to check parts inventory and availability; quickly file and process orders; and access and retrieve technical, warranty, and other documentation. Both field and sales personnel can also be equipped with the ability to deploy short survey instruments, analyze, and view the results.
- **Sharing best practices**: organizations are using EIPs to capture and disseminate the "best practices" of skilled employees to educate other employees who would otherwise have difficulty staying current on new methodologies, products, and services. In some instances, such EIPs are serving in an online training capacity. In others, corporate loyalty, HR, and internal insight can be generated via worker surveys.
- **Research and development (R&D)**: R&D applications run over an EIP and are currently most popular in the hard sciences and manufacturing industries because these organizations have large numbers of research databases worldwide, and they lack a means for researchers to get a comprehensive, organized view of their colleagues' work. However, aspects of market research and the ability to share analysis of results can also be incorporated via EIPs to facilitate and inform collaboration between groups and divisions involved in research on a global basis.

BENEFITS OF EIPS

- **Streamlined and customized information delivery**: EIPs aggregate information relevant to employees' individual roles, inducing the potential to make them more productive. Moreover, they are significantly less expensive than other information-sharing methods such as paper documents, meetings, and training sessions. Presentations, proposals, and research findings posted to the corporate portal can be easily located, no matter where they came from. This reduces or eliminates time spent by employees searching through internal repositories or the web for the information they need to carry out their jobs.

- **Enhanced insight discovery**: predefined reports, tailored to various information needs of the corporation, can alleviate dependence on the IT department to run reports or query data stores. As well, these reports can be updated frequently to reflect changing status and even provide updated data in real-time. Corporate portals with dynamic report-generation and analysis capabilities allow employees to carry out an even wider and more valuable range of business intelligence activities. These range from simply downloading files posted to the portal into spreadsheets for analysis, to drilling down into predefined or published reports, to performing "what-if" analysis using multidimensional OLAP tools. At the next level, the full slate of market research techniques and processes can be accessed and used to further extend analytic capabilities in myriad directions. Finally, data-/web- and text-mining tools can be deployed for highly sophisticated and/or complex projects, or decision support.

- **Collaboration**: EIPs are useful for assisting employees in identifying colleagues working in similar areas and putting them in touch with one another, promoting information-sharing and collaboration that can help prevent duplicated efforts. As well, the interactive nature of more advanced research activities can be exploited via the EIP communication network.

- **Enhanced customer support**: EIPs not only help support internal staff, but also, when extended to the extranet, equip a self-service feature that can help enhance customer support. For example, customers can access the portal to see if their order was shipped, suppliers can check on inventory and shipments, and partners can check where their orders stand in the production line cue. Likewise, customer satisfaction and perception surveys can be readily supported to provide valuable direct customer-facing feedback.

- **Additional sources of revenue**: extended to the extranet, an EIP not only can support a self-service model and help create better customer relations, but also can be used as a source for generating additional revenue. For example, companies can charge suppliers for access to their purchasing data stored in the data warehouse or for key proprietary research results and market measures. Although legal and privacy issues arise, and system security issues emerge, a viable business model is emerging, particularly in large consumer package goods companies which hold copious data in warehouses waiting to be exploited.

PORTALS ARE THE GATEWAY TO RESEARCH COLLABORATION AND DELIVERY

EIPs will be a key feature of market research delivery in the not too distant future. All of the key technological components are in place, and top vendors such as PlumTree have built a remarkable installation base in Global 2000 corporations in a relatively short time. The challenge exists for the market research industry to equip itself as the leader in the management, delivery, and execution of high-value decision support directly to the corporation via the portal gateway. Another option is to align with operational and analytic CRM providers to advance the accessibility and usage of a broad set analytics across the enterprise.

In short, the market research firm must be able to deliver a total research package and solution to the client, across the enterprise, and on a global basis, if needed. Figure 10.4 depicts a general model of a fully empowered knowledge worker as served by an Internet-centric market research provider. As it is clear to see, the vast power and connectivity features of the Internet, fully deployed from a market researcher's point of view, can enable this objective to be realized.

Figure 10.4   Interaction and reporting via corporate portal delivery

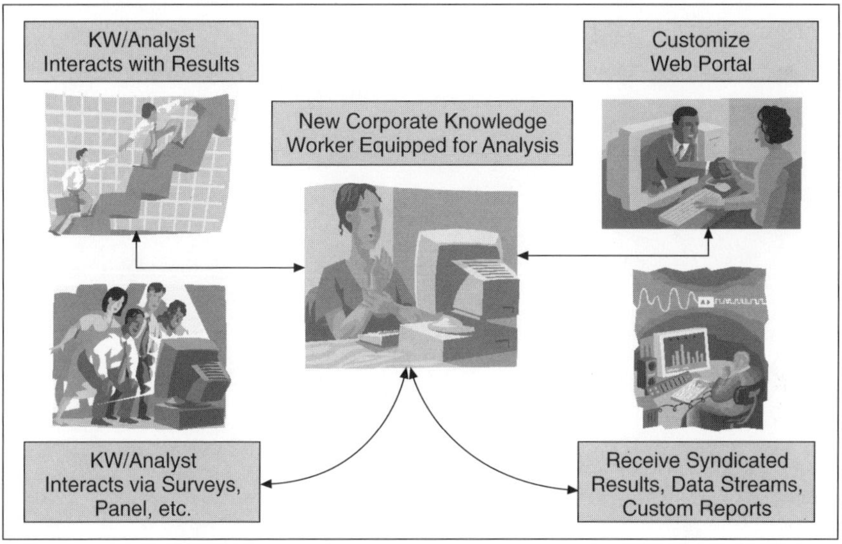

Notes

1   Inmon, W.H., Terdeman, R.H. & Imhoff, C. 2000. *Exploration Warehousing: Turning Business Information into Business Opportunity*. John Wiley & Sons, Inc.: New York, NY.

2   Hall, C. 1999. "Enterprise Information Portals: Hot Air or Hot Technology?".
     Business Intelligence Advisor, Vol. 3, No. 11. Cutter Information Corporation:
     Boston, MA.
3   Plumtree Corporation 2001. "White Paper: Corporate Information Portals,"
     www.plumtree.com.

CHAPTER 11

Scaling the One-to-One Experience

The ability to carry out qualitative market research online – as part of an integrated research system that accommodates both qualitative and quantitative methodologies and results – softens the traditional barriers between the two primary research methodologies while creating the potential for new and creative ways to use them together for research solutions. While much time and energy have been expended on debating the differences between, and relative advantages of, qualitative and quantitative methods, the general consensus among researchers is that both are necessary and vital forms of inquiry. In addition, great value can be gained by a thoughtful combination of both methods when appropriate to the research situation. This approach is often referred to as "mixed methods" and has the potential to be greatly enhanced by a robust and varied online research system.

William Trochim, a professor of marketing at Cornell University, distinguishes between the general *assumptions* involved in undertaking a research project and the *data* that results. At the level of the data, he holds that there is little difference between the qualitative and the quantitative. But to say that qualitative and quantitative data are similar is only partially true. Fundamental differences exist primarily at the level of assumptions about research rather than at the data level. Most market researchers would agree that:

- quantitative research is confirmatory and deductive in nature;
- qualitative research is exploratory and inductive in nature.

Most quantitative research tends to be confirmatory and deductive. But exploratory quantitative research exists, particularly in the area of data-mining and knowledge discovery. And while much qualitative research does tend to be exploratory, it can also be used to confirm very specific deductive hypotheses. Thus, the heart of the quantitative–qualitative debate is philosophical, not methodological.

Simply put, qualitative researchers operate under different epistemological assumptions from quantitative researchers. They tend to see quantification as limited in nature, looking only at small facets of reality that cannot be reduced without losing the importance of the big picture. As Trochim states: "For some qualitative researchers, the best way to understand what's going on is to become immersed in it. Move into the culture or organization you are studying and experience what it is like to be a part of it. Be flexible in your inquiry of people in context. Rather than approaching measurement with the idea of constructing a fixed instrument or set of questions, allow the questions to emerge and change as you become familiar with what you are studying."[1]

Trochim holds that qualitative and quantitative researchers also operate under different ontological assumptions about the world. Many qualitative practitioners tend to believe that perception and experience are uniquely individual and oppose methods that attempt to aggregate across individuals. They would also argue that all research is essentially biased by each researcher's individual perceptions. Thus, no advantage is gained by trying to establish any external or objective validity. The best we can do is interpret our own view of the world and reality.

The significance for market research resides in the fact that great diversity exists among people who consider themselves to be primarily qualitative or primarily quantitative researchers. And, increasingly, we find researchers who are interested in blending the two traditions, attempting to creatively extract the benefits of each.[2] Today, the technical advantages delivered by the enterprise online market research system support and enhance the ability for researchers to explore these new integrated research paths.

- **The integration of methods**: qualitative and quantitative methods often are used together in the same research project. In many cases such integration results in refreshing and deeply informed insights that would not have emerged with a strict "either-or" approach. Since both methods have been used for many years in empirical research and have led to research results that influenced policy, marketing, and business decisions, they are generally both accepted by funding bodies and research clients. As a result, most researchers adopt a pragmatic perspective and will utilize qualitative, quantitative, or mixed-method approaches as they see fit. One particular integrative concept, termed "triangulation," has arisen to account for the combination of qualitative and quantitative methods primarily in sociology, but widely practiced in other areas as well.

- **Triangulation: an integrative research process**: this a process that favors an integration of qualitative and quantitative methods. The term was initially borrowed from the realm of the quantitative psychological. Donald T. Campbell and Donald Fiske, two esteemed social science researchers, proposed to supplement results by the use of different research instruments. According to their seminal article published in the *Psychological Bulletin* in 1959, "multitrait–multimethod matrices" could be constructed using correlation coefficients between scores obtained with a number of different tests. These matrices could then serve as a means toward determining the degree of convergence as an indicator of the validity of research results: This was the first sustained effort to suggest that multiple measures could produce better results.
- **The qualitative perspective**: researchers soon took the multitrait–multimethod (MTMM) concept of Campbell and Fiske, and applied it to a broader methodological framework. Eugene Webb, while teaching advertising research at Northwestern, established a collegial network of professionals in psychology and sociology who were studying attitude measurement and other facets of social behavior. These informal get-togethers with psychology colleagues, Lee Sechrest and Campbell and sociologist William Schwartz, led to a volume that was published in 1966 with Webb as the senior author, entitled *Unobtrusive Measures*. This book further advanced the notion that the collection of data from different sources and their analysis with different techniques would improve the validity of results. Norman Denzin, a dedicated advocate of qualitative methods in social research, picked up on this idea. He advocated – in a book entitled *The Research Act* – that a hypothesis that had survived a series of tests with different methods was more valid than a hypothesis tested only with a single method. Since different methods entail different weaknesses and strengths, Denzin opted for what he called "methodological triangulation" – a complex process of pitting method against method and studying combined results so as to maximize the validity of research efforts in the field. Current practice in marketing research – consciously or unconsciously – makes copious use of these early groundbreaking ideas.[3]
- **The quantitative perspective**: the ability to link and study multiple research perspectives is also possible using Latent Variable Structural Equation Modeling (LVSEM). Although not fully entrenched in the market researcher's toolkit, this powerful set of techniques – that actually encompass well-known and well-used market research methods, such as analysis of variance and covariance, under a general statistical umbrella – permits the exploration and study of models that integrate micro- and macro-level data on key market research concerns, such as consumer

behavior. Since both perspectives have weaknesses, a method that permits the testing of multilevel models and recognizes the mutual interaction and effects that both inner (attitude, concepts, perceptions) and outer factors (behaviors, tests, or measures) have on each other is extremely powerful.

Indeed, both facets are vital to market measures and consumer research. The micro perspective, grounded in psychological research, focuses on variations and characteristics at an individual level. In line with the qualitative viewpoint, this approach takes for granted that a focus on the aggregate masks variations among individual characteristics that are important to understanding difficult-to-measure traits, tendencies, and conceptual thinking. In contrast, the macro perspective, more akin to traditional market research science and thinking, assumes that regularities in social behavior transcend the apparent differences among individuals. Such thinking allows for group-testing, segmentation, profiling, and the like. This approach focuses on aggregate or collective responses – or in some cases aggregate exploration and classification of vast behavioral data sets – and assumes that situational and demographic factors will lead to "anchors" that can be used to describe similar-behaving sets of people.

The capability to combine both levels in an overarching analytical system is bolstered by a research infrastructure that affords the collection of both macro- and micro-level data. This opens the door to interesting new explorations in the market research space, such as:

- using multilevel models to examine the effect of group-level variables (such as social norms and cultural values) on individual beliefs, attitudes, and purchase intentions, as well as the relationships among those constructs;
- estimating a conceptual model to study advertising effects for individuals who saw the same or different advertisements, as well as for differences related to characteristics of the advertisements, the media context in which the ad was placed, and other perceptual or attitudinal responses to the ads;
- using longitudinal studies, via a dedicated online access panel, to track individuals over time to model such aspects as a person's needs or self-esteem on trends in attitude toward consumption produced by repeated exposures to media; an individual's need for stimulation or uniqueness on trends regarding satisfaction with a product over time; or a consumer's brand perception over time and how it changes with usage, product involvement, or evolving needs.

In brief, a whole new avenue is opened to move freely between qualitative and quantitative perspectives and macro- and micro-level explorations. An online market research infrastructure directly supports the ability to merge, filter, integrate, and study data on levels not feasible before.[4]

Criticism of mixed methods has existed since the original MTMM concept of Campbell and Fiske. However, the potential *complementarity* of qualitative and quantitative research methods has generally been realized. Hence, two meanings of triangulation have emerged: (1) as a process of cumulative validation; and/or (2) as a means to produce a more complete picture of the phenomena under study. What is evident is that triangulation is supported by and potentially made more efficient using an integrated online research system. Collaboration and interaction, also characteristic of and enhanced by an online system and its delivery, further emerge as ways to increase the potential complementarity of mixed methods.[5]

ONLINE FOCUS GROUPS

Few market research practitioners would argue with the statement that online qualitative research offers a new and exciting opportunity to conduct research in ways simply not possible before the advent of the Internet. The key phrase missing, here – of course – is: when appropriate. It is the "*when appropriate*" caveat that is the essential point.

Market researchers in general, and those involved with qualitative in particular, are sticklers for method. To most it is the foundation of professionalism and a basis of industry expertise. Indeed, "method" has frequently been at the forefront of discussions regarding all forms of online research. Thus, when we hear "when appropriate," what is really being said is: "when appropriate based on the proper method we, as professionals, determine will end in a gain in quality of results and insights." There is absolutely nothing wrong with this; it is a cornerstone of professionalism in practice. However, sometimes we can overlook the forest for the trees.

There is a distinct difference between doing focus groups online and using enabling (web-based) technology to do focus groups. Doing focus groups online does bring into question whether the method is appropriate and a thoughtful rendering of the strong and weak characteristics carried out by a research professional. But, *using online technology to do focus groups* goes beyond the "when appropriate" discussion. Online technology enables the rapid and integrated collection of data from many sources into one database for analysis. So, the results of online focus groups (OFGs) – when used appropriately – can be meshed and fused with an assortment of other data a client or market research firm may hold. The technology extends the capabilities of the system in a fundamental way. And the result is a more informed, more complete, and one where more useful insights can be delivered directly to the client's desktop, often in multiple forms or levels based on client need – enabling technology to work.

We do not propose to end the methodological discussions for any sorts of market research activities that are being explored using online techniques. Recent experimental research, such as reported by Tom Miller, Director of the ACNielsen Center for Marketing Research at the University of Wisconsin-Madison, is key to further understanding, refining, and utilizing the potential that online research holds for our industry. What we would propose to begin are discussions that will allow market researchers to compete effectively in a world increasingly connected; yet recently fragmented.

Current worldwide events and economic slowdowns have significantly affected the global business community. Corporations have curtailed executive business travel. People, in general, are avoiding airplanes. The airline industry is in upheaval as massive lay-offs occur. Tourism and entertainment meccas, such as Disney World, have been severely affected.

Without trying to profit from tragedy, why would we hesitate to consider the increased use of technology, such as OFGs, to enable us to continue to extend our services globally? Problems of method will exist, but have existed for all new forms of research. However, we all can embrace a move that greatly leverages the use of technology in an integrated and appropriate way to deliver market research services, encourage new and creative approaches, and in the long run, perhaps serve all clients – internationally or locally – better. In reality, this vision is already being enacted around the world, as people, businesses, and governments explore ways to leverage technology with an increased sensitivity to safety.

We are all familiar with the long-term promises of online technology for qualitative research: improved quality of data, increased speed of deployment, and reduced costs. Short-term perspectives usually involve a long list of pros and cons. And most thoughtful practitioners include an evaluation of the effect of online focus groups on clients, moderators, and participants.

As we study any list, we now need to add another component: the safety of doing global qualitative research that may involve extensive travels for any of the groups involved in the effort. While not a pleasant point to add to any list, it nonetheless has become a reality.

Online-enabling technology can connect us across the company and around the world in our efforts to do research. In addition, it can fuse the information – via database, storage, and delivery systems – into a more complete set of data on customers and consumers. Further, systems exist today that enable integrated multi-mode and multi-method research to be completed in one enterprise system. Thus, for example, online focus group members can also participate in a short online survey the results of which can be used to measure against a baseline the client may have. The creative possibilities are fairly open as we explore the ways to best utilize the online infrastructure as an integrating, pervasive system.

Soon, the convergence of voice-over telephony, the Internet, and TV may well make all of our separate processes and systems unnecessary. Multimode or multi-method market research – carried out nationally, internationally, or globally – will be completed using one connected system. Although the need for face-to-face research for individuals and groups will always have a place, a weighing of the pros and cons in the near future will most likely entail a distinctly different list for determining the most appropriate approach to follow.

How OFGs Work

OFGs work by effectively networking all parties involved via the Internet and providing varying levels of access to the communication flow. Thus, a moderator would be able to communicate with everyone, but a group member would not be able to "talk to" the client, for example. The web interface is cleverly portioned out to allow typed communication, the ability to view any number of stimuli, and to link to other areas (such as a website to evaluate or an online survey/form to complete). Figure 11.1 depicts a typical online focus group set-up.

Advantages of OFGs

The advantages of OFGs comprise a long list that includes:

- reduced travel time and costs for clients, moderators, and participants – if business travel is hindered, another advantage emerges: safety;
- increased productivity because less time is spent traveling;
- facility and incentive costs can be reduced;
- participation in the group can take place anywhere an Internet connection and browser is available – OFGs enable a researcher to "reach" and involve participants simultaneously around the world and can be moderated from any location;
- clients can more effectively and efficiently communicate with the moderator online;
- real-time analysis is possible, so clients receive results more quickly – OFGs can accelerate the completion of research studies;
- total time elapsed can be decreased anywhere from 25–50 percent;

Figure 11.1 Online focus groups and discussion boards

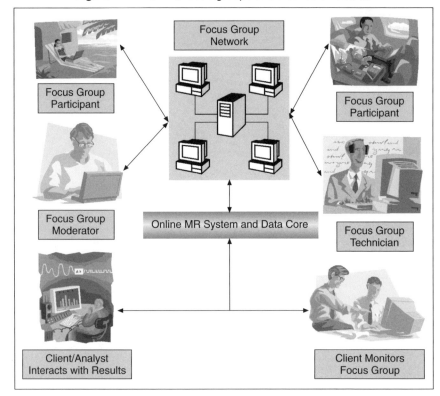

- cutting-edge technology affords the presentation of a variety of stimuli, including pictures, 3D renderings, video, and sounds;
- online surveys can be incorporated as part of the OFG process. Feedback and results occur immediately. Thus, the quantitative exercise drives additional group discussions;
- the ability to do synchronous or asynchronous sessions. Synchronous sessions mimic the traditional approach. Asynchronous sessions allow group members to respond at different times. The asynchronous approach is useful for sophisticated projects where much thought is desired to advance the discussion. Thus, it becomes a "moderated" chat board with a specific purpose;
- OFGs can be effective with small "niche" audiences where there may not be a concentration in any one geographic area.

Issues and Needs

Issues to consider in a discussion of online qualitative methods, particularly focus groups, are quite varied. For example, one that hasn't been addressed adequately is overseas online connectivity. Notably, in countries where local access to ISPs is a toll call, researchers need to realize the access charges along with incentives. Other factors that should be considered when doing OFGs, include:

- a recognition that OFGs may not be appropriate for all studies since not everybody has access to a PC, browser, and Internet connection;
- OFGs also may not be appropriate for certain studies when a product needs to be seen, touched, tasted, or manipulated by the participants. However, some web-based solutions enable any digital file or image to be shown to participants in a secure virtual setting. Thus, the researcher and client can present and receive feedback;
- a common disadvantage of OFGs voiced repeatedly is the inability to see or "hear" the participants, thus subtle body language, inflection cues, and even emotion are eliminated. It is interesting that the online channel mediates the information gathered into a "real-time" data-collection, yet misses the human need to "see, hear, and feel" the focus group in "real-time" (live). However, emotional cues and reactions can be accessed via video streaming, video and/or audio conferencing technology;
- an early disadvantage noted by some was that participants could not be "confirmed" and confidentiality of the sessions could be compromised, although this is less a problem now with passwords, secured sites, and confidentiality statements becoming standard for OFGs;
- slow ISP connections can still wreak havoc as they cause disenchantment or frustration individually or within the group. Some OFGs are now run via global training centers – that is, New Horizons or Executrain – that provide a worldwide standardized computer and connection. Of course, a cost is involved in the use of the facility and to travel there locally;
- with the use of standardized computer centers around the world, theoretical access to a web connection is less of an issue; however, some individuals, particular in a segment located in an emerging market, could be eliminated from participation due to lack of access;
- likewise, participants' lack of keyboard and written communication skills can also handicap their contribution;
- current OFG research has shown that the online channel produces more "frank" comments and strong words, both positive and negative, and impacts on the informational length of sessions. Researchers have concluded that the "anonymity" of the situation fosters this behavior.

Currently, there is a consensus that certain types of OFGs work best: website evaluations, testing of online ads/brands/awareness; pulling together geographically dispersed and hard to locate individuals within a target segment, and new capabilities that allow 3D product manipulation and testing. In addition, many agree that online moderators need new skills. These include technical, multi-tasking skills; real-time coding/transcript analysis training; and training in being responsive to new online group dynamics to best maximize the OFG technique. Since the Internet mediates the experience, these new skills are vital to success. Most will be gained through continual practice and development as OFGs become more common.

Case Study 13
Considerations for Running Global OFGs

Several key considerations must be noted, particularly when running cross-border online focus groups:

- **Adequate access and connection**: participants need proper Internet access and their computers must meet certain specifications for bandwidth and speed of connections. Until bandwidth and connection speed become fairly standardized around the world, this is best addressed as part of the participant screening process.
- **Carefully crafted questions**: athough the official language of computer and IT specialists is most likely English, don't take for granted that every participant speaks English fluently or will understand certain language patterns. Questions should be crafted to ensure comprehension and avoid slang terms, business jargon, or acronyms.
- **Multilanguage groups are feasible**: English-based online software is equipped to handle any language rooted in the Latin alphabet. However, it may be more challenging to find ones that can function in different alphabets (for example, Arabic, Cyrillic, and so on).
- **Know your culture**: cultural differences can result in misunderstandings and misinterpretations. For example, Japan remains a country that communicates very formally. Simply recruiting participants through uninvited e-mails may prove fruitless. Instead, potential Japanese participants prefer a phone call introducing the concept, followed by an informational e-mail.
- **Appropriate incentives**: this can be difficult in an international setting because some cultures are offended by monetary payment. A solid strategy is to discuss with participants during recruiting and offer a choice of incentives.
- **Timing is everything**: if a study utilizes a truly global audience, it is difficult to choose convenient times. Just as in traditional physical focus groups, evening times still tend to work the best.

- **Ensure your customer base is adequately represented**: this is especially vital for consumer-type studies. Currently, IT and computer industries have the greatest online penetration internationally. However, Internet and e-mail communication are quickly emerging in many different countries, population segments, and business sectors. The consensus is that this trend will continue.

Adapted from Trenton Haack. "Considerations for Running Global Online Focus Groups." Article Number: 0573, November 2000, *Quirk's Marketing Research Review*, www.quirks.com.

ONLINE DISCUSSION BOARDS

Online discussion boards (ODBs) are emerging as yet another avenue for companies to collect consumer data. This unstructured data are often surprisingly informative. While discussion boards can be used in a more formalized way – as an extension of traditional focus group techniques – increasingly, clients are interested in what their customer's spontaneous and unrestricted comments can reveal.

A potential problem in analysis of what can be a vast amount of text data is partially alleviated by emerging text-mining tools. These tools, from such companies as Megaputer, employ text algorithms that can parse and categorize text and produce some element of coherence to an otherwise impossible task. In addition, some new media research firms, such as BuzzBack, employ online discussion boards to extend online focus or survey research via an ad hoc consumer or customer panel.

Carolyn Fitzgerald, CEO of BuzzBack in New York City, believes that the ability to recontact online survey or focus group participants to follow up on recent product, service, or advertising evaluations is enhanced by the ability to let the consumer "speak." And the online discussion or chat environment is effective for reaching and gathering insights and information that would normally be missed with traditional methods. This represents a fairly unique method for using the communicative power of the Internet to intentionally blur the lines of research and build an informational relationship with a consumer.

Not surprisingly, clients appear to find the ability to "talk to" consumers literally "on call" about their products or services very appealing. Although traditional and online access panels can accomplish the same goal, clients seem to like the fact that often little or no mediation by a researcher is needed. And, as market research industry lore holds, managers and business executives generally are more influenced by what people (consumers or customers) actually say over reams of statistical analysis and well-supported recommendations.

Key issues and characteristics of ODBs include:

- **Gather unstructured data**: as a method to gather spontaneous, unstructured, and unfiltered data, ODBs are superb, particularly if they are channeled and focused on topics of great interest to the client, such as: "what do you think of my new product?"
- **Track unsolicited opinions, complaints, or perceptions**: business people, in general, put great stock in consumer's actual words. Thus, the ability to see "real" unfiltered feedback is compelling.
- **Difficulties with control**: one issue concerning ODBs is the difficulties in controlling what is shared online. The anonymity factor can have a downside, as certain online communities, portals, chat rooms, and discussion boards have learned.
- **Who is participating?**: along with control issues, online anonymity brings into question the veracity of who actually is messaging. For research purposes, this can be controlled somewhat by careful screening, validation, or the use of online access panels.
- **Build a sense of consumer community**: ODBs can encourage a consumer community that truly provides helpful feedback to a client, as BuzzBack will attest. However, hard line researchers will also be quick to point out that the potential for encouraging a biased yea-saying or nay-saying community can also occur. Once again, careful and judicious management of such a group for research purposes is necessary, as well as the use of advanced text-mining tools to sift through and evaluate large amounts of text data.
- **Do companies want to hear the truth?**: on the other side of the coin about wanting to hear the consumer voice is the fact that companies may not want to hear the truth from customers, for whatever reason. Often this is more political than just a desire to hear only good news. Yet, with the rise in the installation of CRM systems, it is quite likely that companies will be bombarded with the truth as fodder to build better "customer relationships" via the software's solutions.
- **Balancing input with action**: closely aligned with evaluating the value of what consumers or customers are saying is what action to take. Unless managers or executive decision-makers are extremely confident in their ability to take the information gathered from formal or informal ODBs and take action, the wiser course is to engage researchers and analysts to assist in determining cause and effect.

- **Potential to identify and hear consumer beacons**: the IT industry, in particular, has developed great stock in – or some would say simply myths and legends about – first movers in adopting technology innovations. Along the same lines, consumer and packaged goods, retail, automotive, and other service companies also hold to the idea that ODBs can be a source of strong directions via the comments and perceptions of early users. Often, when this type of "driving force" consumer is located or identified, there is a rush by companies to understand why this is occurring and they will try to leverage that knowledge out to the larger customer base to exploit or build trends, fads, or fashions.
- **Viral soft marketing potential**: an outgrowth of identifying beacons, or a separate marketing ploy in its own right, ODBs can become a source of instigating viral marketing campaigns that are enabled easily via the Internet communication network.

ONLINE QUALIQUANT TECHNIQUES

A consistent theme of this book has been the absolute necessity for the market research industry to step up to the technological plate and address growing corporate client needs for global and integrated research services that are both effective and efficient. A number of market research and/or new media firms have made concerted efforts to best leverage the benefits of new technology in this regard. This section of the chapter will focus on some work being done in the area of integrating qualitative and quantitative techniques in new and creative ways. As well, we will focus on a particular compelling protocol developed in the United Kingdom by John S. Pawle of Second Sight International and Peter Cooper of CRAM International Group termed QualiQuant™ Technology. This "best practice" stimulates and supports ideas for further development to best exploit the technology-enabled research system described in this book.

Best Practices: Accelerating Product Innovation and Development Innovation via the Web

Pawle and Cooper[6] recently presented a compelling paper and case study that best exemplifies the potential inherent in combining qualitative and quantitative methods using an online market research-enabling system. After a discussion of the importance of gaining access to the "voice of the customer" and of the reality of the innovation process applied to such marketing processes as new product development, they concluded that a curious dilemma emerges:

- **The traditional process of new product development is decidedly deficient.** It lacks depth and it takes a long time to do it correctly.
- **To do new product development correctly requires using both quantitative and qualitative techniques:** Yet, this is precisely what adds time and cost to projects.

Pawle and Cooper's solution (QualiQuant™) aligns the potential inherent in using quantitative diagnostics (surveys) with qualitative techniques (projective questions, visual imagery, and open-end feedback) to drive a holistic research solution that is accelerated and more cost efficient. Note that this solution can be adapted via traditional forms of research, but the point made is the advantage of utilizing a web/Internet approach. The major objective strives toward improvement in the traditional innovation funnel commonly deployed in product, branding, and advertising efforts.

Figure 11.2 depicts one basic model of combined qualitative and quantitative techniques that represents an extended version of Pawle and Cooper's hierarchy of qualitative techniques. The major characteristics include:

- **The entire continuum of research techniques is available via the online research system:** this includes the advantages afforded for project management, data-collection, and data-interaction and delivery.
- **A variety of qualitative techniques can be combined, streamed, or stacked within one research instrument:** from spontaneous open-ended response to in-depth probing interviews that can be used within an instrument, within a project, or across multiple projects.
- **Analytic diagnostic data can be applied, as well as data appends from a variety of useful sources:** online surveys, as well as third-party data, panel membership/registration data, clickstream, transactional or scanner aggregates can be added to further enrich insight into the consumer.
- **Result/insight delivery can be made directly to the research client for collaboration and additional interaction:** while not a part of this diagram, client delivery is enhanced via a web-based portal that affords interactive analysis or easy collaboration between client and research supplier during the course of research. Finally, delivery via streams, reports, or in-person (static) formats can be achieved.

An Optimum Innovation Tunnel

Pawle and Cooper have developed a rich diagnostic approach to test product ideas (although any sort of brand, advertising, and marketing concepts are applicable candidates as well). Termed as an "optimum innovation funnel" in their paper, the objectives of speed, efficiency, and cost-effectiveness are

Figure 11.2   Mixed-mode (QualiQuant) techniques

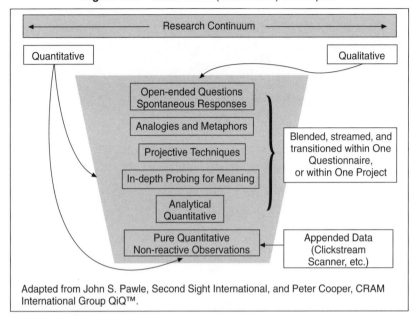

Adapted from John S. Pawle, Second Sight International, and Peter Cooper, CRAM International Group QiQ™.

met while simultaneously and potentially greater insight, direction, and decision support are achieved. This seven-stage process incorporates research at four critical touch points (see Figure 11.3):

- **Research Step 1: Developing a holistic understanding of the consumer**. A wide variety of qualitative and/or quantitative methods can be used to build this most important foundational step in the process. These can include:
    - ethnographic research;
    - observational research;
    - segmentation studies;
    - trend studies;
    - Delphi studies;
    - data-mining of transactional/behavioral databases;
    - exploratory data analysis;
    - knowledge discovery techniques;
    - pretesting structural models, as a baseline for further study or change.
- **Research Step 2: Initial QualiQuant Concept Test**. Tests can be deployed via the web for both rich diagnostic information and rapid turnaround. As Pawle and Cooper emphatically state, the general procedure is to use qualitative techniques more heavily early in the process – prior to any evaluative work – to allow the formation of a solid

basis of understanding. As Research Step 2 is reached, the quick, rapid turnaround of results is more effective and appropriate to avoid the "bogdown" in product innovation that usually develops using traditional strategies. The objective here is to rapidly refine the marketing or product mix for final testing.

- **Research Step 3: Testing the Mix**. Once a finalized mix has been developed, it needs to be fully tested for market potential. Here, as well, a solid foundation based on Research Step 1 will be readily available should weak areas arise in the testing that need to be optimized. Thus, it is not back to square one, but an integrated check based on a rich understanding of the product that can facilitate rapid optimization for retesting.

- **Research Step 4: Tracking**. The final step is to track the progress of brands, relaunches, and extensions via functional and emotional ratings. Thus, even here, "quali-quant" thinking is essential. Plus, if extensive modeling were feasible and completed at Research Step 1, it becomes possible to track changes in the model utilizing Latent Variable Structural Equation Modeling (LVSEM), or simple to perform trend, time series, or data-tracking analyses that can be delivered in continuous or regular updates to the client desktop for further action or insight generation.

Approaches such as those just described will become more and more valuable and accessible as market researchers begin to avail themselves of the tools to meet the needs of corporate global clients. Possibly, incorporation in CRM analytical processes, as well, can further be accommodated. The bottom line, as reflected throughout this book, is that new technologies should not replace traditional market research techniques, procedures, or value-added services. Instead, they should be leveraged to enhance, extend, and create new opportunities to better serve the new global client.

ADVERTISING, BRANDING, AND PERCEPTION STUDIES

One of the best uses of the online medium to emerge recently is the ability to do rapid advertising and brand-testing. While currently limited to online advertising and brand-testing, the efforts and developments underway by companies such as Dynamic Logic, TNSi, and ProActive International are paving the foundation for future uses. For example, utilizing new media online, such as video, audio, and eventually 3D product manipulation, will result in an even greater application of these techniques across a broader online global audience equipped with faster connections and communications. Likewise, wireless access devices can also be pulled into a quick and effective process of testing "on the spot" a variety of advertising, branding, and perception questions.

Figure 11.3   Optimum innovation funnel: ad, product or brand research

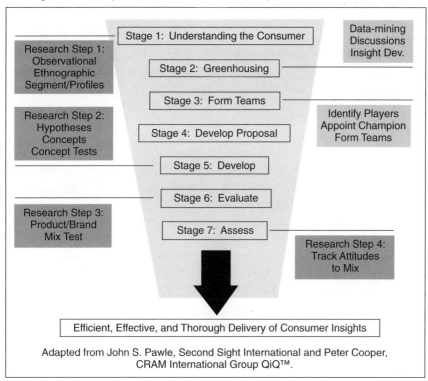

Stage 1: Understanding the Consumer

Data-mining
Discussions
Insight Dev.

Research Step 1:
Observational
Ethnographic
Segment/Profiles

Stage 2: Greenhousing

Stage 3: Form Teams

Identify Players
Appoint Champion
Form Teams

Research Step 2:
Hypotheses
Concepts
Concept Tests

Stage 4: Develop Proposal

Stage 5: Develop

Stage 6: Evaluate

Research Step 3:
Product/Brand
Mix Test

Stage 7: Assess

Research Step 4:
Track Attitudes
to Mix

Efficient, Effective, and Thorough Delivery of Consumer Insights

Adapted from John S. Pawle, Second Sight International and Peter Cooper,
CRAM International Group QiQ™.

Building Global Brands

What role does global-branding play today? If one accepts the definition of a brand as: "a mixture of tangible and intangible attributes, symbolized in a trademark, which, if properly managed, creates influence and generates value,"[7] then global-branding possesses great value in its ability to expand brand awareness on a global basis. For major companies that have an established brand in one country it is the key to leveraging the strength and value inherent in the brand's identity.

For a company, organization, or retailer to achieve global success it requires an understanding of global branding and possessing the capability to explore, study, and research the consumer around the world or in new markets of interest. Although companies can gain knowledge from examining what global strategies worked, what strategies did not work, and what is still working for established global brands, this is not sufficient. Each company striking out on the global path must be able to reach its particular markets, its particular consumers, and its particular segments to best understand them. Enabling research tools and technology that afford the broadest and widest research avenues available and effective ways to centrally manage results and drive actions are vital.

Global Branding and Market Research

Areas of key strategic and marketing research that emerge from the global effort include:

- **Assessing a target market**: one of the first tasks confronting a company is to identify its target market. A global online access panel can provide the answers to numerous business questions, such as product, pricing, location, and promotional unknowns. For example, when a company is working up its product strategy it needs to determine the best marketing mix. Online surveys, appended data from scanner reports, and other transactional data can generate a baseline picture, while – from the consumer side – online qualitative can inform identification of productive strategies. Pricing strategy, for instance, may make or break a new effort. Retailer's pricing strategies need to support overall marketing objectives and policies. The retailer must balance actual consumer demand and the prevailing market price. This requires access to consumers in worldwide markets who can be reached via an online access panel and queried for reliable guidance.

- **Placement and promotion strategies**: a competitive edge can be gained from understanding a new market and employing optimum placement and promotion strategies. Here, market research drives decisions based on the determination of the retailer's size, financial resources, what products to offer, the level of competition, and knowing the target consumer and market. Additional research can also measure promotional strategy success. Once again, access to people to garner this information is enhanced by a robust online system with global capabilities.

- **Brand identification**: product identification begins with interpreting, measuring, and analyzing brand loyalty, brand equity, and the potential effects of global branding. *Brand loyalty* can be measured in three stages: brand recognition, brand preference, and brand insistence. Brand recognition is built through advertising. But awareness does not ensure preference over competitors. To establish brand preference, it is necessary to understand what people prefer, to consistently deliver it, and to gain their trust. When preference is certain, brand insistence takes over and competitors are at a disadvantage. Loyalty measures require an effective system to reach consumers globally and locally, such as through a global consumer access panel, and deploy multimode and multi-method research procedures to verify and track success.

- **Brand equity**: brand equity is also built on brand recognition, brand preference, and brand insistence. Value results from a combination of brand awareness, brand association, and perceived quality. An oft-quoted example is the "Energizer Bunny." When we see an advertisement with a pink bunny playing a bass drum going across the television screen, we know we are watching an Energizer battery commercial. We recognize the Energizer brand because we associate the bunny with the company. We also believe or know, through experience, that the battery is high quality. But our knowledge and/or expectation is also enhanced by the Energizer's status on the battery market. Thus, the three facets of brand awareness, association, and quality contribute to our perception of brand equity. The challenge on a global scale is to be able to manage, test, and measure these facets on new consumers, markets, and cultures in an effective and efficient way
- **Global branding**: often, a company has established and built brand loyalty and brand equity within familiar markets, and needs to know how to replicate this in a global setting. Research provides the answer, but it must be research that can be deployed and managed effectively and efficiently around the world, if needed. It is key that global markets be thoroughly researched, tested, and evaluated or serious errors could occur. With new online technologies and systems for accessing consumers via global panels, and the ability to deploy a broad spectrum of research, what has traditionally been a very difficult task is now eased. Beyond the cost and time efficiencies, the effort formerly spent on logistics and data-collection can now be turned toward meeting the more important needs of the emerging global corporations: guiding, evaluating, and providing insight for branding, advertising, marketing, and strategy decisions.[8]

If a company is truly equipped – via a robust global marketing research component – to carry out a globalization strategy, it will enjoy a much greater potential for success. As mentioned in Part 1 of this book, corporate mergers and consolidations see no let up in the emerging race to globalize. Mergers are forming global powerhouses that require equally powerful consumer insight, market research, analytic capabilities, and decision/strategy support. And a very important facet of this whole picture will be the effective global branding of products and services.

Global branding also requires rapid delivery and dissemination of results. Company executives need global strategic brand management information that will target segments, foster the brand identity or vision, measure brand equity goals, and support brand-building programs. The analysis of customers, competitors, and brands will be consistent and ongoing. Executives and managers need to know what brands are viable, preferred, and working in the new markets. The company needs to know that a brand brings out the best qualities of the intended market. Whatever brand identity the company establishes goes a long way in determining the effectiveness of global brand loyalty.

When a company begins to understand consumer rationale and psychology within a variety of cultural contexts, it will have an inside track to building brand awareness in its targeted global consumer markets. Organizations that have built strong brand equity in new global markets have first identified strategies or tactics that helped them gain their success. Market research has helped them translate their successes to new global venues. It is well known that organizations such as Proctor & Gamble, Visa, and Coca-Cola have built strong global brand equity. They have accomplished this through extensive and thorough research positioned to gain an understanding of how best to build awareness of their products on the global market, and how best to create positive associations in the consumer mind for their product. The efforts of these large multinationals, however, are now the rule, rather than the exception, for virtually all companies engaged in global business activity and expansion. Thus, the emerging need for an enabling online market research system, with global and enterprise-wide capabilities, becomes even stronger.

ONLINE TECHNIQUES FOR TESTING AD AND BRAND AWARENESS AND PERCEPTION

Arno Hummerston, Head of Interactive Solutions, Worldwide, for TNS in the United Kingdom, and Nick Nyhan, CEO of Dynamic Logic in the United States, have each developed a similar innovative online technique for testing ad and brand awareness online. Using a very basic control and test group comparison procedure, the effort has yielded a quick but effective way to deliver quantitative information about the awareness, perception, or effect of an online ad or brand. As Hummerston states: "In analyzing the effects of advertising on the perception of a brand there are numerous issues to understand. Initially the brand perception starting point or benchmark needs to be established in order for the promotional campaign effects to be evaluated. This is accomplished by clarifying the customer's attitudes toward – and opinions of – a brand before the impact of a promotional campaign is introduced. This perception is influenced by historical events that cannot necessarily be qualified, and may be numerous and spread over a long period of time."[9]

Once a campaign is introduced, the effects can be investigated. However, a specific online campaign cannot be viewed in isolation. There will be other forces at work, such as offline promotions and the retention and re-emergence of past attitudes and opinions. It is also important to recognize the lasting effects of a campaign on the perception of a brand, as retention plays an important part in future purchasing decisions. Given this framework for the analysis of brand perception, a process for investigating the brand perception of any number of potential clients can be deployed. Both Nyhan and Hummerston independently developed quite similar approaches.

The objective of an online ad or brand test is to pretest and/or evaluate online and offline advertising campaigns and the resultant brand perception and awareness online. This requires a three-phase survey process: (1) pre-campaign; (2) during campaign; and (3) post-campaign. In order to achieve this the following elements need to be investigated:

- **Audience segmentation**: the audience the advertising message reaches (in terms of gender, age, income, and so on). Has the advertising reached its intended target?
- **Advertising effectiveness**: to what extent does the campaign have the desired influence on the target audience? Are the communication goals being reached according to the way they have been set?
- **Changed brand perceptions**: does the campaign change people's perception of the company, product, or service brands? In what directions?
- **Creativity**: are there specific creative elements that are particularly strong or weak? What is the impact on perceptions of the brand? Does it have the ability to enhance image on key attributes?
- **Ability to drive actions**: its ability to drive people to act. Does it stimulate people to buy and use the advertised products online?

A Typical Research Study Design

Typically, four specific research components are identified that can be incorporated into a study collectively or individually. It is intended that these run over an appropriate period of time, such as six weeks (if this is feasible and suitable). However, the duration of the study can be reduced should deadlines and time scales disallow this.

The four research components are:

- website-recognition testing;
- client-specific online survey;
- click-through survey;
- in-depth online study.

It is also possible to add a campaign pretesting phase that is not described here. Essentially this allows focus group and/or quantitative investigation of the campaign to be used prior to implementation on the advertising host site.

1 **Website-recognition testing**: visitors to a site can be identified by a cookie that is passed to them, and their exposure to the client's banner advertising recorded. By then analyzing the cookies of the visitors to the client's website, it is possible to match the two sets of visitors (those specific visitors and the client website visitors) and track whether the advertisement has had a positive effect in instigating an action. However, there may be a natural incidence of cross-matched visitors that is not related to the exposure of the advertisement. For this reason, those visitors to the specific site that have not been exposed to the advertisement will be tracked similarly. Consequently, the difference in behavior and frequency between those that have been exposed to the advertisement and those that have not can be identified.

This "cross-tracking" usually begins prior to the campaign and continues post-campaign so that the retention effects can be gauged.

2 **Client-specific online survey**: in order to actively and quantitatively investigate the advertising and its effect on the perception of the brand an online survey is needed. This is initiated from the client web pages that run rotated banner advertisements. In order to form a robust view of the effects, two identical surveys are run. The first runs as a control survey and the second as a test survey. The control group consists of visitors who have *not* been exposed to the client's advertisement, while the test group has been served the advertisement on its visit to the site. This method ensures that non-campaign effects are accounted for.

In addition, this methodology is implemented in three stages: pre-campaign, during the campaign, and post-campaign. This ensures that a benchmark is produced in the pre-campaign stage that can be compared to the effects identified throughout the campaign and to the post-campaign period where retention is monitored.

This approach to the online survey is undertaken at the time of the visit to the client site. In order to do so, a pop-up survey is initiated when a visitor leaves the site and the questionnaire is presented immediately. This ensures that the immediate recollection of the page contents is monitored. The longevity of the impact will then be monitored by the post-campaign phase of the study.

It is possible to identify the advertisement type (half-size, full-size, or new skyscraper sizes recently approved by the online industry) and thus track and segment the performance of each.

Question areas for this type of research include:

- demographics;
- attitudes toward advertising on the Internet: use of emotional and functional statements;
- unprompted recollection of ads seen on the client homepage (ever, and at the visit just completed);
- unprompted recall of brands in the industry sector of the advertised brand;
- prompted awareness of the brand;
- prompted awareness of the advertisement;
- advertising content (message, clarity, meaning, style, and functionality);
- call to action: intention to act on advertisement, method of action (purchase, visit to website, and so on), and timing of action;
- offline promotion awareness;
- brand perception: use of emotional and functional statements.

The objectives of the client's campaign are taken into account in developing these question areas.

Generally, some sort of online survey "activator" – usually a small piece of Java code – runs on participating sites for a period of two to four weeks. Each time someone visits the site, the visit is centrally registered. A certain proportion of those visitors are subsequently invited to participate in the survey. This means that a randomly selected sample is generated and ensures the robustness and validity of the study. If somebody who has participated in the research visits the site again during that period of two weeks, and would have qualified again on the basis of the random survey fraction, he or she is *not* given the invitation.

3 **Click-through survey**: a supplementary methodology is often employed that allows the investigation of the click-through behavior and motivations from the advertisements. This survey is instigated once a click-through has been activated. A delay is used on the survey pop-up in order to allow the destination page to be loaded. This ensures that disruption of the visit is minimized. Question areas for this research include:

- demographics;
- advertising content;
- future intent;
- reason for click-through;
- expectations of click-through;
- offline promotion awareness;
- brand perception.

It should be noted that for both online surveys the questionnaire length is kept to a minimum, generally not more than seven to ten minutes.

4. **In-depth, online study**: within the context of this study the intention here is to recruit people from the client website for two separate groups of respondents. Both groups are asked to complete an open-ended questionnaire that consists of two or three key elements regarding the client brand's perception. The respondents are able to view the comments supplied by previous participants, and encouraged to read and comment on these responses.

The first group consists of those who have been presented with an advertisement, and the second of those who have not. The first group generally requires more respondents, as the incidence of those that recall the advertisement will not be 100 percent. This can be easily managed with an online system's management tool.

The questions generally cover the following areas:

- opinion of advertisement;
- comment on the effectiveness;
- impact on the perception of the brand.

This process is usually restricted to take no more than three or four minutes of the respondent's time. Group sizes need to be at least eight people per group. Obviously, the more people that are recruited to respond the better, but a limit is suggested to keep the level of analysis that is required manageable and cost-effective.

Reporting and Delivery

Within a fully equipped online system, as described in this book, results can be delivered in multiple fashion, directly to the corporate client's desktop:

- lists of answers to open-ended questions;
- interactive web reports;
- online reports of all tabulations;
- data for full analysis combined with interactive charts that allow the user to "drill down" to see more detail behind the top-level charts;
- conclusions, interpretations, and recommendations from research supplier and analysts;
- technical description of methodologies used;
- description of statistical analysis conducted on data;
- information on drawn samples;
- information about response, non-response;

- streams of data results linked directly to corporate portal for ongoing, continuous projects, and decision support;
- fully indexed and linked analysis to facilitate easy and quick navigation around key areas of the report;
- comprehensive support information to aid use and understanding.

Figure 11.4 depicts a generic online ad or brand-testing model based on Dynamic Logic's AdIndex™ and TNSi's AdEval™ process.

Figure 11.4 Testing ad and brand perception online

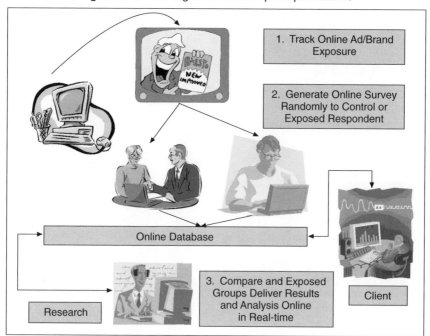

Coda

Part 3 has presented a wide variety of ways to utilize Net-centric research. It has included the benefits, advantages, and issues involved with leveraging enabling technology. The next section proceeds into the realm of the practical. How does an Internet-centric enterprise market research system work? What does it look like? How do you go about evaluating such systems? These questions, and more, are answered in Part 4.

Notes

1   William M.K. Trochim. "Research Methods Knowledge Base," http://trochim.human.cornell.edu/kb/.

2   William M. K. Trochim. "Research Methods Knowledge Base," http://
     trochim.human.cornell.edu/kb/.
3   Kelle, U. 2001. "Sociological Explanations between Micro and Macro and the
     Integration of Qualitative and Quantitative Methods." *Forum Qualitative
     Sozialforschung/Forum: Qualitative Social Research* [online journal], 2(1).
4   MacKenzie, S.B. 2001. "Opportunities for Improving Consumer Research through
     Latent Variable Structural Equation Modeling." *Journal of Consumer Research,
     June 2001* – Vol. 28 Issue No. 1, pp. 159–66 Gainesville, FL.
5   Kelle, U. 2001.
6   Pawle, J.S. & Cooper, P. "New QualiQuant™ Technology: Accelerating Innovation
     on the Web," paper presentation at the ESOMAR Worldwide Internet Conference
     (Net Effects 4), Barcelona, February 2001. ESOMAR: Amsterdam.
7   Clifton, R. & Maughan, E. [Editors] 2000. *The Future of Brands.* New York
     University Press: New York, NY.
8   Davis, S.M. 2000. *Brand Asset Management: Driving Profitable Growth Through
     Your Brands.* Jossey-Bass: San Francisco, CA.
9   Arno Hummerston, TNSi, personal interview, August 2001.

QualiQuant™ is a registered trademark of Cultural Insights, Inc of the USA and CRAM
International of the UK.

PART 4

Leveraging Internet Technology:
A Practical Guide

INTRODUCTION

Part 4 of our book takes a practical tack. As online market research systems grow in complexity of design and function, a detailed evaluation of their many components and capabilities is in order. Chapter 12 provides detailed and pragmatic guidelines for addressing and assessing system functionality, design, breadth, and deployment capacity.

Evaluating Enterprise Online Market Research Software

INTRODUCTION: WHY SOFTWARE MATTERS

I n an industry that is increasingly Net-centric in its orientation, the choice of a market research company's software becomes even more mission critical.

In the case of an enterprise market research software system, complexity is high, as numerous components need to work together seamlessly, completely, and in a logical fashion. Integration with proprietary systems, and other IT systems (for example, accounting databases) is often a requirement.

It is important to *architect* the application with an eye toward full integration of the key participants in the research process, including respondents, customers, research personnel, and project administrators.

Evaluating the "Make-versus-Buy" Decision

In selecting a research tool, a company must first consider the issue of "make versus buy." When making this decision, it is important to realize that past behavior is not always a useful guide for future strategy. Since the advent of the Internet as the primary operating platform of modern business, technologies have incurred massive changes.

An analogy may be helpful. Before the age of enterprise resource planning (ERP), it was commonplace to program one's own accounting software. Legions of COBOL programmers earned their livelihood, and in some cases even prospered, developing custom accounting software for their clients. Today, it is quite exceptional to develop core accounting software given that industrial strength solutions are available from a range of reputable companies who have large ongoing commitments to maintaining state-of-the-art systems.

By the same token, market research companies should not continue to dedicate significant IT resources to develop survey engines or other generic research software. These scarce IT resources are much better used for value-creating activities that can be billed out as professional time. This is discussed in the next section.

How to Maximize Value Creation with Internal IT Staff within MR Firms

Important issues arise in the decision to outsource some or all of the IT-centric activities related to market research software. In some cases, the issues that arise are political and personal, due to the substantial impact on individual personnel who may have long-standing careers with the research supplier.

However, these issues are misguided. They are largely related to viewing the IT department as a cost center rather than as an engine for value-creation. Research firms, as a professional service business, must recognize the tremendous opportunities to use IT talent to better serve customers.

In the Internet Age, research firms with large and talented IT departments should consider themselves blessed. This IT talent creates an unusual opportunity for value-creation that leverages the strengths of the research organization and also serves to embed the research organization into the operational fabric of the operation.

In the coming decades, the IT staff of research firms will be presented with the challenge of operating as quasi-IT consultants, particularly as IT-related deliverables are increasingly *de rigeur* for any research firm that aims to participate in the race for single-vendor global solutions (discussed in the next section). Examples include the following:

- **ERP and SCP integration**: enterprise resource planning (ERP) and supply chain planning (SCP) are increasingly becoming core operations. For example, models for demand-forecasting, product line-up optimization, and pricing are fundamentally dependent on the raw data that feeds the models. Internal IT staff are well-placed to participate in the implementation of proprietary forecasting models that are based on continuous information feeds from various types of longitudinal tracking research; for example, global brand recognition, customer satisfaction, usage and attitude, habits and practices, and economic well-being studies.
- **CRM and sales force automation**: as tracking studies run continuously, rather than on set time intervals, interviews conducted in the field will increasingly include automated procedures for alerting sales personnel of customer issues. This will be possible at the level of the individual

customer, but also at higher levels of aggregation, such as sales district, sales manager, or product line.

- **Human Research Management System (HRMS) integration**: employee satisfaction research should run continuously rather than in batch at set intervals of the year. Data about employees are accessed longitudinally with random sampling done year-round in order to provide management with an ongoing assessment of organizational health. Further, as an option, research data provided by employees can be linked back to the employee's profile allowing management to objectively monitor the health of the entire organization down to the individual employee.

Application Service Provider versus In-house Enterprise Solutions

Research software was historically delivered and installed on an in-house basis. Applications ran on servers that were hosted within the research company's local area network (LAN) and largely served staff within a given location.

The Internet has changed this dynamic completely. Today, research firms are hosting their core software applications on the Internet using the facilities of large co-location providers capable of delivering 100 percent network availability on a global scale. These hosted systems and services are delivered via application service providers (ASPs).

Why research firms MUST outsource server hosting

Research firms need to immediately get out of the business of running data centers. It is woefully outdated and an invitation to disaster. There are two compelling reasons:

- **Network redundancy**: unless your in-house data center happens to be co-located with a redundant network backbone circuit, and maintains one or more back-up power sources, chances are that you have lost your Internet connection at some point in the past year. If you happen to be in the business of conducting your business over the Internet, this is a recipe for the disenfranchisement of would-be advocates of the Net-centric business model. As of this writing, financially viable providers of global data networks include Cable & Wireless, Qwest, NTT, and Telefonica.
- **Security**: the increasing incidents of terrorism and corporate espionage mean that housing one's own servers is a very high business risk. A single server can now hold terabytes of data. The physical box may be no bigger than a television and transported without special equipment. The financial services industry has adopted a certification procedure

called SFAS90. Facilities that cannot pass the SFAS90 standard should be rejected out of hand since the premium for SFAS90 is simply not that great, yet the business risk of not being secure is immeasurable.

Why research firms SHOULD outsource application hosting

- **Shared development cost**: the major application service providers are investing heavily in R&D. GMI, for example, has historically spent at the level of 30 percent of sales on new development, a level comparable to pharmaceutical firms! Research firms historically have a total IT spending of not more than 10 percent of sales, of which only a small fraction is dedicated to new developments.
- **Continuous application support**: research firms who wish to provide a centralized solution for application-hosting have the added task of providing continuous application support. The major ASPs maintain 24/7 application monitoring in line with service level agreements (SLAs) that outline the performance standard.
- **Access to related services**: a hosted application is often bundled with other value-added services that can leverage the economies of scale of a centrally hosted application. For example, GMI provides its licensees with shared use of respondent panel databases and questionnaire programming services.
- **Back-up of core data**: back-up of core data is mission critical. The cost of data-storage is falling precipitously as the cost of mass storage falls by orders of magnitude. The implication is that an ASP can make the most efficient use of back-up resources, filling terabytes of data annually. A mass storage device left unfilled for more than a year is nothing other than money left on the table.

Single Vendor Solutions: The Big Pay-off Modernizing IT Infrastructure

The Holy Grail of any research firm is to be the single vendor solution for a large multinational end-client. To date this goal has been highly elusive. In reality, it is achievable and even desirable for both parties, provided that the benefits of integration outweigh the risk of complacency on the part of the research supplier.

The compelling advantages of single-vendor solutions

There are numerous compelling advantages held by single-vendor solutions. The primary advantages include:

- **Domain expertise**: developing research solutions for a particular niche market requires training the researcher to understand deeply the domain of the end-client. This allows sustained mastery in the form of organizational resources, software tools, research methods, and efficient work processes. Competitive advantage will increasingly come from insight that is differentiated and penetrating. This requires domain expertise, a resource that can only be developed with time, experience, and commitment.

- **Global integration**: as research increasingly involves conducting projects across borders it requires working in global teams. The research supplier that can routinely assign a global project team has this advantage: it can track progress around the world and around the clock. Responsibilities are handed across time zones and the project continually advances while team members maintain sleep patterns that at least vaguely correlate to circadian rhythms.
- **Cultural assimilation**: corporate cultures vary widely between companies. The intense hard-driving culture of one company may be entirely incompatible with the more methodical and risk-averse culture of another. A single vendor solution has the capacity to accommodate both.

The alleged disadvantages of single-vendor solutions
The counter arguments for single-vendor solutions are similarly abundant. Yet, they are increasingly outdated in the Internet Age.

- **Risk of prices increases**: inevitably, single-vendor solutions will lead to a tension toward price pressures or reduced commitment. However, the notion that research suppliers will gouge research buyers is absurd so long as there are a plurality of research firms in the $100 million range. Every major research firm covets the big key account of any competing research firm. The bigger the account, the bigger the target.
- **Risk of lost creativity**: in research, predictability is an asset and consistency is a virtue. Non-validated methods are a siren call beckoning the ambitious and articulate marketing manager to crash a brand into the rocks. Therefore, the idea that research suppliers in single-vendor relationships will be handicapped here is simply wrong.
- **Risk of poor research quality at the local or national level**: historically, research buyers have contracted with multiple firms, even for the same project. Very often this is driven by the search for quality since research networks within global MR firms have historically been woefully inconsistent and non-integrated. Global MR firms with integrated information systems will be well placed to overcome these limitations.

The Case for Having One Data Center for the World

The question of whether or not to run a Net-centric application is really one of timing. In 10 years all modern software will be Net-centric. In moving to a Net-centric business model, there is a compelling logic for having just one data center for the world. Here are some of the key benefits:

- **Increased efficiency via central data storage:** by running analyses on the centrally hosted application, the user also avoids the inefficiency of exporting and downloading a data set for offline analysis. Even in the case of standard formats, there is a time lag associated with exporting data, and then importing data back into a second system. Over the course of a single project, this three-step process of exporting, transmitting, and importing data may consume hours of personnel resources with no apparent value-add whatsoever.
- **Balanced utilization of fixed data center assets via centralized processing:** for certain applications, such as analysis of real-time data, it is desirable to have the processing power of centralized high-performance computer-processing capability. A multi-processor server with abundant memory and a well-designed database engine will surely outperform the typical single-user system. Moreover, in a global research enterprise, it is possible to achieve more balanced usage of centralized computer hardware resources by virtue of time zone differences between the major research markets: Western Europe, Japan, and North America.
- **Cost optimization via remote management:** one risk of having one data center would be the absence of qualified staff for the "night shift." However, for the vast majority of tasks related to managing a server farm, qualified systems administrators can work effectively via secure remote connections. At GMI, a primary data center is housed in New York City with secure remote management done from the US West Coast and Central Europe. This covers the 24 hours of the day, and seven days of the week from just two locations.

CATEGORIES OF EVALUATION

Once the business objective is established, and the question of whether to host the application in-house has been answered, we suggest a thorough 12-step category checklist. Our detailed checklist includes the following:

1 Overall system architecture
2 Project management
3 Questionnaire-authoring
4 Survey engine
5 Translation management
6 Quantitative data-collection
7 Respondent and panel management

8   Sample/quota management
9   Data-processing
10 Reporting and analysis
11 Qualitative research tools
12 Training and technical support

The checklist can be augmented or extended to cover multimode research capabilities demonstrations, as well as integration, based on typical or expected needs of the client (supplier or buyer of research). The final category, costs, will be discussed separately.

Basic Evaluation Checklist for Net-based Market Research Software

A detailed checklist is provided to help guide decisions regarding selection, development/purchase, and deployment of online market research systems. To support the list, a simple rating scheme can be devised to assist in more clearly assessing strengths and weaknesses of competing systems. Note, the guidelines provided here are extremely detailed and thorough in order to cover many types of situations.

In real practice, some of these requirements may or may not be applicable to the particular business objective and may be overdesigned for targeted projects. In addition, other modes or methods will require additional evaluation planning and instrument development. Assignment of weight factors in the computation of an overall utility score is one way to overcome this limitation. Weighting each category, and also weighting each element within each delivers a balanced scorecard.

The authors have prepared, and continue to maintain, a balanced scorecard. The following sections discuss each major focus area and provide a list of the key things to look for in selecting an integrated information system for managing the research enterprise in the Internet Age.

1 Overall System Architecture

The overall system architecture represents the foundation of the platform on which the application and processes are built. It is important to assess whether the application to be implemented will fit the requirements for the future business need.

User interface

The choice of user interface is partially dependent on where the core users are coming from in terms of prior experience with market research software. Here are two important attributes to consider:

- **Balancing power with ease of use**: the application should balance between ease of use and desired functionality. In some cases, a fully graphical user interface is desirable. In other cases, some amount of command language is needed. In the extreme case, the user may desire a fully documented open architecture to allow direct access to raw data.
- **Offline vs. online**: the ability to work on projects offline and online should be considered. Although high-speed Internet connections are increasingly abundant and reliable, there will be situations where an Internet connection is not to be depended upon. In such cases it may be desirable to work offline; for example, authoring of a questionnaire.

Compatibility

Compatibility needs to be reviewed at several levels, including the respondent level, the project manager level, and also within the data center. Poor compatibility at any of these levels will doom an implementation from the outset.

- **Browser compatibility for web surveys**: at the respondent level, surveys should be fully compatible with all, or nearly all, browsers, platforms, and operating systems, including Macs and WebTV. At the very least, browser compatibility should be validated among target respondents.
- **Browser compatibility for internal users**: on the application level, it is possible to be more restrictive in terms of software compatibility. The direction is clearly toward standardizing on Windows and Internet Explorer on the corporate desktop.
- **Application compatibility in the data center**: for companies who intend to host an application in-house, one must assess whether the in-house skill-set is sufficient to manage the entire application, including the operating system, the applications, and the databases.

Data structure

A key challenge with a globally centralized market research management application is to deliver the requirements for performance, flexibility, and robustness simultaneously.

- **Data aggregation**: data from the various sources – online and offline – should stream into one database. In some embodiments, XML or databases may be used to temporarily hold and transport newly collected data before storing in the central data repository. In the ideal situation, data are consolidated in real-time; that is, within seconds of an interview being completed.
- **Robustness and scalability**: the database engine that supports the core of the application should demonstrate robustness and scalability within

the performance level and database size range that is expected during the planned useful life of the software. The vendor should demonstrate good capability in the efficient use of database engines for storing and extracting data.

- **Open database architecture**: for in-house installations, all information should be stored in an open database(s) that can be accessed either via application program interfaces (APIs) or via direct database queries. This added flexibility allows future functionality to accommodate even the most difficult projects, as the situation requires it.

Global capability

The degree to which a system is designed for global work is important to evaluate at the outset. Indeed, many systems on the market today have no reliable global implementation capacity, thereby preventing their users from winning lucrative multi-country research studies. Consider these global criteria:

- **Multilingual**: the ability to use the whole system in multiple languages should be required for a global solution. Western European languages are generally not a problem for any system. However, Asian languages having double-byte character sets can be a challenge. Arabic and Hebrew require right–left display and only a few applications in the world, among them GMI's Net-MR, support this requirement.
- **Multi-currency**: support for multiple currencies may be required. In many cases, surveying may be conducted across multiple nations, requiring reference to multiple currencies. The ability to display data in the national currency of the user is sometimes a requirement even though the data are to be centrally aggregated. The application should make use of central look-up tables for displaying currency-convert values.

Security

The issue of application security is a chapter all by itself, and outside the scope of this book. For a full discussion of system security, contact the authors who maintain a comprehensive security checklist, escalation procedure, and template for service level agreements. For the uninitiated, here are the most important points to consider:

- **Password authentication**: the application must make strict use of password authentication at all levels to prevent unexpected abuse of open interfaces. Even in the case of pop-up interviews, a single-use case ID should be used to prevent unauthorized persons from accessing an interview.

- **Flexible assignment of user rights to different components, modules, or processes**: at the application level, it should be possible to specifically allow or deny access to the various tasks required to manage or use the software. Users should be strongly encouraged to not share accounts.
- **Security of data and system environment**: the application should support the ongoing monitoring of system integrity. A variety of tools are available, including share-ware tools for little or no license fee.
- **Escalation procedures should be agreed and documented**: a centralized application needs to be 100 percent available to 100 percent of the users. Yet, problems will eventually arise. Therefore, an escalation procedure should be agreed upon and documented.

Systems administration
The range of capabilities for system administration is often overlooked during the application planning process. Yet, this is structurally important. Here are several features to look for:

- **Concurrent interview sessions**: in theory, the system should structurally allow an unlimited number of concurrent interview sessions provided that sufficient server capacity is added to host the sessions. This infinite scalability of the data-collection engine is typically accomplished by decoupling data-collection from data-aggregation. For example, an XML questionnaire schema can replicate infinitely to instruct redundant survey engines.
- **Sophisticated usage-reporting and supervisory functions**: at any given time, the systems administrator should have the ability to see who is on the system. The ability to terminate a session, or spontaneously communicate with a user via Internet chat communication, is desirable.
- **Ease of upgrades/patches with minimum/no interruption**: a key advantage of the Internet is that it is possible to upgrade applications without having to distribute a physical object (for example, a CD-ROM). This allows upgrades to be more frequent, and in some cases even client-specific.
- **Back-up of data should be possible with a minimum of interruption**: the data in the database should be backed up at several levels. GMI mirrors data in real-time, backs up incrementally once per day, and backs up all data once per week.

2 Project Management
An enterprise-wide MR management system should have the capability to support project management across the enterprise. Personnel working on any

project should be able to access all details about their projects 24/7 using an Internet connection, secured by one or more authentication measures.

Project design

The application should serve as the central repository for project details including reference numbers, planned sample sources, and quota specifications.

- **Proposal management**: a typical inefficiency in processing proposals is that information is entered multiple times. The preferred solution should prevent redundant entry of information by allowing proposal information to carry forward into actual commissioned projects without re-entering information.
- **Project templates**: for advanced systems, it may be desirable to integrate predefined project templates or the ability to copy project details from a prior project in order to avoid the tedious task of re-entering information.

Scheduling

To increase productivity, it is desirable to integrate the schedule-related details associated with a project into the overall information being stored about the project. Here are some things to look for:

- **Schedule overview**: the user should be able to specify timing requirements and constraints for the project. This information is then part of the central project design and can be used to guide decision-making by personnel who will supervise the completion of the project.
- **Schedule optimization and time-dependent procedures**: for advanced systems, the application can provide increasing amounts of intelligence in terms of automating steps in the implementation of the project, and alerting internal and external clients if issues require intervention.

Resource management

A key challenge in a complex, geographically dispersed organization, with many concurrent projects, is to maintain an overview of the available resources, and see how these resources are being allocated across projects.

- **Resource planning**: the user should be able to specify the resources required for a project and compare this with the available inventory of resources available within the company. At a minimum, this information is used as inputs for budgeting and cost estimation.
- **Optimization**: for advanced systems, the application can also manage the inventory of available resources and provide some amount of verification that resource utilization is both feasible and optimized. For

example, data-processing resources or call center seats may be over-utilized in a given week. The system can then present the user with a range of possible solutions to address the issue.

Contact management/account management

An increasing number of research companies are implementing CRM solutions for improving efficiency of client account management. There are compelling arguments for integrating this functionality directly in the research management application. To that end, here are some things to look for:

*   **Client profile**: the system should maintain a detailed client profile, both by company and by individual. The profiles should also allow the user to create and edit flexible attributes that can be populated at will. In addition, it should be easy for the user to see the client history and also the current projects, and any support requests from the client.
*   **Communication tools**: the ability to efficiently track and manage communication to individuals and groups of individuals is a key strength of the CRM systems. The challenge is to maintain the appropriate level of personalization with scale. The system should provide these capabilities as integrated features that avoid importing and exporting information between incompatible systems.

Project accounting and cost estimation

Integration of basic accounting tools is an optional aspect of a market research management system. In many cases, the functionality for accounting will exist in legacy systems that can be integrated to the rest of the system via APIs. In an integrated scenario, the following capabilities are desirable.

*   **Cost estimation**: the application should provide the means for making cost estimation at the project level. The ability to do "sensitivity analysis," or "what-if" comparisons on various test designs is thereby significantly simplified by avoiding the need for other tools during this phase of project design.
*   **Project accounting**: once the project goes to the field, the system should provide a real-time view of the project cost, including any related costs incurred. This gives the user the most accurate picture of budget impact for running the project.
*   **Invoicing**: an advanced requirement for marketing research management applications is the ability to generate invoices, either internally or externally. By integrating the data from the various sources, the integrated invoicing tool draws on the most up-to-date information. It can also automate the invoicing process, including the possibility of

delivering invoices in an electronic format via e-mail, which can save days or weeks in the billing/collection cycle.

3 Questionnaire-authoring

The authoring tool is likely to be the most heavily used module of any research management application within any suite of research management tools. It is also the area that offers the greatest possibilities for improved researcher productivity. Some key features to look for include:

The overall authoring process

Authoring the questionnaire should incorporate structural attributes that provide the means for efficient questionnaire development. The major structural features to consider include the following:

- **Author once for all modes and all languages**: the user should be able to author once for all languages and modalities. The authoring system should ideally allow the user to author and manage a questionnaire centrally. Logic and quota segments can then be managed centrally without requiring the user to worry about inadvertent and/or temporary inconsistencies between languages or modes (for example, CATI versus web survey).
- **Powerful command set**: writing customized code should now be only very rarely needed. The most advanced CAWI and CATI systems provide a rich command set that perform the vast majority of tasks that might historically have been done with user-written code. Software suppliers should also be willing and able to expand the command set in future versions as part of a program of continuous improvement.
- **Ease of use**: ultimately, regular users of a given system can learn even the most complex tool. The ease of use of the authoring tool is a consideration for shortening the learning curve. Therefore, if the user base is to include project managers, or other periodic non-technical users, ease of use will rank more prominently as a requirement.

Question types

The range of question types that is supported in the authoring tool will vary from system to system, and may even include proprietary questioning techniques. At the core, most systems support the following:

- information-only questions, also known as directives;
- rating scales;
- ranking questions;
- open-ends;

- constant sum;
- grid questions: single and multiple response;
- form questions.

More sophisticated systems go far beyond the core, incorporating other question types such as the following:

- **Conjoint**: has earned renewed popularity in recent years, in part since it is well-suited to self-administered web interviews. Sawtooth Software (Sequim, WA) was the pioneer in commercializing this method, though the algorithms have been broadly reapplied in competing systems. Traditional, Adaptive Conjoint (ACA) and Choice-Based Conjoint (CBC) Conjoint are now available from a plurality of software vendors for both online and offline interviewing.
- **Image association**: some question types provide the ability to associate and group images into categories. For example, this can done via the drag and drop method.
- **Scrollbar question**: in this question type, a sliding scale is used to enter degree of agreement to a horizontal or vertical scale.

Controlling appearance of the questionnaire

The authoring tool should facilitate setting up and managing a consistent user interface. This is particularly desirable for panel-based research where the respondent may expect a consistent experience. Also, it is important for project personnel to not spend endless hours optimizing buttons and colors for a project. Here are some things to look for when selecting an interviewing system:

- **Template management**: use of templates allows a standard look to be applied to a survey. The system should provide the means to set templates for specific pages, as well as per project or globally.
- **Progress bar**: the author should be able to enable the appearance of a progress bar, if desired. If included, the author should also have the ability to change the look and position of the progress bar.
- **Font appearance**: the author should have the ability to define the default font characteristics for question script, code frames, and grids on a project basis, and also on a per-question basis.
- **Navigation buttons**: for the next, previous, and suspend buttons, the author should be able to know whether to use command buttons or graphics. The choice of graphics, for example color, size and form, should also be definable.
- **Question layout**: the user should be able to determine how many questions go on a screen: one or multiple. The appearance of the page should also be definable.

- **Inclusion of open-ends**: the author should have the option to define multiple, other, or specify boxes.

Content management

A significant source of productivity increases can be derived from being able to rapidly find and reapply prepared content that has been previously developed.

- **Question and response library**: the system should provide the means for being able to manage and use questionnaire subcomponents. A simple example of the concept is that a "standard demographic" question block can be defined and used repeatedly, including the corresponding translations. A more sophisticated use is the hierarchical classification of questions allowing a user to search for a set of questions and then apply them either as "copies" of the original question, or as an "inherited" set that is only editable by the question owner.
- **Media library**: the system should have the means to provide central administration of media in an organized manner using a media library that allows project teams to make shared use of previously collected media content. The system should provide the means to search, add, and update images, animations, video, Flash objects, and so on.
- **Sound and recorded voice**: for systems requiring interactive voice response, it is desirable that sound files, for example recorded voice prompts, are loadable from the central authoring system.

Validation

Prior to the start of fieldwork, the survey should be tested. The historical practice of manual testing is no longer practical with modern authoring tools.

- **Automated testing**: the application should provide the means to automatically validate the logic and routing. Typical examples of preventable errors include faulty routing, duplicate variables, and duplicate response codes.
- **Random data-generation**: once the logic has been tested, a further validation step is to evaluate effectiveness of randomization and rotation for projects that require it. This can be done using random data-generation and evaluating response counts.
- **Load testing**: prior to the start of fieldwork, it may be desirable to evaluate impact on server load. Automated tests for server load can provide an indication of total processor and memory utilization during concurrent interviews.

Inspection and approval

Following initial validation of the questionnaire, the client (internal or external) will seek to review and approve the questionnaire. In this case it is desirable to provide a plurality of means for securing client approval.

- **Print**: inevitably, print is still alive and well. Therefore, the system should provide the means to print the questionnaire in a number of views including: (1) as it looks on the screen; or (2) containing all the routing so another person could check the logic.
- **Online**: increasingly, the approval process can be done online. For example, via a client portal interface, a client can review and approve the questionnaire before it is released to the field. In this case the system should provide the ability to make notes directly in the testing module.

Questionnaire import/export

In some cases, questionnaire authoring will be done via external systems; for example, migrating earlier questionnaires from legacy systems or accepting scripts from partner vendors. In this case, to avoid reprogramming, the ability to import from external sources is desirable. Similarly, the ability to generate scripts for use by external systems provides the means to collaborate with interviewing facilities that use incompatible systems.

- **Interfaces to legacy applications**: the ability to import a questionnaire from an external system may be desirable for avoiding recoding. Vendors of major software systems should be prepared to provide migration utilities. An emerging lingua franca is the Triple-S format.
- **Interfaces to Word**: the ability to export or import questionnaire text from MS Word is a desirable feature. Nearly all systems will export to Word; for example, for deployment as paper questionnaires. Reliable importing from Word is more challenging due to limitations of unstructured questionnaire formats.

Questionnaire deployment and triggering

Once a questionnaire is authored, there is a variety of methods for deploying. Integration with CATI and CAPI is discussed in Section 6. For panel-based research, the application should have the means to generate the invitations with user-specific URLs. In addition to CATI, CAPI, IVR, and panel-based web surveys, the alternative scenario, surveys, can also be initiated in a variety of ways:

- Ability to create pop-up surveys: for web surveys, it is desirable to use flexible tools to invite triggering. The triggering logic should be customizable for such parameters as:

- sampling frequency: every *n* person is interviewed;
- targeted pages: respondents are only interviewed if they visit specific pages;
- page count: respondents are interviewed when *n* pages have been viewed;
- non-repeat: respondents are interviewed only if there is no prior participation;
- on exit: respondents are interviewed upon changing to a different URL domain.

  Note that there are a variety of methods for adding the triggering script to web pages. The most common method is manual insertion via an include file. An alternate method is to use a proxy server method that selectively inserts the new code dynamically prior to presenting the page to the user. The limitation of the proxy server method is that it may reduce the peak throughput of the web server due to limitations of the proxy server.

- **Ability to create secure URLs for general distribution**: a generic URL for all respondents is generally not recommended. However, the ability to assign one or more passcodes that are approved for the project is a useful feature that can be used to create access to persons with access to a universal passcode.

Version management

The ability to manage multiple versions of a questionnaire is an important requirement to consider.

- **Live updates of a questionnaire**: a questionnaire may need to be amended even when a study is in the field. The ability to add a new response code, correct a typographical error, or even omit questions should be possible with minimum disruption.
- **Automatic versioning**: as a new version of a questionnaire is put into production, the user should have the ability to save and, if needed, restore a prior version of the questionnaire.
- **Language independent deployment**: translations of a questionnaire are often completed/reviewed at varying rates. Therefore the ability to selectively deploy languages is a desirable feature. A questionnaire that is still in draft is then less likely to be inadvertently put into the field.

4 Survey Engine

The functionality of the core survey engine is largely independent of the mode of data-collection. Whether interviewed by web, in-person or via telephone, the functionality is potentially the same.

Authentication/user identification

Secure hosting of interviews is typically a requirement, particularly for hosting of interviews that include confidential content. However, even for non-confidential interviews, authentication is recommended to enable tracking of activity and customizing the interview experience.

- **Password protection**: the ability to restrict access to authorized users is a key requirement. Password protection, or alternatively a session key that is valid for a particular respondent participating in a single project, can be used to prevent unauthorized access. Transmission of passwords in e-mails is generally not advised.
- **Customization**: upon log-in and authentication, the user experience associated with the interview session can be customized to the preferences of the user. Language preference is the most obvious customization, though other preferences such as color scheme may be adapted to be user-specific.

Session management

While the interview is in progress, the hosted survey should provide a variety of means to assure a high percentage of fully completed interviews. In the event of an incomplete interview, the administrator should have a way to diagnose possible issues based on information collected during the interview.

- **Session recovery:** interviews that are suspended while in progress should provide the ability to return to the same point.
- **Capturing information about interview sessions:** the survey engine should capture interview paradata such as interview duration. In addition, the system should provide the option to capture log file information such as IP address, domain name, browser type, and referring page.
- **Setting of cookies:** the system should provide for the optional use of cookies to prevent repeated completion, or to track future visits. Though not bulletproof, cookies are a means for identifying otherwise anonymous respondents who are not required to authenticate.
- **Termination or blocking of a session:** in some instances termination of a user session may be desired, or to block a particular IP address from participating in an interview. This capability may be applied for situations where there is evidence of "ballot-stuffing;" for example, in a pop-up survey.

Screening

Screening of respondents is widely done, particularly for selecting respondents who cannot be identified via filtered selection according to one or more panel-profiling attributes. The screening ability should consider several capabilities:

- **Customized screen-out messages**: the appropriate handling of screen-outs is an important capability. The system should provide the means to inform respondents why their interviews are being terminated after just a few questions.
- **Differentiated incentives**: respondents who are terminated after just a few questions may still need to be incentivized for their effort in attempting to participate in the interview. Therefore, the ability to set different incentives for persons who have been screened out can be a desirable feature.

Application program interfaces

Application program interfaces (APIs) are critically important in the survey engine; for example, dynamic access to known information allows the interview to avoid asking answers to known questions. It is also a means for delivering data to external systems once data have been collected; for example, to CRM systems. There are a number of considerations:

- **Ability to pipe data from an external API using variables**: in many cases, surveys will be initiated by other systems. A common example is a pop-up interview on a website. In this case, information about the calling website, as well as a respondent ID that has been cookied by the originating website, can be used in the hosted web interview. This avoids having to ask information that may already be known about the respondent.
- **Ability to extract data from a database**: it may be desirable to draw a list of responses from an external database; for example, based on an SQL query. The structure of the SQLSELECT command should comprise information for the server host, authentication information if required, and the query itself. For example, in a customer satisfaction study, this method can be used to query transaction databases to identify the products that were purchased by the respondent in the previous six months.
- **Ability to write back data from an external source during interviewing**: for certain interviewing applications, it may be required to submit information in real-time to a remote system. There are a number of methods for doing this with varying levels of robustness. The most common methods are: (1) HTTP post, which transmits data via the web; (2) remote database calls similar to SQLSELECT described above; and (3) data transmission via e-mail using simple message transfer protocol (SMTP).

Waves, loops, and blocks

The use of waves, loops, and blocks in questionnaires is an important capability for their efficient authoring and fielding. For example, a block of questions on brand satisfaction can be repeated for a series of brands. Similarly, a set of questions can be asked time after time across multiple waves of data-collection. Here are some things to look for:

- **Wave support**: the system should provide the means to use the same questions or questionnaire multiple times within the same project. This is typically done with waves; for example, where the system stores the wave number, together with the response information.
- **Loop support**: a set of questions should be adjustable as a loop of questions. Questions can then be repeated for a set of questions defined as a loop variable. For example, question 1 is "select all brands that apply." Questions 2–5 present a looped series of questions for each brand that was selected in question 1.
- **Block support**: questions should also be clusterable in blocks. Then blocks of questions can be rotated as groups of questions, or randomized within the set of questions, or both. Blocks can also be selected at random. For example, a project has nine concepts to test but each respondent will only see three of the nine, selected at random.

Sorting and displaying responses

There is considerable sophistication in rendering of the response frame. The sophistication of the survey engines continues to increase. Here are some of the most common capabilities that users require in authoring:

- **Sorting the responses**: the system should provide the ability to define the sequence of questions. For example, the ability to display alphabetically codes in a list is widely used to save the respondent time. The challenge is to be able to do this reliably in multiple languages and multiple character sets.
- **Drop-down menu**: the system should provide the option to have a drop-down list: In some cases, for example pop-up interviews, window-size may be severely restricted. In this case a drop-down menu is advisable, particularly if the response list is longer than the length of the screen.
- **Locking positions of responses**: in many cases, responses will be looked at the bottom; for example, other, or none of the above, may be locked at the bottom. In other cases, the most popular/likely brand, or a reference brand, may be locked at the top.
- **Sorting by the most/least selected**: in some advanced cases, it may be desirable to sort by most/least selected. For example, a list of brands may be displayed to the user and selected for "used in past four weeks." In

this case, a particularly low-incidence brand may be given preferred treatment in selection for use in follow-up questions.

- **Inclusive and exclusive piping of responses**: the system should provide the means to select responses to display a response list based on a respondent's previous answers. There are typically two variants: (a) only show responses selected in a previous question; and (b) only show responses not selected in a previous question.
- **Deselecting other responses**: the system should allow a code to be flagged as being mutually exclusive; for example, Don't know and None codes.
- **Copying of responses**: during authoring, it is often desirable to allow the user to copy all response codes or some response codes from a previous question.

Arithmetic functions and system variables

In complex surveys, there is frequently the need to integrate user-defined variables, as well as system-defined variables. Some examples follow:

- **Arithmetic computation**: new variables can be generated via the arithmetic and/or logical evaluations of variables defined earlier in the questionnaire or externally. Random number generation may also be used to create a new variable.
- **String manipulation**: in some cases, the system will need to convert character strings and manipulate sub-strings. Converting from/to upper/lower case is often used to format raw information entered before storing the result.
- **System variables**: examples of system variables include the number of questions answered, numbers of selected responses for each question, and paradata; for example, duration of the interview.

Validation

Validation is critically important for avoiding rework with data-collection. The things to look for are:

- **Preventing missing values**: the application should provide the ability to make any question optional though default mandatory. Mandatory questions should provide incomplete answer prompts.
- **Validation within a range**: the survey engine should provide the means for evaluating within a minimum or maximum, based on a response to a previous question. Similiarly, validation can verify that only valid responses are given, depending on the data type chosen for a particular panelist attribute. For example, a numeric response to the attribute "birth year" would prevent the entry of text. This validation of the attribute

applies in the same way to other data types, such as an e-mail address that checks for a valid e-mail address structure. By associating validation rules to attribute types, the application adds a high level of quality control to the data-collection process, starting with respondent registration, or other forms of profiling of the respondent.

- **Client-side and server-side validation**: in some instances, client-side validation is not enough since client-side Javascript is disabled or otherwise not reliable. In this case, follow-up validation on the server side can prevent errors.

Content protection

There is extensive debate about the effectiveness of content security. Software products such as Alchemedia's Clever Content have been designed for the purposes of preventing users from using screen capture utilities such as SnagIt, or other software such as VNC, to retrieve media that is being presented as stimulus during the online interview process. If strict content protection is important, then the software should provide support for a content protection solution.

Online help

The availability of online help, and convenient access to online support can sometimes be significant in minimizing aborts.

- **Online link to help**: the system should provide an option to include a button or hyperlink (on every survey screen) that links to a help page. For example, the help page may contain instructions on how to complete the survey. Once respondents have viewed the help page they can return to the survey by clicking on a button or hyperlink.
- **Online link to support**: in some cases, it is desirable to provide direct access to live help either via chat interface, or click-to-talk. The perception of live support can also be enhanced via streamed audio instructions using recorded sound.

5 Translation Management

The application should provide a centrally administered utility for managing translations. Given the importance of accurate translations, and often the need to translate questionnaires in context, we expect that human translations will continue to be the norm, and machine translation will continue to be the exception. Therefore, having an automated utility for managing human translation work is critically important for assuring rapid and high-quality translations. There are several things to look for when selecting a translation management utility, either as a stand-alone tool, or as part of an integrated suite of tools.

Translator management

- **Central repository**: the application should include a central repository for information for translators, including: (1) language pairs that translators can conduct; for example, English–German; (2) rates charged by the translator; and (3) contract information about the translator.
- **Translator activity reporting**: the ability to review historical activity by the translators is important for reviewing invoicing accuracy from translators, as well as for evaluating volume of business by vendor, and tracking response time to translation requests.

Translation management

- **Translation tracking**: the system should allow the system administrator to have an overview of the translation requests that are pending, or which have been completed historically using the system.
- **Translation of missing values**: it should be possible to request translations for only the missing texts. For example, brand lists may be pretranslated, and therefore not outsourced.

Translation tool

- **User interface**: the user-interface should allow fast side-by-side translation of source to the target language. In the ideal case, translations are never printed since the ease of use of the online translation tool makes it compelling to translate directly to the screen, even if the translator uses a machine translation tool for a first-pass translation.
- **Productivity tools**: when the translator wins, the customer wins. Therefore, look for productivity-enhancing utilities. For example, the ability to easily copy response frames from source language to target language can avoid unnecessary duplication.
- **Secure access to translations**: access to a translation interface should be password-protected so that it can be secure for access via normal web browsers.

6 Quantitative Data-collection

In addition to the familiar web survey, a Net-centric research management application can also be implemented to accommodate a range of other modes of data-collection, including:

Modalities

The range of data-collection methods is actually increasing. The diversity of such methods in use is somewhat in contrast to earlier forecasts that web-surveying might replace all other modes. The reality is that to achieve acceptable response rates and representativeness, data-collection often accommodates the respondent, accessing them where and when they can be accessed. In some cases, web surveys are not even a viable option to achieve a representative sample. The deployment of Net-centric solutions to a range of data-collection methods should include the following:

- computer-assisted telephone interviewing (CATI);
- computer-assisted personal interviewing (CAPI);
- data-entry;
- interactive voice response (IVR);
- scanning/paper.

Why a Net-centric data-collection saves time and money

Net-centric data-collection can offer significant efficiency advantages over conventional batch processes for data-collection. The main areas where Net-centric data-collection provide efficiency benefits are:

- **Reduced data-processing**: particularly for mixed-mode or multi-site projects, data-collection goes into one database eliminating the traditional need for manual aggregation of data.
- **Tighter quota controls**: as data are collected and merged in real-time across locations, one can monitor progress continuously and avoid over-sampling for certain segments. This eliminates the non-billable cost associated with non-eligible interviews.
- **Centralized version management**: in situations where questionnaires or quotas are changing dynamically while fieldwork is in progress, a key advantage of Net-centric data-collection is the ability to redeploy specifications without human intervention.

Design considerations

The functionality and reliability of Net-centric applications for high-volume data-collection can effectively compete with their traditional peer systems. However, to do so, there are several factors to consider:

- **Speed of data-entry**: a key requirement for CATI, CAPI and data-entry is speed of input. Net-centric applications can introduce a trade-off for speed but this can also be avoided via effective application architecture. A conventional web interface with HTML has the limitation of retransmitting page content each time that HTML information is submitted to the web server. This can significantly impact data-entry speed. The alternate methods for speed involve either: (1) client-server architecture with a PC-based application for data-entry and data submitted in the background via a TCP/IP connection; or (2) applet or thin client application; for example, Java or Flash, that captures data at the browser level and periodically transmits data to the central server. GMI's Net-MR uses method (2) because it avoids the need for locally installed software to run the data-entry application.

- **Robustness**: related to speed, a further requirement is robustness, especially as it relates to the ability to store and transmit collected results. In a continuous data-collection environment, an intermittent Internet connection presents a high risk to productivity. This risk can be mitigated via redundant Internet connections. It can also be mitigated via the use of software solutions that are capable of queuing respondent information and caching collected results. Once again, a thin client (for example, using Java or other operator-side applications) provides the means for buffering input and output to accommodate an intermittent Internet connection.

Within the next few years it is highly probable that Internet speed and robustness will be of such a high quality that the current trade-offs will approach nil and the true benefits of the Net-centric architecture will be increasingly apparent. In the meantime, architecting the system to accommodate the lingering trade-offs is the answer.

7 Respondent and Panel Management

Respondent and panel management is increasingly important as random digit dial (RDD) telephone samples lose their viability as a primary source of sample. The care and feeding of panels are part art and part science. Therefore, selection of a suitable tool that applies best practice and automates routine tasks is an important consideration in architecting a system for enterprise-wide research management.

Attribute and profile management

The traditional model for panel data structures is that new attributes are endlessly added to a single flat table. The result is a very inefficient data structure with vast numbers of empty fields stored in a single table. Worse, when new unforeseen attributes are added, the data structure needs to be changed. There is a better way of using relational data structures. Here is what to look for:

- **Dynamic assignment of panel attributes and panelist attributes**: systems administrators need to have the ability to assign new attributes to either the panel or the panelist. This ability to create new attributes and assign values to those attributes allows the user to search according to user-defined attributes (for example, the average number of cigarettes smoked per day), in addition to predefined attributes (for example, family name).

- **Hierarchical attributes**: the ability to accommodate hierarchical attributes may be important. For example, we may want to assign various attributes not just to a panelist, or to a panel, but also at an intermediate level such as "Household." This makes it possible to select respondents having some household attribute, such as "number of cats in the household."

- **Historical attributes**: in some cases it is desirable to be able to sample or filter on the basis of historical attributes. For example, we may want to search for "Newlyweds;" that is, respondents who were not married one year ago but are married now. The classification of newlywed may still be validated in an interview, yet screening costs can be dramatically reduced via target sampling according to this historical attribute.

Data import

- **Flexible import specifications**: the application should integrate a flexible tool for importing externally supplied data. This import tool can then define settings for field delimiters, field sequence, field widths, and whether or not validation is to be done for imported fields.

- **De-duplication of data**: as data are being imported, it is desirable to automate de-duplication based on predefined criteria. Therefore, the ability to append data based on known values (for example, an e-mail address) allows the user to import supplemental data where available without creating new panel members that are duplicates of existing panel members.

- **Automated validation**: the ability to perform validations on imported data is an important function. The validation rules that are applied to data entered into a registration form can be similarly applied to the import process. In this way, panel records with erroneous e-mail addresses or impossible birth dates can be caught and corrected before they cause issues elsewhere in the system.

Incentive management

Incentive management is an important area for any panel application. Increasingly, respondents expect to be incentivized for their time. Therefore, the ability to award targeted incentives to respondents in an efficient manner is a competitive advantage.

- **Points-based account management**: in most cases, the objective of the panel is to secure repeated participation in research. Therefore, an incentive program based on points is highly desirable. GMI uses Marketpoints for its GlobalTestMarket panel. Harris Interactive introduced HIPoints for its managed panel. Similar points-based schemes are in use throughout the industry and include a novel system developed by Luth Research of San Diego that allows respondents to also earn points based on the interviewing activity of persons whom they have referred into the panel.
- **Rule management for incentive awards**: incentive awards may in fact be cost-optimized by demographic grouping, or even down to the level of the individual respondent who may have unique preferences. The application should offer the ability to assign rules for incentives based on consistent rules that are optimized for the panel. For example, respondents in Russia may be offered an incentive that is different or less costly than respondents in the United Kingdom or Japan.
- **Rule management for gift conversion**: the level of accrued points will vary significantly between respondents, depending on many factors such as length of membership, frequency of participation, and size of incentives awarded each time. However, the terms and conditions for converting points will typically need to be standardized.

Respondent portal management

For some panel projects, it will be desirable to allow panel members to manage their own details related to the panel. The ability to manage content via a respondent portal is one way to keep the panel members engaged and interested in participating in future interviews, especially online self-administered interviews that tend to have high attrition rates.

- **Registration forms**: the ability to author one or more registration forms for an online panel is an important requirement. In the ideal embodiment, all of the attribute information, including validation properties, is automatically embedded in the panel management tool.
- **Incentive history**: questions about incentive history are unavoidable. Therefore, we strongly recommend that any respondent portal include a tool that allows panel members to review their incentive history, as well as a request for payment of incentives if the requirements for payment have been met; for example, they have enough points.
- **Account management**: the users should be able to conveniently unsubscribe or manage routine tasks such as updating their e-mail address

Quality control and fraud detection

The issue of quality control and fraud detection must be dealt with when considering selection of a panel management tool. The reality is that there are many opportunistic individuals who will seek the vulnerability of any system, and especially a new system that is sponsored by a well-endowed research firm. Here are some things to look for in a research management system:

- **Duplicate detection**: the ability to automatically detect duplicates is an important feature. This allows the system to automatically inspect the information about a new respondent and alert customer service personnel if two persons living in the same home have registered in the same panel. The administrator can decide whether to contact the latter respondent, or similarly, to assign a common household ID.
- **Quality scoring**: the ability to assign a quality score to respondents via an automated formula is highly desirable. For example, GMI uses word count for answers to open-ends as a key factor in assessing panelist quality. The argument is that logically engaged respondents will spend more time than persons who are motivated exclusive by an incentive.

Mail management

In the case of online panels, mail-out of invites is typically a required capability. Though mundane, it is more complex than may be immediately apparent to the casual observer. Here are the things to expect:

- **Mail formatting**: the mail format should be highly flexible, allowing the use of multiple variables such as respondent information and system variables. Meta-variables such as "Salutation" are language-dependent and adjust the structure of title and name depending on the language (for example, Asian languages put the family name before the given name.).
- **Mail-out of e-mails**: the ability to send out vast amounts of e-mails is an increasingly important requirement. Response times are a direct function of the mail-out engine. If prime time (7–11 p.m.) is to be hit in any given time zone, then it is important to be able to deliver messages within minutes. A throughput of 50,000 per hour is a reasonable minimum for an Enterprise application.
- **Queue management**: in some cases it may be desirable to cancel e-mails that are in the queue; that is, when invites are sent inadvertently, or with errors. In this case it is strongly desired to have a tool that lets the user access the queue and remove mails before they are actually sent by the mail-out engine.
- **Delayed mailing**: in some instances, it may be desirable to schedule a mail-out to occur at a certain time of day. Multiple waves of invitations

can be scheduled in advance. For example, sample sources that may be more expensive can be staggered to occur after a less-expensive sample.

- **Paced mailing**: a variant of delayed mailing is the system of paced mailing. In this case, the mail-out engine first initiates a "heartbeat ping" to the remote server that is to host the surveying application. If the ping time is above some acceptable level, it stops attempting to mail for some set interval. This method is well suited for situations where the receiving survey engine has questionable scalability/availability.
- **Scheduled reminders**: reminders can also be prescheduled to occur on set intervals of days. These reminders are sent to panelists who are within quota segments that are not filled. In an ideal embodiment, reminders are sent out with a "tapered" pace; that is, sending reminders in a quantity that is proportional to the amount needed rather than reminding all eligible respondents.
- **Bounce-back processing**: the panel management tool should include a solution for bounce-back processing. The system administrator can set the number of failed attempts that are to be attempted before marking the panelist as non-active.
- **Mail-out with attachments**: attachments can at times be a requirement for newsletters or invites. As research and CRM become increasingly melded into a linked process, the ability to include attachments will take on more importance.

Statistics and reporting on panelists and panels

The panel management tool should streamline the process for generating real-time or static reports for panel counts. This allows the panel owner to efficiently deal with the periodic requests for information about panel growth, panel counts, response rates, and demographic profile. Some typical reports include:

- **Panel counts**: counts by country, with cross-tables for age and gender would be a typical consumer panel summary. The ability to report panel counts by time period is a further report that is a likely requirement in most panel systems. Advanced systems and more options for flexible reporting.
- **Response rates**: the ability to monitor response rates is an important diagnostic of panel health. A steep fall in response rates can indicate both the need for more proactive "care and feeding." It may also be an indication for a need to purge non-responsive panelists.

The preferred solution is to be able to generate reports in a flexible manner.

Customer service

The efficient processing of inbound inquiries from panelists is an area where significant efficiency gains can be derived via automation of work processes.

- **Standardized messages**: most panelist inquiries are mundane inquiries related to lost passwords and inquiries for accessing a particular project. For these situations it can be desirable to have a repository of standard messages that are pre-translated in the case of multilingual panels.
- **Queuing and message-routing**: the panel management application should have the ability to pass respondent e-mails on to predesignated persons depending on project/language. For example, a non-German speaker should not be able to access German customer service inquiries.

User management

User management for a panel may vary widely from panel to panel. Therefore, some special features are suggested for panel-user management, including:

- **Access privileges**: the restrictions of which users can access which features for which panel are the core of user management. A customer service person may be restricted to using just a handful of tools, and perhaps even restricted to a single language. By contrast, a panel owner may have full authority over a given panel, yet may have more limited authority over a panel managed by a colleague who is managing a similar panel in a neighboring country, or related subject area.
- **User settings**: the ability to define user preferences and settings is a core feature that can be used to customize the unique requirements; for example, by country or language. A French person working with a US panel may be easily confused by differences in language, date display, or currency values. By using user settings, one can effectively overcome the cultural difference, thereby allowing both respondents and internal users to see the world in a familiar way.

8 Sample/Quota Management

Probably the single most important feature of any panel management system is the caliber of the tools for filtering and sampling respondents. Inevitably, there are historical norms within any company about what a system should do, or look like. Yet, there are some recurring points that any industrial strength panel system must offer:

Selection

- **Filtering**: the system should allow complex Boolean logic (AND, OR, and NOT), including nested logic (with multiple layers of parentheses) in order to precisely define the target group. The ability to save these filters into a named filter also saves time for future reference to the required filter.
- **Sample frequency**: a classic issue with sample management is the issue of "over-fishing." Therefore, the filtering tool should include the option of filtering on the basis of criteria for survey frequency, or data of the most recent interview. This allows the user to sample respondents that not only combine some target profile for demographic, technographic, or psychographic attributes, but who also have not been interviewed in the past 90 days.

Deployment

- **Loading and managing sample to a live study**: a key feature is the ability to add a new sample to a live project. A sample should also be reassignable across modalities. A sample that may start as being for a self-administered web survey can be dynamically reassigned to other modes; for example, CATI.
- **Oversampling**: the ability to oversample by quota segment is strongly advised. This capability provides the means to set oversampling ratios at varying levels. For example, in consumer panels, young males have a notoriously lower response rate in managed panels when compared to older women.

Control

- **Ability to use quota information in the survey engine**: for certain studies, for example brand awareness, it is desirable to reference quota status during an interview. This system variable for quota cell status may have the property of "filled" or "unfilled," or may refer to the actual numeric value for the quota cell. Special functions may also present or rank a response set based on most or least selected; for example, to increase the probability of filling quotas in a balanced way.
- **E-mail alert upon quota completion**: in some cases it may be desirable to inform a project manager or an external client when a quota segment has been reached.

9 Data-processing

Historically, data-processing is done offline using PC-based software such as Quantum. This method is not compatible with the Net-centric model since Quantum works with data in a batch process rather than in real-time.

Data preparation

Preparation of the raw data so that it can be used for analysis can be done concurrent to data-collection.

- **Data-editing**: the ability to remove cases or edit raw data is a key requirement. Therefore, it is desirable that the tool can efficiently identify and remove cases that may be incomplete or may have implausible answers suggesting non-valid data. Additionally, the ability to select faulty interviews and edit raw data is a further requirement for avoiding the need to download and re-import raw data prior to web-based data delivery.
- **Weighting**: in some cases, a representative data set cannot be collected. Therefore, the ability to weight data to population or percentage weights is desirable. In addition, it may be a requirement to generate complex weight factors and re-import the weight factors via an online interface that matches the weight factor with the case ID.
- **Computed and recoded variables**: this is typically done offline using Quantum; computing and recoding can be efficiently done online. This has the added advantage that the user-defined variable can be updated as new raw data are received in the system.

Coding of open-ends

Coding of open-ends is historically done offline by using products such as Verbastat. A new generation of coding solutions such as Ascribe from Language Logic is a leading-edge solution that ports the coding process to the web via a "coding portal" that provides the means to efficiently code open-ends entirely via a web-based application. Here are the key things to look for in a coding system:

- **Integration with data-collection**: in the ideal mode it should be possible to do coding even as data are being collected. This allows raw uncoded information to be rapidly converted. The Net-centric model also means that multiple coders can work on a shared central data set without risk of duplicated effort. A project leader can also evaluate the open-ends and gauge whether additional closed responses should be added to the questionnaire.
- **Review of the raw text responses**: the user should have the ability to print out, export, or display verbatim responses.
- **Efficient tools for preparation of the code plan**: after reviewing the raw codes it is desirable to be able to execute automated coding of open-ends via keyword/phrase matching. Advanced systems allow the ability to combined Boolean operators such as AND, OR, and NOT, as well as nest expressions in parentheses.

- **Security for coder portal**: in cases where a coder portal will be used for providing access to the system for external coders, password protection for use by external coders is recommended. Coders can be authorized to access certain projects and certain languages.
- **Multiple language versions**: the coder portal should be multilingual, allowing coders to work in their native language rather than navigate foreign menu prompts; for example, an English application for a German–French translation creates unnecessary complexity for the coding personnel.
- **Integration with translation management**: in some cases, coding of open-ends will be done only from translated texts. This assures the highest level of consistency for coding. Therefore, it is desirable to have the ability to translate open-ended responses during and after data collection.

Import/Export

In many cases, data-collection, analysis, reporting, and presentation will still proceed via conventional systems that are not Net-centric. In these cases, it is desirable to efficiently transfer content between systems. Several items are to be considered:

- **Easy export of analyses/charts to Microsoft Word, PowerPoint, or Excel**: for the foreseeable future, presentations and attachments will be in Microsoft formats. Therefore the ability to transfer raw analysis into a Microsoft format is a requirement. In the preferred embodiment, content is generated into a Microsoft-native format rather than a static image.
- **Exports to standard formats for raw data**: delivery of a raw data file is a typical deliverable at the end of a data-collection project. Net-centric systems can make this step relatively effortless since there are no files to merge. Typical export formats include ASCII, Column Binary, Excel, Surveycraft, Quantum, Espri, SPSS, SAS, Column Binary, and triple-S.

10 Reporting and Analysis

The range of reporting analysis possibilities via Net-centric tools is increasing dramatically. Within three to five years the majority of all analysis of market research data will be viewed and analyzed using web-based tools. For an integrated market research management system, several capabilities should be evaluated.

Types of output

The conventional desktop output can increasingly be implemented online. This includes:

- **Snapshot reporting**: the ability to quickly and easily view the number of completes, incompletes, and other statistics on a live project.
- **Overview reporting**: the system generates summary counts and statistics that are appropriate for the question type. A ranking question is presented with a sorted table of means, whereas an open-ended numeric field question presents an arithmetic summary; for example, mean, standard deviation, minimum, and maximum.
- **Charting**: the user defines the variables to be charted and the output format to be generated.
- **Cross-tabulation**: the user defines page, column, and raw variables to be generated. In advanced systems the user can define a banner with multiple variables, including nested variables.
- **Frequency counts**: the ability to run and print frequency counts of all data.
- **Export of cases**: the ability to run a listing of case data, with or without filters on the data.

Additional analysis options

- **Drill-down**: in many instances it is desirable for the user to see the "why" behind the "what." The drill-down method provides the user the means to see: (1) raw data; (2) respondent demographic data; or (3) a summary report for all questions filtered on respondents within the selected cross-table cell.
- **Significance testing**: the system should provide the means to generate a t-test and/or Chi Square at various confidence intervals.
- **Custom weighting**: in some instances, users may want to assign their own user-defined weighting algorithm.
- **Customization of graphical output**: the traditional method of creating charts and graphs in Excel is essentially out of date. Modern web applications now provide the ability to prepare and manage presentation-ready graphics directly in the web-based application.
- **Sorting of responses**: the ability to display the response frame sorted in a way that is intuitive to the viewer may be desirable. For example, displaying the response frame alphabetically, or sorted by frequency, may be preferred.
- **Hiding null values**: in cases where there is a very long response frame with low incidences, or even no incidences during a reporting period, it may be desirable to suppress responses in the response frame.
- **Showing incomplete questionnaires**: research purists may prefer to not show incomplete interviews. In some cases, it is in fact desirable to show partial interviews.

Client data-delivery options

The range of ways to deliver data is increasing to reflect the differentiated ways that data are put into use, and also differing levels of time-sensitivity.

- **Client portals**: provide the ability to allow clients to access a customized portal or website that provides a secure view of the data that the client is approved to view. Permissions for functionality, filters, and variables can all be set, and even be made time-dependent to expire on a set timing.
- **Printed reports**: the traditional printed tome was supposed to go away. Unfortunately, it hasn't. Therefore the ability to generate a printed report is still a requirement.
- **E-mail-based reports**: there is an increasing trend toward push-based data delivery. Rather than going to a website to retrieve information, preprocessed reports are generated and sent to eligible subscribers on a predefined distribution list.
- **Wireless reporting**: there have been some attempts at delivering top line reports and quota reports via WAP and SMS. Though not widely used, it is a further example of push-based data-delivery.

11 Qualitative Research Tools

The core application is described in the previous applications. However, for certain implementations, an expanded set of functions may be desirable to integrate other forms of research that can penetrate more deeply into the "why behind the what." For example, respondents who answered in a particular way to a quantitative interview can be selected to participate in a qualitative research project. Alternatively, members in a panel can be invited directly into a qualitative research project.

Online focus groups

In some cases, a moderated focus group session is the preferred tool for more deeply exploring issues. An online focus group can be executed in a variety of ways, including chat-based communication. This method is used in Net-FOCUS of GMI, and also available from iTracks. The alternative method is to use moderated videoconferences such as what is available from ActiveGroup and FocusVision.

Online discussion boards

A further variant for qualitative data-collection is the online discussion board. The online discussion board is essentially moderated but not in real-time. Respondents interact in a moderated bulletin board but do so at their leisure. The result is that the discussion board can run for days or weeks with the moderator periodically injecting a comment or question to keep the discussion focused and engaged.

QualiQuant interviewing techniques

A key limitation of most qualitative research methods is the inability to execute large numbers of interviews due to the constraint of needing sufficient moderator talent to interact with the respondents. QualiQuant methods seek to overcome this issue by allowing the respondent to engage in various self-administered question types without requiring a moderator.

12 Training and Technical Support

The resources available to support users in using and mastering the tools are something to evaluate carefully when evaluating alternative solutions. Here are some key resources to look for when selecting a solution.

- **Technical support**: the availability of technical support is a critical must-have. Free technical support on a 24-hours-a-day basis means that the software vendor is strongly incentivized to make sure that the tools are reliable and easy to use.
- **Documentation**: the documentation should provide a descriptive and instructional resource for self-guided problem-solving. Inclusion of extensive screen captures with step-by-step examples and a detailed table of contents (or index) is also a must-have.
- **Training programs**: a sophisticated software application is often difficult to master on an auto-tutorial basis. Therefore, access to training programs is a capability to expect. Training may be provided by the company itself, or by third-party training vendors.
- **Service bureau support**: in some instances, mastering a tool will not come fast enough to meet the demands of the business. In those situations, it can be strongly desirable to be able to outsource routine activities such as questionnaire-programming or preparation of tabulation reports.
- **IT consulting**: for certain types of projects there may be a business need for customized solutions that require IT resources that are not readily available in-house. In this situation it may be desirable to be able to draw on IT resources directly from the software vendor.

Final Consideration: Costs

The final category offers a review of the major cost categories. Total cost of ownership has to be considered by evaluating all of the various costs that contribute to the operating cost of the market research management system.

Cost categories

In formulating a budget and assessing the costs, here are the key categories to consider:

- **Set-up costs**: some software licenses include a one-time set-up cost. This amount can sometimes be negotiated away since it is largely a fee to recover the pre-sell and start-up cost. Set-up costs would typically be amortized over the license term.
- **Software license fees**: this amount is alternatively known as service fees and applies to situations where the user is "renting" rather than owning the software. It is typically assessed on a regular time interval; for example, annual.
- **Usage fees**: for hosted applications it is commonplace to charge a transaction fee such as a rate per question answered, or a rate per interview.
- **Support costs**: whether you depend on internal support personnel, or external support personnel, there is a cost. An in-house system will have a higher cost for technical support, server maintenance, back-up, and monitoring versus a hosted system.
- **Hardware costs**: hosted systems almost invariably include hardware as part of the offer. In-house systems therefore must factor in the total cost of purchasing, shipping, configuring, and installing new hardware.
- **Network and data center costs**: if the application is to be hosted in a facility that is managed by the licensee, there will be some costs related to the data center. These costs can be economized by carefully evaluating the choice between fixed costs and variable costs, depending on volume levels. In many cases a higher fixed cost, in the form of dedicated bandwidth. provides lower overall costs for a given volume of data transfer.
- **Training costs**: the costs of training personnel vary widely. Day rates for in-house training ranges from $750–2,500. These costs should be factored into the cost forecast, particularly if a large number of personnel will require training.
- **IT consulting**: In some cases, a customization cost may be required to adapt the application to the required capability.

Contractual considerations

In drafting a contract with a software provider there are many considerations beyond the specific financial terms. Here are some of the most common issues to consider.

- **Term and termination**: often overlooked, term and termination are important to consider. A shorter term, with the ability to terminate without cause is the most favorable to the licensee.

- **Service-level agreement (SLA)**: reference to a service-level agreement is strongly advised, especially for hosted applications. The SLA spells out the terms and conditions related to application availability, response time, and support. It also specifies the corresponding penalties if certain criteria are not met on a consistent basis.
- **Protecting against provider insolvency**: even the largest and best funded providers are not immune to becoming over-extended. In the year 2001, the failures of giants such as Enron and Exodus Communications show the risks associated with depending on a service provider. To overcome this risk, most software vendors will agree to a clause that transfers intellectual property rights to the licensee, thereby providing the basis for moving to a new provider with reasonable continuity.
- **Governing law**: in the event of a legal dispute, cross-border licensing agreements can have the added complexity and risk of dealing in foreign law, or worse, litigating in foreign costs. The buyer of software is often in a position to dictate venue, and can at least recommend a neutral major city such as Geneva or London.

QUALIFICATION PROCEDURES FOR AN ONLINE MARKET RESEARCH TOOL

There is no one right way to qualify a research tool. Based on our experience in participating in the qualification process in numerous software evaluations, we provide the following:

- **Request for proposal (RFP)**: an initial RFP is desirable and recommended. The preparation of an RFP assures that the participating vendors will provide a targeted proposal that specifically addresses the strategic and tactical requirements. At the RFP stage, vendors can be eliminated from the process on the basis of core functionality, cost, or other criteria.
- **Demonstration phase**: a demonstration of the suppliers' software is the next phase. This is an opportunity to evaluate the application's ease of use, the quality and responsiveness of the personnel, and to gauge the accuracy of the proposal. Applications that are visibly unstable, or do not match the description of the proposal can be eliminated from the process at this stage.
- **Pilot project**: the software can be evaluated on a pilot basis. Most software vendors will offer this at little or no cost. The benefit of this is mutual since the lower risk of the buyer, the higher the level of initial commitment for the implementation. The pilot project can be used to identify systems that are functionally inadequate, or poorly supported.

- **Initial implementation**: implementation of the application is a key phase, often contingent on some kind of financial commitment.
- **Validation and acceptance**: once the application is implemented, some period of validation and acceptance is required. The application's stability and scalability can be gauged during this period. Where possible, record the system performance and compare it over time in order to track the impact of increased number of users, or increased data in the database.
- **Rollout**: after some initial acceptance criteria have been achieved, rollout can proceed rapidly. Web-based implementation has the huge advantage that rollout is essentially a function of providing two things: (1) access to the system in the form of a user ID and word; and (2) training in the use of the system, either via formal training or self-serve training resources.

Some Practical Advice in Qualifying Research Software

- Set up clear success criteria at the start of the project: it is important to set measurable success criteria for the system implementation. These should be based on the business objectives, planned usage, and timing constraints related to the implementation. In some cases, a phased approach is required, meaning that success criteria may in fact be increasingly stretched and broadened over time.
- Identify a sponsor *and* a project leader: the most successful implementations of research software we have seen have had both a sponsor and a project manager. The sponsor is typically the senior executive with sole authority to disburse funds to deliver the project through its initial implementation. A project leader has tactical oversight over the implementation and reports to the sponsor on matters related to the system implementation and related issues.
- Define milestones: in order to make sure that objectives of the software supplier are closely aligned with your own, we recommend using milestones during the implementation. In case of customization projects, this is absolutely critical.
- Ask the last question first: where possible, use the pilot project to test out the more difficult features of the required system. If this means that the pilot project is not gratis, so be it, since the reduced implementation risk justifies the investment. The masters of this process have used pilot projects to complete real projects.

In summary, the selection process for research management software is one that can benefit from a stationary approach. Done right, you won't have to do it too often.

PART 5

A Vision for the Future

INTRODUCTION

Our book concludes with two very different scenarios for the global market research industry, followed by some reasonable observations about the state of the industry in the near future. The rapid pace of change evident in business today makes predictions particularly difficult. Couple this with our human predilection for thinking linearly, and such forecasts are many times way off the mark. Thus, we have attempted, through the use of opposing scenarios, to take the current industry situation to two logical end points. The truth is most likely somewhere in between.

Our predictions center mainly on the structural changes that are appearing on the landscape of business, and how this will affect the collection, analysis, and dissemination of results. We feel strongly that what market research offers is valuable now and will continue to be valuable in the future – this will not change. What will change, however, is the way we "do" market research, and this falls right in line with the initial thesis of the book: that the Internet is a pervasive force that is affecting us in monumentally subtle and simple ways, in addition to the more radical ones. Everyone – from Manuel Castells, the esteemed University of California, Berkeley, "sociologist of the Internet," to top executives in leadership roles around the world, to the project managers, analysts, and clients involved in the day-to-day details of market research – is affected. Thus, our observations reflect this underlying trend and the many ways it will blossom into business, strategic, and human impacts and changes.

CHAPTER 13

Outlook and Forecast

FOR WHOM THE BELL TOLLS: TWO SCENARIOS FOR THE GLOBAL MARKET RESEARCH INDUSTRY

Scenario 1: Global Market Research Firms Resist Technology and Are Severely Challenged

The global market research industry, although appearing to keep pace by mergers and consolidations, has refused to alter traditional practices and ways of doing things. This has severely hindered efforts to meet the needs and challenges presented by the new global client. New technologies, such as the wireless Internet, shatter the use of the RDD technique that market research has so long favored. Worse yet, phone survey completion rates are dismally low, as most phones around the world contain privacy blocking technologies that prevent unwanted calls – and unwelcome interruptions to surveys have fallen into this category. Surveys via mobile phones, while promising at first, degenerate quickly as people on the move tire of having to stop everything to answer survey questions. Mail surveys become suspect due to same outbreaks of bioterrorism, as people exercise caution by refusing to open mail they do not expect or recognize. In addition, privacy legislation in California finally sweeps the United States and begins to approach strict European standards. Domestic and global market research become very expensive propositions. Local and global clients cannot justify the cost, regardless of long-term relationships and respect for the insight, skill, and analytic expertise of their market research partners. In addition, corporate needs and demands are moving faster and faster, and are becoming broader and broader. The market research industry cannot keep up.

CRM software companies, teamed now with consultants from new media, online research, and the "big five," have realized that their CRM systems can work, if supported by analytic talent and change management. SiebelSoft – as the new merged giant is known – for example, leverages 75 percent of seats it installs across the enterprise into newly termed "analytic knowledge software." Training, change management, and cultural adoption practices are remaking the corporate landscape into a knowledge organization. Market research, per se, is very rare, as multiple technology-based and innovative analytic solutions can be customized – and delivered via the CRM infrastructure – so that everyone in the organization is an analyst. Through a clever combination of automated, templated, and customized analytic solutions – supported by vertical, research, and OD experts from new media and the "big five" consulting firms – what traditionally was done by global market research firms is now done in-house via solutions adapted to the individual or the department. No longer constrained, but liberated by the communicative power of the Internet, the corporate information factory allows knowledge workers to collaborate, interact, and work with data, knowledge, and information with anyone around the world.

A few market research firms – now called "scientific data-collection and delivery houses" in deference to their statistical heritage – carry on with time-honored tracking studies, in-home panels, and specialized syndicated research. But, by and large, the industry has become a very small and specialized component of the business information industry. With the pervasive sharing and access to data and information available in many forms, large BI firms – using integrated technology and an Internet-based platform – have taken over nearly all forms of what we once knew as market research.

Scenario 2: Global Market Research Firms Embrace Technology and Leverage Information Technology for Global Competitive Advantage

Market research firms, though slow on the uptake, quickly realized that investments in technology were necessary for survival. With expensive CRM software systems failing to deliver what was promised, and many installations sitting partially unused, leading global market research firms – along with their smaller, but able, cousins in the new media and online research arena – moved aggressively to fill the analytic void with new, faster, and more efficient solutions, and leveraged the industry's strongest assets: analytic expertise, insight delivery, and marketing and executive decision support. Business practices were stepped up that preserved the best that market research had to offer, but now delivered in a cost-effective, timely fashion via an online-enabling market research system. Database linkages and mediating architectures were developed that allowed all traditional forms of market research – as well as new QualiQuant methodologies, behavioral data integration, CRM analytics, and data-mining – to be deployed using an online system. In addition, a wide variety of reports, data result streams, and desktop analytical capabilities are now delivered directly to the corporate desktop. Market research firms begin to populate the innovation quadrant (see Figure 13.1), thus enhancing and extending the ability to deliver the gamut of products and services: from raw data to sophisticated, powerful, and insightful executive decision support.

Figure **13.1** Innovation quadrants

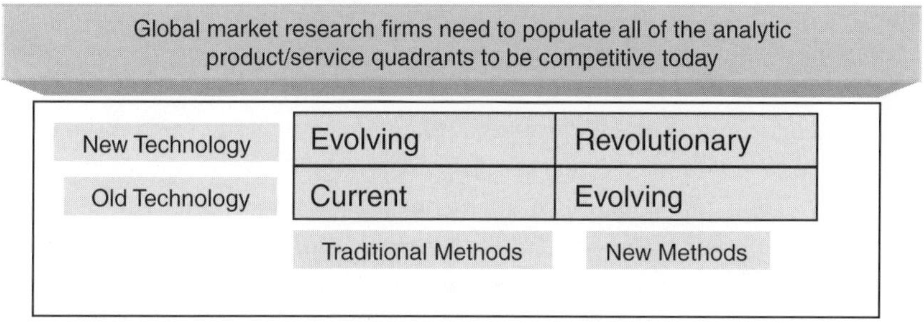

Global market research firms need to populate all of the analytic product/service quadrants to be competitive today

	Traditional Methods	New Methods
New Technology	Evolving	Revolutionary
Old Technology	Current	Evolving

Market research firms, now equipped to operate on a global scale and to reach consumers, clients, and customers around the world, can concentrate on unparalleled high-value delivery of data, services, and products. Although it has been a long road, the industry has begun to assert itself as the primary provider of BI and information around the world. Global clients rely on mission critical deliverables. Market research firms have gobbled up consultants and CRM software companies while also extending specialized services. Knowledge management and insight delivery have become the driving forces of the industry. Research and researchers are now embedded in the corporate knowledge factory as advance scouts, trainers, change agents, analysts, and trusted guides.

The business information industry, as it is now called, readily supports so-called "scientific data-collection and delivery houses" – in deference to their statistical heritage – that carry on with time-honored tracking studies, in-home panels, and specialized syndicated research using traditional techniques, such as phone and mail. But, by and large, the industry has become technologically enabled, renamed, and wholly integrated into the business intelligence, market measurement, and consumer insight stream that runs continuously and in every corner of the world. What with the pervasive sharing and access to data and information available in many forms, large global BI firms – using integrated technology and a Net-based platform – enable nearly all forms of what we now know as market research.

FIVE PREDICTIONS FOR MARKET RESEARCH PRACTICE IN 2005

What will be the state of the market research industry in 2005? While predictions are always fraught with danger, even when well informed by a study of the past and present, we believe that five reasonable observations – based on the comprehensive frames of reference we have employed – can be advanced. All have to do with structural changes in the way market research is done. Throughout the book we have presented many concepts, ideas, and example of evolving methods, practices, and procedures that are fostered by embracing an integrative and collaborative technology mindset. But to forward these as predictions would be unwise, except to say that the fundamental value that traditional market research brings to the table will most likely still be the same in 2005 as it is today.

Our sense is that these structural changes will form the fundamental platform for the practice of market research to evolve into a compelling and vital marketing support and customer intelligence function driving business growth, development, and success. Technology alone is a naive solution. To believe that CRM analytics and the study of behavioral data on consumers will tell you about customer's feelings, perceptions, motivations, and awareness – all foundational forces driving customer satisfaction, relationships, loyalty, and ultimately return on investment – is not only misguided, it is dangerous. Technology as an enabling force that supports increased communication, information collection, dissemination, and learning, however, is extremely valuable. Thus, our predictions focus on these aspects.

1   Internet-based market research will be the standard for quantitative multi-country consumer research. Research suppliers who have not fully embraced the Internet will have lost out, or sold out, to more Net-savvy competitors. Global 500 firms will increasingly adopt a single-source model for selection of research suppliers. Technology is about efficiency and effectiveness. A Net-centric architecture clearly supports this. While most traditional techniques will not disappear, we will see a gradual blending and shifting of processes and methods moved to the online channel. As well, we will see highly effective offline methodologies tied into the Internet-centric system, such as through the use of Net-CAPI and Net-CATI solutions.

Global 500 corporations are already in the process of developing and deploying CRM, SCM, and enterprise application integration (EAI) solutions for the expressed purpose of achieving and enhancing global efficiency, enterprise standardization, and corporate collaboration. Market research must be equipped to be part of this solution. The only way to do this will be through exploring, investing, and adopting ways to move the best of what the industry has to offer to a Net-centric platform. The alternative is the dissolution of the industry or the gradual displacement of the market research function by tech-driven solutions that are essentially engaged in reinventing the wheel.

For the large global clients of research and business information, a single-source solution will increasingly become the partnership of choice. As the Internet brings consumers and markets together, the ability for research providers – in multiple capacities: primary, secondary, information management/delivery, and syndicated research – to afford research across borders and the enterprise will become a requirement. Further, new "global" consumers and markets will appear that will demand another level of research exploration, understanding, and insight delivery to commence. Internet-centric systems and processes will then be mandatory for any firm expecting to be competitive.

2 Multi-channel data-collection using Internet-based data consolidation will streamline traditional research and enable new market research techniques, methods, and business processes.

Online marketplaces dealing in perishable commodity services – such as call center hours – emerge. Once a foundational, scaleable architecture is achieved, the real work of taking the extensive expertise and marketing knowledge the industry has accumulated and putting it to work in an efficient, usable, and compelling form can begin. Companies, with the support of sizeable partners and investors, are already attempting to take the combined marketing wisdom, knowledge, and expertise of global corporate leaders and transfer it to online systems capable of driving improved and efficient marketing systems. Emmperative, for example, has developed a streamlined, integrated, and networked system that takes the combined corporate marketing history, knowledge, and best practices of P&G – one of their primary investors – and transferred it into an online system joined across the enterprise and around the world for Global 2000 clients. This is just the beginning of a revolution in the use of enabling technology that will become even more evident in the next few years.

Market research must and will join the knowledge management and business information revolution. As data are integrated from multiple channels – and easily accessed via components specifically developed for market research – new techniques, methods, and business processes will naturally appear. In addition, ways to move commodity services – such as call centers, interviewing, and syndicated tracking studies – to forms that improve cost-effectiveness and support measurable ROI will emerge.

3 The mobile and wireless Internet will accelerate the growth of the Internet in emerging markets, enabling increasingly representative research to be conducted, particularly by using pre-profiled panels of respondents. Already this is occurring in countries that exhibit substantial usage of wireless devices and have a strong foundation in doing phone research, such as Scandinavia. Research efforts underway there will form the foundation for future efforts around the world. As mobile and wireless communications become ubiquitous, the data collected will be increasingly concentrated in single-source databases, accessible as an integrated whole, rather than the current silos of data prevalent today. As well, pre-profiled and customized global respondent panels will appear, as market researchers locate the appropriate and preferred way to contact individuals to carry out research, not only in countries or regions, but also around the world.

Of primary importance, however, is the ability for the data to be collected and sourced as a data stream, via a single data store enhanced by meta data layers. This will result in the possibility of constructing representative global access panels. Some panelists may respond only via wireless; others by fixed-line phones, on the Internet, or via iTV. Regardless, the panel will be used as a representative cross-sectional panel or as a source to do targeted surveys or research. The ability of market research firms to leverage their expertise and leadership in this capacity will define a large part of their success in capturing a premier place in the corporate business information industry and in taking control of a vital and unique contribution to global marketing, advertising, and sales success.

4 The analysis of research results will be conducted via web-based applications accessing centrally stored data, effectively replacing the desktop analyzer using locally stored data. Work on building exploration data warehouses, data stores, and data marts to afford efficient and real-time access to data across the enterprise is already under way. The continuing development of a mediating architecture – based on meta data concepts and solutions – will continue to enhance the development of flexible and powerful systems that can utilize many forms of data. The primary goal, not achieved yet, is to achieve dynamic interaction with customers to provide richer, deeper client relationships across all relationship channels. The role of market research will be to provide powerful insights into consumer and marketing behavior patterns, propensities, preferences, feelings, and attitudes.

To fully integrate market research enterprise solutions into corporate network infrastructures, corporations will present new requirements to market research providers for capacity and connectivity via rules-based processes that enable cross-channel synchronization and real-time customer interaction. This emerging technical architecture includes an enterprise application integration (EAI) solution, in which middleware provides for the sharing of applications and data to ensure data consistency across databases and to support multiple end-user devices and interfaces related to the market research function.

In order to provide real-time analysis and dissemination of customer data, technical solutions such as a "customer data store" or a "marketing information database" are being explored. This architecture provides a data storage core dedicated to amassing current customer information that is drawn from real-time data from operational and Net-centric research systems; historical data from the data warehouse; and stored results from QualiQuant market research. This can then support rich, value-added analysis to leverage improved interactions with customers. The "customer data store" concept, for example, provides for more intelligent, streamlined processing. Scoring, rules, filters, original research results (qualitative and quantitative), and predictive/descriptive data-mining techniques are applied to real-time data – focusing only on information that has been identified as having potential value (versus batch-scoring/batch data feeds of everything). This scalable approach is more flexible, allowing "learning about" learning based on changes in data attributes, business rules, and more qualitative features that provoke and invoke marketer's experience and insight.

5 Consumer data will be closely integrated into global enterprise computing systems, thereby further blurring the lines between market research, CRM, and business intelligence. A new mega-merger phase will emerge linking CRM, BI, and MR firms into powerhouse companies that are global and Net-centric. Behavioral data on consumers will continue to accumulate and become part of increasingly complete stores of accessible data. As a result, all facets of information gathered about consumers and customers will be fair game for analysis. The triad of key functions undergirding marketing, sales, and advertising – market research, CRM, and business intelligence tools – will blend into one complete system that supports and enhances data-collection, data analysis, and data delivery, as well as supporting higher levels of collaborative, insight-generation, decision-guidance, and knowledge management processes. To use the analogy of a fully functioning human system, the digital nervous system (CRM) will have a brain (market research) and a sensory system (BI tools) – specialized components each delivering its own unique value, while blended into a complex, interrelated structure.

Solutions, such as the ability to map individual customers to densely informed hierarchical segment models, will arise that will enable personalization, customization, and relationships to thrive without infringing on individual privacy. Just as today a successful, in-person, sales/service person can combine observation, a few questions, and intuition (literally, working with generalized internal experience maps to guide decisions and actions) to build a solid customer relationship and outcome – technology-driven analytics will support frontline service people in the future. This is only possible, however, with all of the elements – network communications, analytics, software linkages, data-mining, and market research information – in close harmony.

As a result of the conceptual and functional changes increasingly sought in the race to understand and relate to the customer, mergers involving CRM, MR, and BI companies will appear. Further driving this mega-merger phase will be the adoption of a Net-centric infrastructure that will enable global systems to be effectively deployed and used. Thus, we will finally see the time when the "wolf and the lamb feed together, and the lion eats straw like the ox."

CONCLUSION

The market research industry stands poised at the precipice of great change. The winds stirred by the Internet and enabling technologies, significant new competitors, and the pressing global needs of clients are relentlessly at work reshaping the industry, forcing it to break the mold of past practice, habits, and thinking. In particular, the rapid convergence of business globalization and the ubiquitous use of *technology-driven solutions* is demanding the formation of global market research organizations equipped to serve as leaders, expert guides, and solution providers in the emerging global business information industry.

Enabling technologies offer a dizzying array of opportunities for market researchers to respond to a tremendous gap that exists in efforts to hear and understand customers and consumers. The market research industry must recognize this need, adapt to technological innovations, and work diligently to leverage market research's greatest strengths. A failure to exert leadership, take action, or remedy the situation will result in an industry that is relegated to a sideline and secondary role, as a component of larger, faster, and more efficient technology-driven solutions that provide superior business intelligence tools, marketing automation processes, consumer feedback mechanisms, and customer relationship management improvements.

Research Instruments

EXECUTIVE INTERVIEW GUIDE

Market Research in the Internet Age

1. What are the major trends (short and long term) affecting your firm today?
2. What aspects of your business currently involve using the Internet or web-based tools for market research or CRM analytics? [For example, do you use the Internet only for web surveys, or for other modes of research, too? Do you have a separate customer intelligence division or embed this function across divisions, and so on?]
3. What do you feel are the most important aspects of your value proposition?
   a. What are the factors that are most important to your clients?
   b. How does the Internet and online-enabling technology help you in delivering the most important aspects of your value proposition and the things that are most important to your clients?
4. Now I'd like to talk about your global mindset. Do you see the future direction of your company moving toward (continued) global expansion, or toward developing new or existing services, specialties or methodologies, or both?
5. Which of the following do you perceive your company to be the closest to, in terms of what you do, clients you serve or seek, or in business goals/objectives? How does the market research or customer analytics function fit into your solution:
   a. New media research companies, such as Diameter, CyberTarget, DynamicLogic, heavily or exclusively using technology?
   b. CRM/eCRM software providers, such as Siebel, SAP, PeopleSoft?

    c. Syndicated research/consulting firms, such as Forrester, Media Metrix/Jupiter, IDC?

    d. "Big five" consulting firms, technology integration, and strategic/business services?

    e. Web-analytics firms, such as NetGenesis, Accrue?

    f. Database companies, such as Oracle, Microsoft?

    g. Pure-play online MR firms, such as Harris Interactive, Greenfield Online?

    h. Top 25 global market research firms?

6. What do you see the future of (global) MR (or customer intelligence-gathering) to be in 2005? Has that changed in the last year?

ONLINE SURVEY INSTRUMENT

Online Survey for Marketing Practitioners and Market Researchers
Market Research in the Internet Age

Invitation

Welcome to an online survey for marketing and market research professionals. Your input is appreciated, as a significant facet of our book will be shaped by your professional opinions, attitudes, and perceptions regarding:

- trends affecting you today;
- aspects of work involving Internet or web-based tools/techniques;
- important success factors related to Internet or Web-based tools/techniques;
- perceived competitors;
- information about your company.

The survey should only take about 15–20 minutes to complete. At the end, you will be asked to send us your e-mail address so we can notify you if you have won a free copy of our book: Market Research in the Internet Age. *This is entirely optional, of course, and you are under no obligation to do so.*

Thank you for contributing your expert thinking and time to this study.

Filter:	Are you a research supplier? Or are you a research client?
Part 1:	Trends affecting you today
Part 2:	Aspects of work involving Internet or web-based tools/techniques
Part 3:	Important success factors related to Internet or web-based tools/techniques.
Part 4:	Perceived competitors

Part 5:   Firmagraphic information
Last screen: Thank you and request for e-mail to share results

PART 1: TRENDS AFFECTING YOU TODAY

Q1:   Considering all aspects necessary to manage your firm, what trends
          have an impact on your firm today? Please select a response from
          1 to 5, where 1 is low impact and 5 is high impact: [Randomize
          order GRID: 1 = Low Impact; 5 = High Impact, DK and RF.]
     1. Pervasiveness of the Internet.
     2. The trend toward globalization of business.
     3. The consolidation of market research providers.
     4. Online research becoming more important/requested by clients.
     5. The emergence of global access panels.
     6. Availability of enterprise-grade software to do market research.
     7. Consulting firms appearing as competitors for market research.
     8. Application service providers offering research services to end-
        clients.
     9. Request for continuous research/information delivered directly
        to the desktop.
     10. Declining cooperation rates for telephone-interviewing.
     11. Growth of syndicated firms, such as Forrester and Jupiter
         Media Metrix.
     12. End-client deployment of CRM/eCRM software solutions.
     13. End-client deployment of business intelligence tools (for
         example, Microstrategy and SAS).
     14. End-client demand for data-/web-mining solutions.
     15. End-client demand for an integrated and total view of the
         customer.
     16. Clients more eager to know influential and important factors
         that affect their business.
     17. The emergence of single-source relationships between the MR
         supplier and end-client.
     18. Demand for rapid turnaround of data-collection and results via
         online portals.

Q1A: Considering the trends you identified as "high impact," please rank
         them in the order that is likely to have the greatest impact on the
         future growth of your company? [Ranking questions: randomize
         order checklist, carry over those trends rated 4 or 5 from Q1.]

PART 2: ASPECTS OF WORK INVOLVING INTERNET OR WEB-BASED TOOLS/TECHNIQUES

Q2:   What market research services that your firm currently deliver involve the use of the Internet or web-based tools? [Multiple responses allowed: checklist.]

- ❑ Web surveys (CAWI)
- ❑ Focus groups (OFG)
- ❑ Discussion boards
- ❑ Consumer panels
- ❑ Professional panels
- ❑ CAPI
- ❑ CATI (using the web)
- ❑ Data delivery
- ❑ Report-publishing
- ❑ Data-mining
- ❑ None (skip to Part 4)

Q2A: Considering all of the projects your firm will complete this year, what percent do you estimate will be done online? And in 2005? [2-column GRID response]

1. 0 – 10%
2. 11 – 24%
3. 25 – 49%
4. 50 – 75%
5. 76 – 90%
6. 91 – 100%
7. Can't say or Don't know

Q2B: What do you estimate is the percentage of mixed-mode (online/ offline in one project) research completed this year? In 2005? [2-column GRID response]

1. 0 – 10%
2. 11 – 24%
3. 25 – 49%
4. 50 – 75%
5. 76 – 90%
6. 91 – 100%
7. Can't say or Don't know

Q2C: Based on the experience with your clients, what would you say are the key motivators driving clients to suggest, implement, or request either online or mixed-mode solutions? [Open end, text.]

PART 3: IMPORTANT SUCCESS FACTORS RELATED TO INTERNET OR WEB-BASED TOOLS OR TECHNIQUES

Q3:   How *important* are Internet and web-based research techniques/ tools in delivering important aspects of your firm's value proposition to your clients? Please rate the degree of importance with the following: [Randomize order: 2-stage column GRID (Important to my firm – Important to clients): 1 = Not at all Important; 3 = Very Important.]:

❏ The ability to deploy and manage multiple modes of research.
❏ The ability to integrate data from multiple modes of research.
❏ Improving the speed of fieldwork.
❏ Real-time reporting.
❏ Advanced analytics, including detailed behavioral data, such as clickstream data.
❏ Reducing research cost.
❏ Increasing research productivity.
❏ Enabling delivery of results to client desktops.
❏ Advancing perceived high-value services, such as: insight, recommendations, and counsel for decisions.

Q3A: How *effective* are Internet and web-based research techniques/tools in delivering important aspects of your firm's value proposition to your clients? Please rate the degree of effectiveness with the following [Carry over responses rated 4 or 5 from Q3 – Randomize order – 2-stage column GRID (Important to my firm – Important to clients): 1 = Ineffective; 2 = Effective; 3 = Very Effective.]:

❏ The ability to deploy and manage multiple modes of research.
❏ The ability to integrate data from multiple modes of research.
❏ Improving the speed of fieldwork.
❏ Real-time reporting.
❏ Advanced analytics, including detailed behavioral data, such as clickstream data.
❏ Reducing research cost.
❏ Increasing research productivity.
❏ Enabling delivery of results to client desktops.
❏ Advancing perceived high-value services, such as: insight, recommendations, and counsel for decisions.

Q3B: What challenges do you encounter when attempting to deliver Internet and/or web-based research to clients? [Open end, text.]

Q3C: Are you aware of the following firms that provide online research
        services and tools? [Rotate prompted awareness list – checklist Yes
        or No.]

        ❑ CFMC: servant and mentor
        ❑ FIRM: confirm it
        ❑ GMI: Net-MR
        ❑ MarketTools: zTelligence
        ❑ NIPO
        ❑ PTT
        ❑ SPSS: dimensions
        ❑ Other

PART 4: PERCEIVED COMPETITORS

Q4:   Which of the following do you perceive your company to be closest
        to, in terms of what you do, clients you seek or serve, or in business
        goals/objectives? [Rotate checklist – Multiple responses allowed.]

        ❑ New media research companies – such as Diameter, Dynamic
           Logic, Cyber Target – heavily or exclusively using technology.
        ❑ CRM/eCRM software or solution providers, such as Siebel,
           SAP, PeopleSoft, e.Piphany, Onyx, Vignette, or Broadvision.
        ❑ Syndicated research/analyst firms, such as Forrester or Jupiter
           Media Metrix.
        ❑ Web analytic firms, such as NetGenesis, Accrue, or
           WebSideStory.
        ❑ Database companies, such as Oracle and Microsoft.
        ❑ Firms heavily invested in online research, such as DMS, Harris
           Interactive, and Greenfield Online.
        ❑ "Big five" consulting firms, combining technology integration
           and strategic/business services.
        ❑ Business intelligence software firms, such as Business Objects,
           Cognos, Hyperion, or Sagent.
        ❑ Top 25–50 traditional market research firm (global,
           international, or national).

Q4A: Why? (Describe the characteristics in common, synergies, and so
        on, for those chosen.) [Carry over responses checked in Q4 – Open
        end, text.]

PART 5: FIRMAGRAPHIC INFORMATION

Q5:   Please provide the following information about your company [One-page form style.]:

❑   Company Name: [Text response.]
❑   Your Title and Function: [Double standard drop-down lists]
❑   Company Size: [Double-standard drop-down list for number of FTE and 2000 & 2001 estimated revenue categories.]
❑   Company Locations: [How many: discrete number and where, standard drop-down list of countries.]
❑   Target Markets: [Standard drop-down list of vertical industries.]
❑   Primary methods/types of research delivered [Modified ESOMAR list.]

Q5A: Do you have a dedicated FTE person or Division exclusively devoted to e-research (web-based research) [Yes or No. If Yes, continue to Q5B. If No, skip to Q5C.]

Q5B: How many persons are currently involved in online research in your company? [Discrete numbers 1 – 50 or more? – skip to last-page request for e-mail notification of results.]

❑   Sales or account management
❑   Production or project management
❑   Data-processing personnel
❑   IT/Data center personnel
❑   Research personnel

Q5C: Is e-research embedded throughout the organization, rather than the responsibility of a particular individual or group? [Yes or No. If Yes, skip to last-page request for e-mail notification of results. If No, continue to Q5D.]

Q5D.1: Is online data-collection outsourced? [If None, skip to last-page request for e-mail notification of results.]

❑   Yes, all
❑   Yes, about half
❑   Yes, some
❑   None

Q5D.2: Is offline data-collection outsourced? [If None, skip to last-page request for e-mail notification of results.]

- ❑ Yes, all
- ❑ Yes, about half
- ❑ Yes, some
- ❑ None

Q5E: Who do you generally outsource to? [Open end, text. When completed, continue to last-page request for e-mail notification of results.]

List of Firms Providing Executive Interviewees and Information

1. ABT Associates – US
2. ACNielsen – US/UK
3. Advertising Research Foundation – US
4. BAI Global – US
5. BMW NA – US
6. BuzzBack – US
7. CLT Research – US
8. Comscore Networks – US
9. Diameter/DoubleClick – US
10. digiMine – US
11. DMS/AOL – US
12. Dynamic Logic – US
13. E.Consultancy.com – UK
14. Emmperative – US
15. e.Piphany – US
16. ESOMAR
17. GfK Group AG – Germany
18. Harris Interactive – US
19. IBM – US
20. IBOPE Group – Brazil
21. Information Builders – US
22. Information Resources International – US
23. Intage – JAPAN
24. Ipsos-Reid Group – Canada
25. Knowledge Networks – US
26. Korn Ferry International – US
27. Marketing Evolution – US
28. Market Research Association

29. MarketTools – US
30. Microsoft – US
31. NFO World Group – US
32. Nokia – UK/Finland
33. NOP World Group – US
34. Opinion Research Corporation – US
35. Pepsi – US
36. PricewaterhouseCoopers – US
37. Quaero, LLC – US
38. Research Lab – Norway
39. RFL Communications – US
40. Ronin International – US
41. SAS – US
42. Scient – US
43. Siebel – US
44. SLP Infoware – France
45. Talyor Nelson Sofres PLC – UK
46. The Kantar Group – UK
47. Tower Group/Reuters – US
48. Tribal DDB – US
49. True Audience – US
50. Universitaet Erlangen-Nuernberg – Germany
51. Viacom – US
52. WebMiner – US
53. WebSideStory – US
54. Wharton School of Business, The University of Pennsylvania – US
55. Yahoo! Europe – UK

Glossary

A

Acquiescent response set: A biasing condition that can be set up by a series of questions that beg a "YES" response.

Advertising development research: Investigations done prior to launching a campaign, to input into the creative process. Usually helps to define the audience and its interests.

Advertising effectiveness research: Most often, research done to measure ad awareness and remembrance and day-after recall. Pre- and post-advertising surveys are two common types.

Aided recall: A typical awareness measure. Also called prompted recall. Usually asked after unaided questions. "Have you ever heard of Company X as a provider of word-processing software?"

Ambiguous question: One that implies multiple questions or could be answered correctly in at least two different ways. Usually a design mistake.

Analytical matrix: A cross-tabulation form or format where the headings are categories. For example: age categories (over or under 40) are the headings, and the rows are possible answers. Sometimes used in focus group analysis where vertical columns are separate groups and horizontal rows are responses to each question. Allows looking across columns for consistency or differences.

ANOVA (ANalysis Of VAriance): A statistical test used with interval data (see definition) to determine if multiple samples come from populations with equal means. In other words, is there a statistically significant variance? Like Chi Square, ANOVA tests for significant variation between groups or samples. However, ANOVA requires interval data and signifies differences in sample means.

API (Application Program (or Protocol) Interface: A form of middleware that enables legacy systems or differing systems to "speak" to each other. A very important component of application integration.

ASP (application service provider): Increasingly, a company that hosts a co-located solution to strict, high-quality, and rigorous standards. As emerging software solutions become increasingly complex and unaffordable, ASPs fill an essential gap by providing critical competitive services that are affordable, scaleable, and continuously updated.

Audit: A review of specific aspects of a market, such as products on store shelves, to determine the number of facings and competitive mix, or a complete advertising audit. Also a broad-based survey, such as a market audit, intended to determine a wide range of basic market facts about a product category.

Awareness: A basic marketing measure. Companies, brands, products, new concepts all must establish awareness prior to purchase.

Awareness and attitude research: A fundamental type of marketing research often used as a baseline for tracking companies' positions in the market. Measures awareness of the company and competitors and attitudes toward the company or product.

B

Back-to-back focus groups: Focus group research where one session occurs shortly after the other and on the same day.

Banner point: The column or heading over a data set in a computer cross-tab table. Vertical headings that describe data breakouts. For example: college grads, income over $50,000, design engineers. Similar to a column on a spreadsheet.

Base, sample base, base over: The number over which percentages, averages or other findings are calculated. For example, positives or negatives about a specific company will often be based over those who are aware of the company. Often a subset of the entire sample.

Baseline: An initial research project against which future changes are benchmarked.

Benchmark: A tracking wave or survey designed to measure against the previous baseline. All repetitions of a given study after the first are benchmarks. Also used to describe the ability to measure one company against an industry standard or its own past measures.

Benefit segmentation: Breaking out specific subsets of a population based on their needs or desires rather than on measurements such as lifestyle or demographics.

Bimodal distribution: Different from the familiar bell-shaped curve or normal distribution. Bimodal means that there are two modes of responding instead of having the data cluster around a central point. A bimodal distribution might be seen in a population where people either strongly prefer a product or strongly reject a product – half the population might be rating the product 1–2–3 on a 10-point scale, and the other half of the population might be rating it 8–9–10.

Bias: The research equivalent of sin. Clients and researchers are consistently on the lookout for anything that can corrupt or "bias" data and lead to erroneous conclusions.

Blind study: Research where the sponsor/client/brand is masked from respondents or researchers.

Brand preference and awareness research: Studies conducted to determine the awareness of specific brands or companies and the degree to which the purchasing population prefers or doesn't prefer a specific product.

Briefing: Typically the process of orienting data-collection personnel (interviewers) on a new project.

Business convergence: The gradual evolution of business toward a truly customer-centric focus. Highly touted by consultants, the actual emergence of convergence has been slow. It is more likely to be seen first in the business-to-business sector, as whole industries move supply chains online into one system.

Business Intelligence (BI): Business intelligence in the broadest sense is any information that is used for corporate strategy, planning, or decision-making. BI tools have emerged as those data analytic tools, usually fairly limited OLAP tools, or highly sophisticated data-mining templated solutions that attempt to achieve that goal. Rather late to the party have been the "bread and butter" of BI, which are the standard tools of market research, just now emerging on the Net-centric playground.

C

Call record sheets: A paper and pencil method of tracking results of calls made to homes or businesses. Not the actual survey but a record of terminations, those who were not at home, attempts, language barriers, refusals, and so on. Becoming less common as CATI (see definition) systems automate this record-keeping.

Callback: Recontacting a respondent to clarify or verify survey information. Done to check quality, correct errors, or expand an initial finding.

Categorical data: Responses that have no numeric relationship to one another. For example, categorizing respondents as brown-eyed, blue-eyed or green-eyed. Same as nominal data.

CAPI (computer-aided personal interviewing): Questionnaires are shown on a computer screen, and the questioning is directed to some degree by computer. Results are usually entered directly into a computer database. CAPI interviews are generally administered by a human interviewer, though self-administered CAPI is increasingly being applied.

CATI (computer-aided telephone interviewing): Questionnaires are shown on a computer screen, and the questioning is directed to some degree by computer. Results are usually entered directly into a computer database. Can be administered solely by computer, or the computer can aid a human interviewer.

Cell: Often used to refer to a subset of a survey sample or experimental design. "Since there are only 10 males in the cell, the sample base is too small to draw a conclusion."

Central location test (CLT): Using a central site for conducting interviews. May be either a convenience sample such as traffic in a shopping mall or pre-recruited to specific criteria and invited to an interviewing location.

Central tendency, measures of: there are three basic indicators: mean or average, mode (most common), and median. The median is the middle response. For example, if there are 19 responses, the median is the tenth response up from the lowest or the tenth down from the highest.

Chi Square: A test of statistical significance used for analyzing frequency distributions or contingency tables.

Choice modeling: A related technique to conjoint, used when there is a strong need for the results to map closely to actual market response. Also called discrete choice analysis.

Clarify: An interviewing process used to improve the quality and clarity of data for open-ended questions. For example, "Tell me more about what you meant by your response."

Classification/classification questions: Demographics. Questions asking respondents' characteristics. Typically occur later in a questionnaire. Ask for responses to questions such as age, income, household size, dollars spent in a product category, and so on.

Cleaning/data cleaning: The process of taking survey computer printouts and checking data for logical consistency or error. Increasingly automated by computer. Also, dual entry of data and comparing records to eliminate mistakes.

Clickstream: Proceeding through websites across the Net leaves a "trail" of information that can be analyzed. Essentially, every "click" results in some sort of standard information-sharing as "packets" of data circulate and move around the Internet. This "clickstream" can be analyzed for a "traffic report" on an individual's Internet behavior or aggregated up for analysis.

Closed-ended: A question with a fixed response set. Perhaps a rating scale, "yes" or "no" choices, and so on. As opposed to an open-ended, free-responding question where the respondent's verbatim answers are recorded.

Cluster/cluster analysis: Techniques designed to classify individuals into a relatively small number of exclusive groups. A goal of cluster analysis is to maximize likeness within groups and differences between them to create an understandable topology of the market.

Co-op/co-op fee: Money or gifts given to respondents for their participation. A gratuity or honorarium.

Codebook: A set of question responses and their associated computer code numbers. Used to assign categories to answers given to each question on a survey questionnaire.

Coding: The process of categorizing survey responses for computer analysis.

Completions: The number of interviews completed to date.

Concept test: Research designed to investigate market responses to new ideas or their implementations.

Conclusions/recommendations/interpretations: Typically, a section of a research report that gives the researchers' perspectives on the findings separate from specific data results.

Confidentiality: Masking the sponsorship of market research to avoid bias and protect the client's interests. Sometimes called "blind" research. Also, protecting the identity of respondents.

Confirmation: The process of ensuring recruited participants will show up. May involve phone calls and/or letters. Used for focus groups and other pre-recruited research.

Confirmation letter: A letter sent to a respondent to confirm that they will in fact attend the central location test, focus group, or other research session.

Conjoint analysis: Sometimes called feature trade-off analysis. However, conjoint is a special type of trade-off analysis. A method for establishing respondents' utilities or evaluations based on the preferences they express for combinations of product attributes and features. Price is typically one of the attributes included.

Content analysis: The process of extracting and organizing the key elements from verbatim responses. Typically, these responses are then coded and computer analyzed.

Control group: The opposite of the experimental group. They are kept separate from the group that receives some sort of experimental treatment and are used as a base against which changes can be measured or tested.

Copy-testing: Research to determine the degree of understanding, impact, awareness, and credibility that ad copy generates.

Correspondence analysis: Maps results using categorical data such as "name anyone" responses. Generally more flexible and easier on respondents than classic multidimensional scaling.

Cost per interview/CPI: The dollar cost of completing an interview in a survey research project.

CRISP-DM (cross-industry standard platform for data-mining): A thorough template for designing, running, and completing a data-mining project.

CRM (customer relationship management): A form of corporate software solution that has emerged from older systems, attempting to tie all customer-facing information and data into one place. Current incarnations have an operational and an analytic component, as it is increasingly apparent that CRM is more than just software. In addition, CRM is leading the charge toward full enterprise application integration (see EAI), as software providers are vying to be the common platform for usage across the corporation and around the world.

Cross-tabulation: A typical technique used to display research data, similar to a spreadsheet. Used as a basis for analyzing most surveys. Cross-tabs normally sort responses by type (young, aware, heavy users) and display the results in a data matrix.

Customer voice management (CVM): Very early entrant in the CRM solution space. CVM attempts to remedy the weaknesses inherent in contemporary CRM software solutions, mainly by delivering standard market research capabilities, such as surveys, interviews, feedback services, and polls, into a CRM system. The tiny differentiating component is that CVM is inherently Net-centric to match the CRM architecture.

D

DAR (day after recall): The awareness or message content recalled within 24 hours. Normally a measure used for television or radio advertising.

Data-collection: Also called field work or interviewing. The process of actually collecting market research data.

Data entry: Entering survey data into a database so that it can be analyzed. May be done from a CATI terminal or entered from paper records and questionnaires.

Data-mining: An inductive, atomistic analysis approach that works best with extremely large data sets. Frequently held as a promising solution, data- and web-mining has shown to require quite advanced skills, enough to make it less than routine for market research, CRM, and statistical use.

Data warehouse: Originally, data warehouses emerged as a way to store all essential corporate data. But as accessibility and the desire to maximize the use of collected data appeared as a mission-critical effort, data warehouses have been forced to adapt. Operational and analytic (or customer) data stores now exist, as well as data marts built specifically for a typical analytic function (auditing, for example). Evolving currently are exploratory data warehouses, designed to accommodate "ad hoc" analyses. Integration and a specific way for all of the data collections to "talk to" one another has emerged as a leading preoccupation in the corporate data arena.

Demand bias: Research corruption created when respondents know or suspect that researchers have a particular agenda. One example of demand bias is the effect of knowing who is sponsoring the research.

Demographics: The characteristics of respondents participating in research. Typical examples include age, income, sex, and so on.

Depth interview: A form of qualitative research. Typically trades out sample size for delving deeper into the subject matter. Used to determine underlying causes and motivations.

Descriptive data analysis: As opposed to statistical testing. Observing findings, data distributions, and relationships between data without applying statistical tests. Reporting and summarizing on these observed findings.

Diadic: Paired or face-to-face. An example of a diadic design would be a paired comparison taste test where two versions of a new french fry might be tested against each other. As opposed to monadic where one version of the french fry would be tested independently of any comparison.

Diary: The record kept by a respondent of purchase behavior, likes and dislikes, and so on, over a period of time. Typically diaries are a product of research panels who create them.

Dichotomous question: A question that has only two possible responses. An example might be, "Will you vote for candidate A or candidate B?"

Disconnect/termination/midway termination/partial: When a respondent ceases to be involved in the survey and quits the process.

Discussion guide: Typically five to 10 pages of questions used in a focus group. The questions proceed in chronological order. Discussion guide design is usually worked out between the researchers and the client prior to conducting groups.

Disk-by-mail: A newer research technique where a self-prompting questionnaire is sent to respondents on floppy disk. Respondents use the disk to answer the survey on their computer and send the completed disks back to the researchers.

Distribution: The pattern and frequency of responses to a given question.

DK: Common research shorthand for "don't know." The response a person gives when they don't have any other answer.

Door-to-door interviewing: The older practice of going into neighborhoods and to individuals' homes to interview them in some sort of systematic fashion. The Gallup Poll was originally conducted in respondents' homes.

Double-barreled question: Example: "What did you like about the new product, and how would you improve it?" Also known as: ambiguous question.

Drawing a sample: The process of determining in a random or systematic fashion who will be candidates to participate in research.

Dual moderator focus group: A technique using two researchers to conduct group interviews. Typically used for complex or difficult topics to provide greater depth, breadth, and quality of information.

E

Eager respondents: The market research equivalent of groupies. People who are repeatedly willing to participate in research. Normally to be avoided, as eager respondents may tend to become "experts" or give atypical responses.

EAI (enterprise application integration): Literally, one fully integrated system comprising all the software needed for a business. EAI has emerged as a lofty goal to tie together all information-gathering, collecting, and dissemination under one rubric to afford the most efficient and effective usage of data. Many software and IT-related business firms are converging on this "solution," increasingly looking at the Internet as the enabling platform to achieve this.

Early adopter: Also called innovators. Those people who tend to try new ideas or products early in the adoption cycle. Frequently a target for research since they often set the tone for later behavior in the marketplace.

E-business: A focus on moving all business to the Internet-centric platform. Ultimately, all business will be e-business, in the sense that all business information will flow on a common, Net-centric system.

Editing: The review of questionnaire responses prior to coding and entering them into a database. A quality control check to make certain that all questions are answered and questionnaire logic has been followed.

EIP (enterprise information portals): Also known as corporate information portals, corporate knowledge portals, or simply portals. This technology affords the dissemination of information directly to the corporate knowledge worker, while allowing interaction and collaboration on a wide array of business processes.

EMM (enterprise marketing management): A budding corporate-wide technology solution to automate and improve the marketing function via Net-centric deployment and dissemination of marketing/sales-specific information, knowledge, and data.

Enterprise software: Whether a software solution is "enterprise" or not depends on the definition on "enterprise." However, the goal is to literally provide a robust solution that equips the whole corporation in a specific functional area, or in the grandest sense, every single area of corporate information-gathering, storage, and dissemination is brought together under one common system.

ERP (enterprise resource planning): Predates CRM software (see CRM), as the supplier of a software solution that integrates all "back-office" processes into one holistic system. ERP, as are CRM, companies are all moving in the same direction: toward EAI (see EAI), or a total, integrated software system for all corporate data-collection, storage, and dissemination needs.

Evocative imaging: A focus group technique that uses a series of pictorial representations to explore intangible but highly influential associations with brand.

Evoked set: The set of choices that are salient or kept in mind for purchase. For example, from the multitude of laundry detergents available in the grocery store, the evoked set is the two or three brands the buyer may remember and actually be considering for purchase.

Exhibit cards: Cards given to respondents to aid them in answering. May list choices or provide a trigger to elicit response.

Experimental design: Research designed to follow classic laboratory or experimental techniques. Normally consists of a control group that does not receive the experimental treatment and one or more experimental groups that do. The underlying assumption is that if the experimental treatment has an effect, there will be a statistically significant difference in the experimental group when compared to the control.

Exploratory research: Research typically conducted early in a research program. Designed to uncover basic viewpoints, perceptions, behaviors, attitudes, and so on in a market place. Intended either to produce results that may be actionable or lead to additional research.

F

Face validity: Acceptance of a measure or technique simply on the basis of whether it appears to be valid.

Factor analysis: A data-reduction technique intended to trim the range of characteristics or findings to their underlying structure, dimensions, or factors.

Feasibility study: Typically, research done early in the process to determine the likelihood some new concept, product, or idea may have potential. Often similar to exploratory research.

Field edit: The process of editing questionnaires as they are collected, typically on a paper and pencil survey. Done by a supervisor, clerical staff, or the interviewers themselves.

Field research or field work: Also referred to as data-collection or interviewing. The process of collecting the data used in market research. To "field" is to put a research project into the data-collection phase.

Field service: A supplier of data-collection services.

Field supervisor: Typically, the person who is charged with managing and ensuring the quality of the data-collection process.

Focus group research: A research discussion composed of eight to 14 participants, directed by one or two moderators for the purpose of developing a group interaction around the topics of interest. Typically conducted in a focus group facility equipped with a one-way mirror for observation and with video-recording capabilities. Can also be conducted online for participation from varied parts of the globe or for accessing some specialized respondents.

Funnel design or funnel sequencing: The design of questionnaires in a manner that narrows questions/topics down from the general and unaided to more detailed specific or aided areas of investigation. Considered to be one aspect of quality questionnaire design.

G

Gap analysis: A method for finding the difference between importance and performance ratings in order to concentrate improvements on problem areas.

Global access panels: An increasingly viable and much-needed tool for corporate research. Global panels built and managed via an online system afford unprecedented control, efficiency, effectiveness, and coverage. They are rapidly becoming mandatory for market research firms wishing to serve large worldwide clients with a single source solution.

H

Halo effect: The result of a dominant reputation on an unrelated topic. For example, a manufacturer may be perceived to have a presence in a product area where it doesn't actually compete.

Hand tab/manual tabulation: The process of enumerating survey responses by counting as opposed to using computer automation.

Hawthorne effect: The phenomena of behavior changing simply by being observed. Typically considered to be a bias that can be introduced by conducting research.

Honorarium: Same as co-op fee.

Hosted solution: A software service or solution that is "hosted" or co-located by a provider. Also known as an application service provider (see ASP), hosting provides a slew of benefits as software architectures and solutions become increasingly complex and prohibitively expensive to build in-house.

HTTP (hypertext transfer protocol): The original method developed to send "packets" of information across the Net. Still robust and the standard after many years.

Hypothesis: Operational guesses being tested or examined for truth by research.

I

Image/reputation: The perceptions in the market place about a brand, company, product category, and so on.

In-home placement: A research technique requiring repeated use and experience with a product under investigation. Typically conducted under natural conditions – "in-home."

Incidence: The occurrence of a behavior in the population. For example, the incidence of personal computer users in the population at large may be 20 percent. Frequently, incidence has a strong effect on the cost of conducting research. Low incidence research is usually more expensive.

Industrial or business-to-business research: Investigations involving commercial enterprises, selling one to the other, as opposed to consumer marketing research.

Interaction: The effect two variables may have on each other that does not occur independently. Increasing heat and humidity will have a different effect on perspiration from increasing either one alone.

Intercept: The process of approaching customer foot traffic, asking screening questions, and including qualified respondents in a research interview.

Internet-centric: Briefly, any technology that uses standard TCP/IP transmissions to send information back and forth on the Internet. For market research, this affords anything "Net," such as Net-MR, Net-CAPI, Net-CATI, Net-Focus, Net-IVR, and Net-discussion boards.

Interval data: Responses having a known, fixed distance from each other. A ruler with small divisions is the perfect tool for collecting interval data. See "nominal" and "ordinal" data for contrast.

Item non-response: The "don't knows" or "refusals related to specific questions on a survey.

ITSP: Internet telephone service provider.

K

Knowledge management (KM): A key, but evolving, corporate initiative. KM currently holds a wide range of definitions, but essentially is a system – often Net-enabled – that affords the control, dissemination, and usage of information, both structured and unstructured. Some very early providers, such as Emmperative, are emerging in the marketing space (see EMM).

L

Language barrier: What it sounds like. Typically, in door-to-door or telephone-interviewing, those instances in which a non-English-speaking respondent is contacted and that respondent is recorded as being un-interviewable.

List order bias: The learning effect originally described by Ebbinghaus. People are generally inclined to remember or focus more on list items at the beginning and end – and less on the middle items on a list.

List rotation: The process of randomizing the starting point when reading a survey list. Intended to minimize the effect of list order bias.

Loaded question: One that begs or influences a specific response as opposed to an objective or well-designed question.

Longitudinal research: Research tracking attitudes, viewpoints, behaviors, and so on over a period of time.

M

Mail questionnaires: Surveys sent to respondents through the mail, which they fill out and return to the research organization.

Mall intercept: The research process of interviewing traffic in shopping malls where customers are available to participate.

Marginal: An early, partial computer run used to examine the basic frequency distributions in the data. Often used to help determine appropriate banner points for cross-tabulation and as part of the data-cleaning process.

Market research: Linking the customer, consumer, and public with the marketer through information that is used to identify and define marketing opportunities and problems. Market research generates, refines, and evaluates marketing actions, monitors marketing performance, and improves the understanding of marketing. Market research specifies the information required to address issues, designs the methods for collecting information, and manages and implements data-collection, analyzes results, and communicates the findings and their implications.

Market share: That portion of the market purchasing a particular brand, supplier, or company. For example, shortly after introduction, Microsoft had an 80 percent market share in word-processing programs for the Macintosh.

Market simulation: The research technique of statistically modeling an actual market situation. Variables are controlled and the effects of a new product introduction, advertising, pricing changes, and so on, can be measured in an experimental environment. To the degree possible this environment simulates an actual market situation.

Mean: One measure of central tendency. The average. Descriptive statistics.

Median: Another measure of central tendency, the response in the middle. If there are 19 responses, it is the tenth one from either end.

Message (as in ad message): Content recalled when respondents are probed to ask for their recollections.

Mixed-mode data-collection: The use of a number of modes of research collection within one research project or study. This approach, though intuitively attractive and academically proven, is only now becoming feasible with the emergence of Net-centric research management, collection, and deployment systems.

Mode: Another measure of central tendency. The most common response.

Moderator: A person or persons asking questions and directing the discussion in a focus group.

Monadic: A design in which a single product or concept is exposed to the respondent. As opposed to diadic in which two options or new products might be proposed, or triadic in which three would be compared to each other.

Monitoring: The process of listening in, coaching, and managing interviewers as they collect data on the phone.

Multimethod research: The use of a number of methods of research (qualitative and quantitative) within one research project or study. This approach, though intuitively attractive and academically proven, is only now becoming feasible with the emergence of Net-centric research management, collection, and deployment systems.

Multiple mentions: A question where more than one response is recorded per respondent.

Multivariate research methods: Advanced procedures that have emerged to bridge the gap from market research to CRM analytics and in some cases, data-mining. These include:

> **CART** (classification and regression trees): A very powerful set of segmenting, classifying, and predicting tools.
>
> **Kohonen networks**: A multidimensional cluster analysis (see cluster analysis), also quite difficult to understand.
>
> **Neural networks**: Essentially non-linear regression procedures that can fit and measure just about any data set. The difficulty emerges in the interpretation stage, as neural networks offer no guidance or understanding concerning their predictions.
>
> **PCR** (principal components/regression): Useful for customer satisfaction, loyalty, and profitability research problems.
>
> **PLS** (partial least squares): Affords the ability to model causal chains; however, not at the level of SEM.
>
> **SEM** (structural equation modeling): A technique that allows a researcher to quantify hypotheses and concepts. Also known as LV (latent variable) SEM.

N

NA/not applicable/not answerable/no answer: Questions for which there is no response given. Also item non-response.

Natural observation: The technique of conducting research in the least obtrusive way possible. One example might be observing shopping behavior in stores without directly asking questions of shoppers.

New media: Media that use the Internet or are constructed from the ground up to be Internet-centric (see Internet-centric). This includes all of the media we see and hear currently on the Net.

Nominal data: Responses that have no numeric relationship to one another. For example, categorizing respondents as brown-eyed, blue-eyed or green-eyed. Same as categorical data.

Non-response bias: The effect of a set of respondents refusing or choosing not to participate in research. Typically larger for self-administered or mail-out surveys.

Normal distribution: A bell-shaped curve or tendency of responses to distribute themselves around a central point. An underlying basis for many forms of statistical tests comparing central tendency.

Not-at-home: A record of a contact. Attempting to conduct an interview in which no respondent was available at the location.

O

Observers: Typically clients: those who have an opportunity to watch and listen to focus group research (online or offline).

OLAP (online analytical processing): Essentially, OLAP is a pre-built cross-tabulation table (or cube, if in three dimensions) that is pre-configured to be easily accessible from a data warehouse or store. OLAP emerged along with ERP solutions in the late 1980s and as a BI tool thereafter. Although the concept is sound, OLAP solutions are rather restricted to common business templates that use historical data. They are not a substitute for most of the common statistical and research procedures in use by the market research industry.

Omnibus survey: Also called piggyback survey. Research in which multiple clients share the cost of conducting research. Subscribers usually receive the portion of the information that is collected specifically for them.

One-way mirror: The mirrors used in focus group facilities. One way they are a mirror and the other way a window to allow observation of groups.

Online research: A group of data-collection techniques, including surveys on a web page or an online service, e-mail surveys, and focus groups conducted online.

Open-ended: As in open-ended questions. Those questions that allow respondents to verbalize reactions in their own words. Contrast with closed-ended.

Ordinal data: Findings that can be categorized as greater than or less than. Cannot be referred to as twice as large, half the size, or some similar mathematical comparison as can interval or ratio data. For example, ranking toothpastes from most to least desirable would be a way of creating an ordinal scale or ordinal data.

Outlier: Atypical data occurring at the tails of a normal distribution. Frequently outliers are removed to minimize their effects. For example, in research where 300 interviews are conducted and 299 respondents buy less than five times a week, the one respondent who is purchasing 30 times a week may be removed to suppress his excessive weight in measures of central tendency such as means or averages.

P

Paired comparison: When two products, concepts or candidates are tested head-to-head. Typically, serving order or comparison order is rotated to avoid first order bias.

Pantry check: A type of audit. The process of either looking in or asking a respondent to look in the refrigerator or pantry to determine brands or products currently on hand, as opposed to depending on respondents' recollections. Eliminates pressure to say, "I drink Michelob," when the refrigerator is full of Busch.

Participants: Typically used to describe those who attend or contribute to focus group discussions.

Penetration/market penetration: A measure of use, market share, or dominance. The degree to which a product is used, experienced, or known by a population.

Phone-mail-phone (also phone-fax-phone): A technique of calling and qualifying respondents, then sending them a questionnaire that might be lengthy or cumbersome by phone. When they've had a chance to complete the questionnaire, they are called back and their information is collected over the phone.

Piggyback: Also referred to as omnibus. Research shared by multiple clients. Subscribers get their data inexpensively by sharing costs.

Placement: Giving a respondent a product to use for a specified time. Usually followed by a phone call or visit to gather reactions.

Plus one dialing: The process of adding one to a number selected at random from a directory. Used to include unlisted numbers in the sample.

Poll: Most often used for political research in which the electorate's likely behavior is investigated. Often asks "horse race" kinds of questions about candidates or ballot measures.

Population: Any complete group sharing some common set of characteristics. Samples are drawn from populations. For instance, we may draw a sample of grocery shoppers from the population of all grocery shoppers. Usually considered synonymous with "universe."

Pre-coding: The process of determining and appending computer codes to questionnaires prior to conducting interviews. Used to accelerate data-processing for paper and pencil or computer-aided interviewing.

Predictive dialing: A computer technique for finding working telephone numbers where a respondent is available to be interviewed. Used to increase interviewing efficiency and minimize "dialing drudgery."

Pre-recruit: Contacting individuals by phone or in person and asking them to participate in research scheduled for a future date.

Presentation: Typically, the final step in the research process when results, conclusions, and interpretations are presented to the research sponsor.

Pretest: Interviews conducted to determine the effectiveness of the questionnaire design and to finalize the budget.

Primary data: Information collected directly from a respondent population as opposed to secondary or published data.

Probing: When asking open-ended questions, the process of requesting additional responses. Asking "what else?" Not the same as clarifying, which asks respondents to expand a previous response.

Prompting: Also referred to as aiding. The process of reading lists or names and asking if a respondent now recalls having heard of the brand, company, and so on.

Proprietary research: Most market research is proprietary. That is, owned by and exclusively for the client who purchased the research.

PSTN: Public service telephone network.

Psychographics: Lifestyle investigations. You may be familiar with VALS as an example of psychographic research. Used to segment markets based on values, attitudes, and lifestyles rather than product benefits or direct needs.

Purchaser/purchase influencer: Person who places the order or buys the product. An influencer recommends or specifies what is to be purchased.

Q

Qualifying/qualifying questions: Questions used to find those who have the characteristics required to participate or respond to the research.

Qualitative data: Findings that are not projectable to the population as a whole. A respondent's verbatim response is a good example of qualitative data.

Quantitative data: Any result that is inherently numerical and projectable to the population.

Quota: The number and kind of respondent from whom completed interviews must be obtained in order to satisfy the requirements of a study. For example, 100 design engineers, 100 engineering managers, and 100 purchasing agents might be the three quotas necessary to complete a 300-respondent engineering market study.

R

Random digit dialing (RDD): Using a computer and algorithms to generate a truly random, non-directory-based sample.

Ranking: Putting in order from most to least or least to most without regard for the specific size of the interval between ranked items.

Rating: The process of having respondents assign specific values to the characteristics. For example: "On a scale from one to 10, rate the importance of ease of use."

Real-time tracking: An ongoing monitor with data produced on a continuous basis. Real-time analysis and reporting are also possible with an online system.

Recruiting: The process of qualifying and inviting research participants. Used for pre-recruited central location test and focus groups.

Referral: Asking others to name potentially qualified respondents who can be contacted to participate in research.

Refusals: Respondents who choose not to participate in research.

Reliability: Reliability is the similarity of results provided by independent but comparable measures of the same characteristic. For example, one measure of reliability would be splitting a sample in half and comparing the results, one to the other.

Research design: The stated structure and process of conducting a research project. Includes specifications, schedule, and budget.

Research methods: How the research is conducted. Also, a section in a research report detailing the process. At minimum, should allow for replication of the project.

Research proposal/recommendation: The document describing the design, schedule, and budget for conducting a research project.

Research specifications: Design characteristics of proposed research.

Respondents: Those who participate in research.

Response rate: The percentage of potential respondents with whom completed questionnaires are accomplished. For example: the "return rate" of mailed-out questionnaires. The percent of qualified computer users called who finish the interview. Typically, ineligible members of the sample are excluded from the denominator.

S

Sample: The group of respondents derived from a population. Analogous to a spoonful of soup compared to the pot.

Sample size: The number of elements (names, phone numbers) drawn from the population.

Sampling: The process of selecting subjects from a population or universe for inclusion in research. Following are common sampling methods:

> **Census**: When all members of a target population are included or surveyed. Eating the whole pot of soup.
>
> **Cluster sample**: Samples drawn in a cluster so the researcher can collect information from that cluster. Used to reduce costs. For example, sales districts are randomly chosen and then all buyers within the chosen district are interviewed.
>
> **Convenience sample**: Sample that is easy to acquire but is not a valid representation of the population. One example is interviewing shopping mall traffic as opposed to taking a pure, scientific random sample. Lower cost and lack of need for extreme rigor are often good motivations for using convenience samples.
>
> **Disproportionate stratified sample**: Appropriate method when certain segments of a population are seen as more important than others, as varying more, or as more expensive to sample. For example, a health insurance company surveys its corporate customers, oversampling firms with larger memberships to reflect their true influence.
>
> **Heterogeneous sample**: Includes a high degree of variance. A general population sample would be heterogeneous in that there would be lots of variation in ages, incomes, educational levels, and so on.
>
> **Homogeneous sample**: Tends to have less variance. An example might be design engineers. Most are male, in a certain age group, and have similar educational backgrounds
>
> **Judgment or purposive sample**: Non-probability method used when a target population is judged to be like the true population. Effective for exploratory research, this method is often used to pretest surveys or develop focus group discussion guides.
>
> **Non-probability sample**: Any sample where the likelihood of a particular element or characteristic being included cannot be determined. There is no way to ensure this type of sample is representative.
>
> **Probability sample**: A sample in which each population element has an equal and known opportunity to be included. This knowledge permits statements of sampling error and estimates of precision. Also called random sample.
>
> **Proportionate stratified sample**: Selected so each stratum is in proportion to the actual occurrence. If 25 percent of registered voters live in a particular county, the final sample would contain 25 percent from that county.
>
> **Random/random sample**: Process of ensuring there is no systematic bias in the way potential respondents are selected for inclusion in the research.

Snowball sample: Normally used for hard-to-find populations. Initial respondents are selected through a particular sampling method and referrals are recruited during the interview. For example, you wish to interview individuals who live in log cabins, so during the interview with the qualified respondent you ask for names of others they know who live in log cabins.

Stratified sample: A two-step probability sample where the initial population is divided into unique subsets. Each is then randomly sampled. Quotas may be set.

Systematic random sample: A probability sample obtained by beginning at a random starting point and then selecting every nth entry. Can be more efficient than pure random sampling; however, problems arise if there is a cycle in the data that relates to the interval between respondents.

Sampling error: The variation that could occur when drawing a sample of a given size from a population of given size.

Sampling frame: A procedure or list of elements (cities, institutions, individuals) from which the sample will be drawn. Could be subscription lists from four different trade journals, or a list of people who have inquired about laser printers in the past 12 months.

Scalability: When referring to data-collection and dissemination systems, scalability means the ability to handle increasing data demands. The Net-centric platform has emerged as the golden solution since it affords essentially unlimited scalability using its platform.

Scales: A series of graded values used to measure responses. Following are common types:

Agree–disagree scale: a variation of a bipolar scale. Opposite labels are applied, such as "disagree strongly" at one end and "agree strongly" at the other. The respondent is asked to indicate level of agreement.

Bipolar adjective scale: Labels of opposite meaning are only attached to the two ends of the scale. Generates interval level data by forcing respondents to look at the numbered points as equal widths.

Binary scale: Nominal measurements that have only two possible values. Do you own a car: yes or no?

Comparative scale: Requires the respondent to make a series of relative or comparative judgments rather than a series of independent ones. Rating scales.

Constant sum scale: Ratio scale where respondents are asked to divide a specific number of points among a smaller number of alternatives according to set criteria (for example, preference, importance, aesthetic appeal). Multiple points are given to alternatives most preferred.

Constant sum paired comparison scale: When a constant sum scale is combined with a paired comparison scale, a ratio-scaled paired comparison is possible.

Direct qualification: Requires a direct number or ratio answer. For example, how many printers do you have in your division?

Dollar metric (graded paired comparison) **scale**: Interval scale used to collect paired preference plus the monetary value by which it is preferred. The scale pairs two products and asks for the respondent's preference. Once the decision is made, the respondent is asked how much extra they would pay to get their preference. Results can be used to predict market share for each brand, but cannot be a direct representation of actual market strength.

Equal width interval scale: Respondents are asked to indicate which category they fit into using a scale that usually has four to eight divisions of equal distance. When the interval between categories becomes unequal (0, 1–2, 3–15, 16–99, and so on), the data fall to ordinal level.

Forced ranking scale: Ordinal scale where respondents are asked to rank objects or things. Used to learn attitudes or preferences. For example: "Please rank the following seven brands in terms of your preference, with 1 being most preferred."

Interval scale: A numeric scale where the extent of difference between any two points is a legitimate basis of comparison. Note, however, the ratio between values is meaningless and zero is an arbitrary point on the scale. In addition to nominal and ordinal level, calculations can determine means and standard deviations. Good for measuring attitudes or preferences.

Likert summated scale: Gauges attitudes. All points on the scale are labeled, and the respondent is asked several related questions; then a total score is calculated. A Likert scale might look like: dislike strongly (–2), dislike (–1), neutral (0), like (+1), like strongly (+2).

Metric scale: A ratio or interval scale.

Multiple-choice scale: The respondent is read a list and selects the option that best fits. Often used for collecting demographic information.

Multidimensional scale: Measures respondents' perceptions of the similarity of objects and preferences among these objects. Relationships are plotted in multidimensional space and displayed on two-dimensional maps. One of the several mapping routines similar to Rating Scales.

Nominal scale: Numbers are used solely to identify or label, with no meaning in terms of amount. For instance: 1 = IBM, 2 = Canon, 3 = HP. Good only for calculating frequencies.

Non-metric scale: Refers to nominal or ordinal scales.

Ordinal scale: Respondents are confronted with 10 factors and asked to rank them in order of importance. Assigned numbers imply some ordering of the objects (less than to greater than). Can calculate frequencies, medians, and percentiles.

Paired comparison scale: Respondents consider preferences two alternatives at a time. The advantage is that individual decisions are made as simple as possible. The downside is that this scale can become unwieldy – 15 products generate 105 paired comparisons.

Ratio scale: A scale that encompasses order, a constant unit of measurement, and an absolute zero. Examples are scales for reporting length, weight, or number of objects. Can perform all statistics of lower level scales, plus coefficient of variation.

Reference alternative scale: Also called a fractionation or magnitude scale. Has respondents compare to a reference alternative (X) while applying a given criterion.

If X = \$100, how much would you pay for A, B, and C? Problem is X tends to influence the results, so the constant sum scale is typically used as an alternative.

Semantic differential scale: Respondents choose the category that best fits them, based on labels or semantics describing each option. This is an ordinal level scale, so it is not possible to measure the difference between categories.

SCM (supply chain management): Software solutions that tie together all supply chain functions into one integrated system, most often Net-based.

Screener: The questionnaire used to qualify and recruit participants for focus group research.

Screening: The process of contacting, qualifying, and inviting respondents to participate in additional research.

Secondary data: Any information collected from intermediate sources. Industry figures, databases, library sources, and so on, are examples of secondary data.

Segmentation: Splitting up a population into subsets based on common characteristics. Examples might be product requirements, needs, age, income, education, product preference, and so on.

Selective perception: A biasing effect common to all observation. The process of observing only part of the pertinent data available for analysis. Selective perception may cause focus group observers to develop a set of beliefs based on only part of the information.

Self-administered questionnaire: An instrument the respondent fills out. A questionnaire not administered by an interviewer.

SFA (sales force automation): The original CRM solution, which has quickly evolved into more complex and holistic CRM architectures.

Sign-off: The form used to check out respondents as they leave focus groups. Verifies they have received payment and agreed to protect confidentiality.

Simulation: See also "market simulation." A replication of market conditions to allow drawing conclusions about what is likely to happen under the conditions created in the simulation environment.

Skew: A non-symmetrical distribution. If, for example, most respondents on a 10-point scale rated the product a nine or 10, we would describe that distribution as "skewed."

Skip pattern: The logical organization of an interview so questions are asked only of those who fit certain criteria. Other respondents are directed elsewhere in the questionnaire, depending on the criteria they meet.

SMS (short messaging system): Currently a favorite on wireless/mobile phones.

Sponsor: The client or organization paying for the research.

SQL (structured query language): A programming language used for accessing data from a data warehouse or store.

Statistical test: Measures of significance applied to data collected using probability sampling. Used to determine if the null hypothesis (there is no difference) may be rejected and in fact there is some reliable difference between two sets of data.

SUGGING (selling under the guise of research): Pretending to conduct market research for the purpose of selling goods or services. An unethical and dishonest practice that undermines respondent cooperation for future research.

Syndicated research: Research with multiple sponsors or sold to multiple audiences. Similar to omnibus or piggyback research.

T

T-test: A statistical test comparing the distribution of two means for the purpose of determining whether they are significantly different, one from the other.

Tab or code and tab: The process of tabulating or calculating survey responses. Can be done manually, by computer, or a combination of both.

Taste test: Research designed to compare food products to each other. A test of palatability, desirability, and preference.

Telephone interview: Survey research conducted over phone lines.

Terminate/midway term: Interviews in which the respondent chooses not to complete the interview and is unwilling to continue with the process.

Test market: A clearly identified town or geographic region in which a new or improved product or change in marketing elements is tested to see if in fact the new approach is viable for introduction across a wider area.

Test product: Any new or existing product being included in the research process.

Theoretical error: An estimate of the difference between survey results on a specific variable and the long-run mean of that variable if the entire population were measured. The typical standard in research is a 95 percent confidence level, where in 95 of 100 samples we are sure the true mean falls within the stated range. For instance, suppose a stated 95 percent confidence interval from a sample of 200 is plus or minus 6.9 percent. This means that if we repeatedly draw samples of 200 from the given "universe," on 95 out of 100 occasions, we would not expect results to vary by more than plus or minus 6.9 percentage points from the results shown.

Top-of-mind awareness (also called "tip-of-the-tongue"): First mentioned recall of vendor names, brands, products, ideas, services, and so on.

Total unaided recall: All of those recalls or mentions a respondent can volunteer when asked to identify a brand, company, message, and so on.

Tracking study: Research that repeatedly measures the same variables and determines their changes over time.

Transcript: The verbatim or nearly verbatim accounting of respondent comments in personal interviews or focus groups.

Triadic: A design for three-part product or concept comparison. See also monadic and diadic.

Triangulation: In market research (and social science), a method that uses multiple forms of research to enhance the validity and robustness of a conclusion. Both qualitative and quantitative practitioners use triangulation, and increasingly, a mixture of qualitative/quantitative is emerging, as well, supported elegantly by online research systems.

U

Universe: The entire group about which some information is desired and obtained through a sample. Usually considered synonymous with "population."

V

Validity: The extent to which research actually measures what it says it does.

Variance (S2): The degree to which data are distributed away from or vary from the center or mean. Related measures are standard deviation, standard error, and "product moments."

Verbatim: Respondents' true and actual verbalizations.

Verification: (1) The process of determining if respondents did give the answers recorded on a questionnaire. Typically, response verification is accomplished by calling back a subset of the sample. (2) List verification: the process of cleaning and completing lists such as customer or mailing lists.

Verified data: Data entered into a computer database multiple times as a way of ensuring accuracy of entry. "Verifying 100%" means dual entry of all responses and comparing both data sets for anomalies.

W

WAP: Wireless application protocol.

Wave: An instance of a tracking study. Multiple waves are conducted over time.

Weighting: Process of increasing or decreasing data by the proportion of segments in a sample or by a known multiplier. Often used to "fix" non-representative samples.

XYZ

XML (extended markup language): Essentially, a way for inserting/extending a semantic layer between the business and technical user of data. XML, it is hoped, will provide the necessary framework for data that will allow a "common" language to emerge, thus simplifying and/or enhancing data-integration efforts. For market research, this will provide an unparalleled opportunity.

Z

Z-test: Statistical test of the central tendency of two percentages or means to determine where they are significantly different from each other. When the sample is larger than 30 respondents, Z-tests and T-tests are identical.

Index

Strong, E.K. xvi
Structured Query Language 169, 299
Struse, Doss 87, 108
Supply Chain Management 299
Swaminathan, Vinodh 35, 41

T

TACODA Systems 86, 109
Taylor Nelson Sofres PLC x
Taori, Norio 82, 107
Taste test 286, 300
The Kantar Group 280
Tomei, Bob 104
Total Research 12, 81, 191
Tower Group/Reuters 280
Tribal DDB 93, 94, 113, 280
True Audience 86, 87, 280

U

United States Rubber and Swift &
   Company xvi
Universitaet Erlangen-Nuernberg 280
University of California at Berkeley xviii

V

Viacom 280

Virtual Surveys 9, 37, 41
VNU 8, 29
Vossos, Tolis 83, 85

W

WebMiner 280
WebSideStory 91, 108, 276, 280
Weighting 132, 135, 145, 175, 227, 252,
   258, 301
Wendt, Laura 94
Wharton School of Business, The
   University of Pennsylvania 280
White, Percival xvi
Wireless 3, 23, 52, 94, 101, 110, 132,
   152, 161, 163–165, 167, 208, 223, 255,
   263, 268, 299, 301
Wireless Application Protocol (WAP)
   165, 255, 301
WPP 8, 29, 104

X

XML: Extended Markup Language 166,
   169, 228, 230, 301

Y

Yahoo! 22, 94, 112, 280